MW01122513

HIGH-RISK PATROL

ABOUT THE AUTHOR

Gerald W. Garner, a veteran of more than forty years in law enforcement, is chief of police for the city of Greeley, Colorado. He holds a master's degree in Administration of Justice and has authored seven books on a variety of law enforcement subjects. He has published more than 200 magazine and journal articles on law enforcement topics, many of them dealing with the subject of officer safety and street survival. He teaches widely on policing.

Garner's considerable law enforcement experience spans three states and ranges from time spent as a patrolman and street sergeant to roles as an academy director and watch commander. He also has served as a field training officer and field training supervisor. He additionally has worked as a consultant on police procedural and use of force issues.

Second Edition

HIGH-RISK PATROL

Reducing the Danger to You

By

GERALD W. GARNER

Police Chief
Greeley Police Department
Greeley, Colorado

CHARLES C THOMAS • PUBLISHER, LTD.
Springfield • Illinois • U.S.A.

Published and Distributed Throughout the World by

CHARLES C THOMAS • PUBLISHER, LTD.
2600 South First Street
Springfield, Illinois 62794-9265

© 2011 by CHARLES C THOMAS • PUBLISHER, LTD.

ISBN 978-0-398-08618-3 (hard)
ISBN 978-0-398-08619-0 (paper)
ISBN 978-0-398-08620-6 (ebook)

Library of Congress Catalog Card Number: 2010034346

With THOMAS BOOKS *careful attention is given to all details of manufacturing
and design. It is the Publisher's desire to present books that are satisfactory as to their
physical qualities and artistic possibilities and appropriate for their particular use.*
THOMAS BOOKS *will be true to those laws of quality that assure a good name
and good will.*

Printed in the United States of America
MM-R-3

Library of Congress Cataloging in Publication Data

Garner, Gerald W.
　　High-risk patrol : reducing the danger to you / by Gerald W. Garner. – 2nd
　ed.
　　　　p. cm.
　　Includes index.
　　ISBN 978-0-398-08618-3 (hard)–ISBN 978-0-398-08619-0 (pbk.)
　　1. Police patrol. 2. Police–Violence against–Prevention. 3. Law enforce-
　ment–Safety measures. 4. Police patrol–United States. I. Title.

HV8080.P2G37 2011
363.2'32–dc22　　　　　　　　　　　　　　　　　　　　2010034346

Dedicated to the officers
Who have died,
And in their dying,
Taught others to live.

SPECIAL NOTE

This book presents practical, proven, commonsense suggestions for responding to the dangers that threaten police officers. They work. But there are alternative means for handling these hazards that under certain circumstances may also work. As a result, the author and publisher accept no responsibility for harm to persons or property resulting from utilization of tactics and procedures suggested in this text.

PREFACE

- A big-city uniformed patrolman, 15 years on the job, stops a vehicle containing a known robbery suspect. He saunters up to the driver's door and is fatally shot for his carelessness.
- A sheriff's deputy in a rural Texas county chases down a speeder on an isolated country road. After contacting the driver, he turns to get his summons book from his patrol car. This momentary lapse is all the wanted fugitive needs to shoot the deputy in the back. The officer dies.
- Two officers—longtime car partners—take a drunk into custody and place him, unsearched and unhandcuffed, in the car seat behind them. Each relies on the other to do something neither actually does. And both die needlessly when the drunk produces a handgun.
- A rookie officer stops by the corner drugstore for a quick purchase. Her mind in neutral and her thoughts of officer safety suppressed, she walks into a robbery in progress. Stunned, she draws her weapon without clear-cut plan or purpose. She is subsequently killed by a shotgun-wielding lookout she never even saw.

American police officers killed—murdered—in the line of duty. Officers have been dying with frightening regularity on the paved streets, dirt roads, cluttered apartment landings, and spotless living room carpets of the nation for a long time now. They were dying violent deaths long before anyone thought about formal, organized training in something called officer survival.

Unfortunately, they are still dying violently today even after the last three decades' long-overdue emphasis on police field survival skills. It is obvious that more work—a lot more work—will be needed if the nation's peace officers are to reach their potential as guardians of the public while they simultaneously protect themselves from criminal violence. Fortunately, it is a job that *can* be done. It must be.

This book goes a long way toward helping the individual police officer do that vital job. It is designed and intended to help him or her *survive*. It provides a general orientation for survival, and it details the specifics the intelli-

gent police professional must master to survive the many types of potentially risky situations he will be exposed to over a career. As it must if it is to be
really helpful, the book delves into the down-and-dirty, nuts-and-bolts details
of everything from searching a prisoner to searching a building; arresting a
300-pound outlaw biker or a surly teenager. The volume is painstakingly
thorough in its approach to officer survival. The officer who reads it can
afford to be no less thorough as he applies its practical information to the
street situations he encounters.

But a printed narrative, no matter how careful and comprehensive, can
only do so much. It can emphasize important principles in such areas as
firearms use and self-defense, but it cannot teach complete physical skills,
and it cannot instill nearly automatic motor responses. As a result, the wise
student of officer survival will supplement this book with personal exposure
to skilled, hands-on training in such areas as marksmanship, pursuit driving,
come-alongs, and other physical tactics and techniques. By meshing that
experience with what he reads here, the safety-conscious police practitioner
can become the skilled professional he must be to survive and stay healthy,
both physically and emotionally. He can, in sum, drastically reduce the personal risks of high-risk patrol.

G.W.G.

INTRODUCTION

This book has a singular purpose: helping the contemporary police officer hang onto his or her life in a world that can turn suddenly deadly. It shows the reader what high-risk patrol really is and then spells out exactly what he must do to counter those risks successfully. It discusses his personal preparations for risk reduction, including mental attitude as well as physical skills and training.

Nineteen chapters show the safety-minded police person how to do everything from handling traffic stops to surviving felony encounters; getting out of a domestic violence call alive to surviving an ambush attack. Some "special" dangers are also discussed, including off-duty confrontations and the emotional hazards of the job.

The practical police officer should find the book's layout of particular value. At the end of each vital chapter, a quick and concise "Risk Reduction Checklist" is presented. These chapter summaries are excellent for review and merit rereading by the police professional intent on surviving to a healthy retirement.

The book includes ample evidence of what can go fatally wrong when officers meet danger. Culled from the "Law Enforcement Officers Killed and Assaulted" reports put together by the Federal Bureau of Investigation, these tragic but sadly informative accounts of police deaths are found throughout the text. Every account is true. These anecdotes accompany each chapter and contribute to an Appendix at the end of the book. Each one makes a point by way of grim example. Yet every tragedy described can help to save the life of an alert police reader who might otherwise have become one more statistic.

Key points on officer survival appear in more than one chapter. This is as it should be, inasmuch as something as central to officer safety as "obtain needed backup" is quite relevant to the safe handling of more than one kind of risky assignment. The repetition is both intentional and reinforcing to the careful student of field survival skills.

The information contained in this text is as current as the morning's head-lines and as relevant as the obituary for a fallen comrade. This, then, is HIGH-RISK PATROL. Its purpose for existing is REDUCING THE DAN-GER TO YOU.

CONTENTS

HIGH-RISK PATROL

Chapter 1

WHAT IS HIGH-RISK PATROL?

Just what is a high-risk patrol assignment? Simply put, it is one in which the potential for you to be injured or killed is high. High, that is, if you fail to take some practical, commonsense precautions and apply sound officer safety tactics of the kind described in these pages.

The average police officer would have little trouble identifying certain calls or assignments as obviously hazardous ones:

- The reported sniper on a downtown roof.
- The man with a gun in the neighborhood bar.
- The shots fired call in a crowded shopping mall.

But would that same, average officer also recognize as potentially dangerous the following situations:

- An elderly man acting strangely in a local park.
- A stoned, teenage kid sitting on a bus bench.
- A reported argument between a landlord and his female tenant.

Each of the last three scenarios described here is potentially hazardous. Each *has* resulted in the violent death of a police officer. Each represents a real-life threat to you.

Just how dangerous is your world out there? Dangerous enough, according to some very reliable, revealing, and sobering statistics. Each year the Uniform Crime Reports Section of the Federal Bureau of Investigation produces a comprehensive report of violence and mayhem directed against American law enforcement officers. It is called "Law Enforcement Officers Killed and Assaulted," and that is exactly what it reports on an annual basis.

WHAT THE STATISTICS SAY

It makes it a bit easier to understand what high-risk patrol really is when you take a look at police officer fatalities and how those officers died. In the sample year of 2008, for instance, 41 police officers were murdered in the United States, according to the FBI report. Twenty-two of the murdered officers were employed by municipal police departments. Of that total, 12 worked for agencies serving cities of 250,000 people or more.

In 2008, line-of-duty deaths occurred in 19 states. The South, the nation's most populous region, saw 20 officers killed. Nine officers were slain in the West, nine in the Midwest, and three in the Northeast.

Of the 41 officers killed in 2008, 37 were male and four were female. Some 30 of the victim officers were White, nine were Black, one was as American Indian or Alaskan native, and the race of one was not provided. The average age of the officers killed was 39 years, and the average length of service was 10 years. Of the 41 officers murdered in 2008, 27 were assigned to vehicle patrol.

What were the officers doing when killed? Nine were fatally attacked during arrest situations. Eight died during traffic stops or pursuits. Seven were slain while handling suspicious persons or circumstances, and seven were murdered while involved in tactical situations, such as a barricaded offender. Six officers died in ambush scenarios, and two died while doing investigative work, such as surveillance or interview. One officer was killed while handling a prisoner, and one died after responding to a disturbance call.

In 2008, 35 of the 41 victim officers were killed with firearms. Of these, 25 were shot with handguns. Four officers were killed with their own weapons. Of the 41 murdered, 32 were wearing body armor at the time of the fatal attack.

When did these officers become victims? More died in January than any other month. The deadliest day was Friday. The most dangerous time period in 2008 was between midnight and 4 a.m.

The FBI figures make it plain that making or attempting arrests and handling traffic matters are definitely big parts of what contribute to high-risk patrol for you. There is more to it than that, however. As any veteran law enforcement officer will tell you, life-threatening, gut-wrenching, heart-stopping danger can turn up anywhere and at any time. A grave threat to your life really can materialize in the form of the stoned kid on the bus bench or the little old man "acting weird" in a local park. Either of these troubled people may attempt mightily to kill you, the rescuer. Whether he succeeds will greatly depend on how prepared you are to face danger when it arrives with little or no warning. That success will turn to a considerable degree on the mental and physical preparations you have made in advance to defend your life with every reasonable means at your disposal. In the end, your success (or your opponent's) may depend on who is best prepared to win the struggle at hand, whether that struggle amounts to a matching of wits and street savvy, a contest of survival tactics and techniques, a test of physical strength and agility, a match of skills with deadly weapons, or all of these.

CAUTION VS. PARANOIA

At the same time, you must see to it that your survival conditioning as a competent street cop never strays into *unrealistic* fears of impending destruction. Being careful does not mean the same thing as being hopelessly paranoid. The former is just good street sense; the latter will make you dysfunctional. No normal person can live sanely while seeing threats everywhere, every moment. Being survival conscious does not require that you see a cop killer behind every tree. Being survival smart DOES require that you recognize the fact that there are people out there who are willing, even anxious, to hurt you. It requires that you realize that these threats to your well-being can materialize when you least expect them.

Condensed into a concise formula for street survival, your motto for reducing the danger of high-risk patrol might look something like this:

I will be prepared.
I will be alert.
I will win.
I will not give up.
I will survive.

High-risk patrol, then, can be found in virtually any call you respond to, any contact you initiate, any individual who approaches you. High-risk patrol tactics are appropriate for you to initiate when you pick up a chronic drunk from the corner bar. They are entirely in order when you retrieve a runaway, teenage hitchhiker off of the interstate. They are absolutely a must when you transport the town's "harmless old crank" to the mental health facility.

MISTAKES TO AVOID

But exactly what are these high-risk patrol tactics, anyway? Just what procedures and techniques should you rely on when the chips are down and potential danger looms? It might be helpful to first examine what sound high-risk patrol tactics are NOT. To know what to do when split-seconds count, it is worth examining the pitfalls you should at all costs avoid. And how do you find out where these traps lurk? You ask the police professionals who have been there and back. When you query experienced street cops and supervisors about what to *avoid* doing in order to stay alive and healthy on the street, you come up with some pretty strong (and strongly felt) answers.

How, then, do these veterans suggest you go about getting yourself killed? It's easy:

1. **Don't Ask for Help.** You have a much better chance to be a hero when you handle dangerous people or situations solo.
2. **Take Things for Granted.** Assume someone else has searched for weapons or loaded the patrol car's shotgun. It saves time and effort if you let somebody else sweat the details.
3. **Don't Study Your Job.** When you are off-duty, you are off-duty. Don't waste your time reading professional publications or learning how to do your job better and safer.
4. **Ask for Trouble.** Picking a fight helps build your reputation as a macho man (or woman.) Take the offensive. Let everybody else worry about the consequences.
5. **Stay Out of Shape.** After all, it takes a lot of weight to push folks around. And if you are obviously in poor shape, the boss won't expect you to take on unreasonable tasks, like chasing creeps and climbing fences.
6. **Keep a Bad Mental Attitude.** Don't strain your gray matter worrying about that officer safety nonsense. After all, if somebody wants you, he's going to get you, and there is nothing you can do about it.
7. **Don't Worry About Handcuffing.** If you scare them bad enough, they won't need handcuffs. Save the cuffs for the really bad dudes.
8. **Don't Worry About Equipment.** Firearms are tough–they'll fire with very little maintenance. Don't waste time on leather gear, flashlights, and the like. They'll work. If they don't, you can always replace them later.
9. **Don't Worry About Their Hands.** Watch their eyes, their facial muscles, or whatever else catches your fancy. But they won't hurt you with their hands.
10. **Searching Is for Sissies.** Take him to the station and then let *him* empty his pockets. You can't hurt yourself on needles, blades, and the like if you keep your hands off of these filthy people.
11. **Catch a Few Winks When It's Quiet.** You can't stay sharp for the Big Call if you are not refreshed and fully rested. A good "cooping"

spot is a cop's best friend.

12. **Patrol Time Is Daydream Time.** There's a lot of wasted time to be killed out there. It's a good time for figuring out some answers to those financial woes, supervisor hassles, and romantic entanglements. After all, it helps to keep your mind off what you are doing.

The "dirty dozen" tricks listed here definitely should further your efforts if you are dead set on getting yourself hurt or killed. They are definitely *not* the way to stay healthy on high-risk patrol.

The way to survive high-risk patrol is to be better than the opposition. The way you get better and stay that way is to have some idea what your potential opponent is going to do before he does and what you can do to successfully counter him. This book will help you prepare for the dangers of high-risk patrol.

Those very vital preparations are examined next.

A RISK REDUCTION CHECKLIST FOR HIGH-RISK PATROL

1. Take a look at the numbers for what they can teach you about how and why cops die.
2. You must make both physical and mental preparations to protect yourself.
3. Being careful does not require you to become paranoid.
4. Your personal formula for street survival includes preparedness, alertness, and a determination to win.
5. Be conscious of the list of officer safety errors you must avoid in order to stay safe.
6. Your personal goal is always to be better than the opposition.

A 37-year-old state trooper with 11 years of police experience was killed by gunfire at about 5:30 p.m. after stopping a vehicle whose driver had earlier failed to pay for gasoline. A struggle began when the trooper attempted to handcuff the 27-year-old suspect and the man got control of the officer's handgun. The officer was hit by two rounds in the chest but wounded his assailant in the hand with a backup .38-caliber handgun before dying. The assailant fled and was arrested by backup officers.

* * * * *

A 30-year-old sheriff's deputy with 8 years of law enforcement experience was beaten to death in a 9 p.m. incident while on duty in a jail infirmary. A male inmate became irate when he was refused medication. He subsequently picked up an oxygen tank and repeatedly struck the officer with it. The unarmed officer died at the scene.

* * * * *

A federal agent was killed at about 6 a.m. while attempting to serve an arrest warrant with a multi-agency arrest team. After knocking at the front door of a residence and seeing the wanted party run in the other direction, the officers used a battering ram to open the door and entered. The agent, who was the first one through the door, was hit with a single round fired from a .38-caliber revolver by the suspect's wife. The round hit the agent in the chest above his body armor.

* * * * *

A sergeant was killed at about 11:30 a.m. while responding to a radio report of an armed robbery at a bank. The 11-year veteran spotted a vehicle matching the description of one seen at the robbery. The vehicle stopped and an adult male wielding a semiautomatic rifle exited. The rounds he fired struck the sergeant in several places, including the abdomen. The murderer fled and was later killed by another officer.

* * * * *

A state trooper stopped a motorist for a registration violation and asked him to step out of his vehicle. The man complied and accompanied the officer to the front of the patrol car. The trooper asked for permission to frisk the man for weapons, and the subject stated that he had a gun. A struggle began, and the man pulled a semiautomatic handgun and shot the officer three times. A round that entered above the officer's vest killed him.

Chapter 2

PERSONAL PREPARATIONS
FOR RISK REDUCTION

Let's face the facts. When it comes to surviving on the street, you only have two options. You can opt to do whatever is necessary to stay alive. Or not.

Another fact of police life for you to face up to is this one: The best way to survive a dangerous confrontation is to keep it from occurring in the first place. You do that by utilizing everything you have learned about field survival to keep a potential attacker from ever getting the opening he will need to lay you low. By preventing him from ever feeling he has the advantage, you may be able to keep him from trying his luck. If he is foolish enough (or drunk enough or high enough) to try it anyway, what you know about tactics, procedures, positioning, cover, and a dozen other officer survival details will help ensure that he loses his ill-advised contest with you. That is the way it has to be.

The key for you, of course, is to know what to do and how to do it when your life is on the line. By knowing what needs doing and how to get it done, you will be more confident in your own abilities. As any pro coach will tell you, that is a big part of winning. By being both knowledgeable *and* confident, you will be able to reduce significantly the number of street encounters that get to the really hazardous stage. Bolstered by your technical skills as well as by confidence in yourself, you will be much less likely to overreact or not react at all in a dangerous situation. All of this will help you survive, both physically and emotionally.

Recognizing danger is a very big part of your job. But danger recognition is only part of your task. Knowing what to do to eliminate or significantly reduce the risks to *you* is equally vital. Both danger recognition and an effective response to the hazards you identify are skills you must apply consistently to EVERY situation you encounter, not just the ones clearly labeled as dangerous from the start. That's what a *total* officer survival package is made up of.

All too many otherwise good cops have components missing from their personal survival packages. Their oversights can get them killed. Example: A 40-year-old metropolitan police officer responded to a domestic dispute at approximately 1 a.m. Although it was the second time police had been to that address within 2 hours, the 16-year veteran cancelled a responding back-up unit shortly after he arrived on-scene. Seconds later, a 33-year-old male grabbed the officer's sidearm from its holster and shot him fatally in the neck and head. The murderer fled the area and killed a pursuing police dog and wounded its handler before dying in a storm of returned gunfire. The dead officer was an experienced cop. But missing from his "survival gear," at least on this particular occasion, was the ability to recognize potential danger, use backups properly, take a good position, and apply proper weapon retention skills. His shortcomings cost him his life.

Sometimes a personal survival package is missing some very basic items, such as a sensible regard for officer positioning and good, me-oriented survival sense. Example: A 33-year-old officer, 12 years on the job, made a 4 a.m. contact with a pedestrian he suspected of carrying stolen items. The post-shooting investigation showed that all the suspect had to do was pull a .22-caliber handgun, reach INSIDE the patrol car, and blast away at the still-seated policeman. The officer died of wounds to the chest and abdomen. A survival package lacking the most basic officer safety skills contributed again to the "officers killed" statistics.

SURVIVAL SKILLS

The preceding chapter of this book discussed some of the mental as well as physical abilities you must master to stay alive on the streets today. It also noted that there are a number of bad habits you must avoid and specific skills you must possess to stay a step ahead of those who would hurt you. This chapter and several that follow examine those specific skills in detail. They include the following:

1. Use of cover
2. Positioning and contact
3. Use of verbal commands
4. Weaponless defense and control tactics
5. Firearms use and retention
6. Handcuffing techniques
7. Body search techniques

8. Use of impact weapons
9. Use of lighting
10. Building search skills
11. Approach to a downed subject
12. Role of the cover officer
13. Communication on scene

While these officer survival skills will, for convenience and clarity, be discussed separately here, you must remember that all of them must be integrated in practice into a single, effective package of threat reduction procedures to be followed on the street. For instance, here the use of verbal commands, positioning and contact, handcuffing techniques, and search guidelines will be dealt with one at a time. But in applying them on the job, you will mesh these physical skills and preparations into one, smooth-functioning operation without even thinking about it. That's what risk reduction is all about at the nitty-gritty level.

Now, about all of those things you will need to survive. . . .

Use of Cover

Cover. It's what you'll want to be hiding safely behind if somebody is intent on blowing a hole through you. But it is more than that.

Cover is not the same thing as concealment. Adequate cover will shield you from whatever your opponent may elect to fire in your direction. Cover may be anything from a telephone pole to the exterior wall of a building to the engine compartment of your patrol vehicle. Concealment, in contrast, protects you from little more than the hostile glances of your adversary. It may consist of no more than a bush, a cardboard box, or a thin office partition.

What constitutes adequate cover and what is merely concealment can vary according to what sort of threat you are presented with. Flattening yourself against the outside wall to one side of an apartment house door may provide you with suitable cover if you are seeking a subject armed with a handgun. But such positioning may prove woefully inadequate cover if your opponent is armed with a .308-caliber rifle loaded with armor-piercing rounds. Cover, then, is a relative thing. Presented with more than one cover possibility equally accessible to you, it makes good officer survival sense for you to select the most solid cover available: a thick-trunked tree is better than a skinny one, a concrete retaining wall is preferable to a wooden fence, and so on.

Every year in this country, police officers are murdered within a very few feet of good cover. Perhaps they had no chance to get there. Perhaps events took them by surprise. But perhaps they never recognized cover for what it was and likewise failed to realize its crucial importance to their continued survival.

Whenever you go in harm's way, you *must* be aware of the cover possibilities around you. *Any* cover is better than standing in the open and slugging it out with gunfire with an armed opponent, particularly one who is behind cover himself. No matter how quick and good a shot you are, you are much better off firing from behind cover. Get there, if possible. Then concentrate on neutralizing your attacker.

How to shoot from behind cover is a subject better taught under the tutelage of a skilled firearms instructor than in the pages of a book. Suffice to say that you must expose as little of yourself as possible while acquiring a target and directing gunfire upon it. Look quick and get yourself back behind cover. Never peep from exactly the same spot twice. Watch out for back-lighting–a light source behind you that makes you a crisp target for your opponent. And whatever else you do, get in plenty of realistic training experience at the practice range beforehand so you will know in a crisis what works well for you and what doesn't.

Be aware that not everything that looks like good cover really is. Don't be too intent on staying with a patrol vehicle that is drawing fire if there is better cover readily at hand. If you do decide to stay with the car, remember that staying crouched beside a wheel or the engine compartment is your best bet assuming that your adversary's position is not elevated enough to allow him to shoot over the car and down on your position.

Cover. Never stop thinking about making it available to yourself even as you deprive your potential enemy of its benefits. Cover may be your major advantage in a life-threatening situation where you will need every advantage you can grasp. Don't neglect it.

Positioning and Contact

Where you place yourself in relation to those you deal with on the street has a lot to do with your survival potential as a police officer today. This positioning is directly related to what you already know about cover–you want to have some available for yourself while you, to the extent possible, deprive your adversary of it. That means, for example, that on the street you at least initially keep your patrol car's hood between you and a suspicious person you are stopping. You stay ready to go to better cover until you can see your subject's empty hands clear of his clothing. You keep watching his hands throughout the contact.

Good positioning requires that, at least until you begin to take him into physical custody, you keep any individual that you are in contact with well beyond an arm's reach of your body. You are best protected if the standing subject is a good 5 or 6 feet distant. Move if you have to, or order him to, in order to maintain that buffer zone.

Stand at a side angle to your contact that permits you to keep your holster side turned away from him and thereby out of sight for a quick takeaway. Use your peripheral vision to alert you to any movements that may infringe on your safety buffer zone of personal space. Always remain aware of the position of your weapon in relation to those you are near, even if the individual or individuals appear harmless enough.

Do not try to watch and control multiple suspects by yourself, particularly if they are belligerent, intoxicated, or stoned. Call as much help as you need and try to keep the contact nonconfrontational until you are ready to act. Don't allow subjects to maneuver their way behind you. Don't stand between two subjects either. Consider keeping your back to a solid object, such as a building, wall, or even a vehicle, whenever feasible. And do not turn your back, even briefly, to a suspicious subject you have contacted. At the conclusion of the contact, try to allow him to move away from you, not the other way around. Stand your ground and keep your eyes on him until he has moved well past having a shot at assaulting you.

Do not approach a subject at all if you have reason to believe he is armed. Whether he is walking, standing, or seated in a vehicle or elsewhere, *first* seek cover for yourself before you do anything else. Then, unholster your weapon and issue a verbal challenge or command. Just what you will want to include in that verbal command is the next topic for discussion.

Use of Verbal Commands

A couple of quick and easy rules: 1. Do not say anything that won't have immediate, compelling meaning to the person you are addressing. 2. Mean what you say. The whole business of verbal commands is no more complicated than that.

Talking can be a totally consuming act. It can distract you from other vital things you need to be doing, such as covering a suspect and getting a good sight picture in case you need it. For that reason, you want to do as little talking as possible in getting your job done during a confrontation. Cursing, "macho talk," and detailed threats of impending violence may only aggravate and challenge a drunk or drugged or just plain mean subject. Instead, say what you must in as few words as possible and as directly as you can: "Police! Don't move! Lay the gun down or you will be shot!"

There it is. Simple and to the point. There is a very clear and real threat of sudden death if the subject does not meet your terms immediately. Yet no time or effort is wasted through needless name-calling or goading. The choice is a clear one. The ball is in your opponent's court. Whether he stays healthy or not is up to him.

Speak in a loud, firm voice. Don't beg him to comply with your demands. TELL him to. Tell him in a manner that says you fully expect immediate compliance. *You* are in charge, and you want it to be obvious.

Admittedly, smack in the middle of an adrenaline rush might not be the easiest time for you to get the oral communication duties accomplished without screaming at the target(s) of your attentions. But the advantages to be gained from staying forceful yet in control make the effort you put out well worth it.

Weaponless Defense and Control Tactics

This is another of the absolutely essential skills that only competent, hands-on instruction can teach you. There are, however, some concepts about defense and control that can guide you in your on-the-street application of the physical skills you master at the hands of a good physical tactics instructor. First of all, don't concern yourself with learning half a dozen or more different moves, throws, blocks, and other means to accomplish the exact same thing. Master a technique that you like and feel comfortable with and stick with it. Having a lot of different ways to accomplish the same thing is fine for the skilled hand-to-hand tactics instructor who may practice for hours virtually every day. But if you are anything like the average officer, you *won't* practice anywhere near that often. As a result, get good with what you do know and stay with what works for you. It is far better to have one weapon takeaway move that you have learned and practiced thoroughly than six such maneuvers that you are not really all that familiar with or good at.

Second, know when hand-to-hand tactics are appropriate. You would not, for example, want to go up against a man armed with a knife with only your bare hands if you had other options available. Options such as a sidearm. Options such as a strategic withdrawal until help is at hand.

Third, know your limitations in employing weaponless defense and control tactics. The martial arts are terrific for exercise and keeping in shape. But unless you are the reincarnation of Bruce Lee, you would not want to go up against a roomful of big, strong opponents with only your knowledge of Kung Fu or whatever. Or up against even one offender who is displaying a firearm. A little knowledge can be a dangerous thing. Don't get in over your head.

Fourth, don't perform any defense or attack maneuver half-heartedly. If someone is attacking you, it is your duty to yourself and your peers to do everything legally within your power to stop his unlawful actions. If that means you must injure or temporarily disable someone who is attempting to injure or kill you, so be it. Make certain your well-being is truly at risk. Then do whatever you must to neutralize the threat with an appropriate amount of force.

Be sure your on-the-mat instruction includes a good comealong, but don't get too exotic here. A comealong focused on wrist pressure looks better to a critical public and probably works just as well as some sort of grasp around the neck or thumb poke behind the ear. Remember that in police work it is not only *what* you are doing but what it *looks* like you are doing that can be important. Restrain when you must but restrain with proper restraint, so to speak. Don't get carried away in the emotion of the moment and contribute to the bank account of a hungry police malpractice lawyer. That's a part of officer survival, too.

Finally, know that nothing you may learn in the way of weaponless defense and control tactics requires that you grapple endlessly with a resisting suspect. Even if you are in relatively good shape, your strength and resultant ability to continue struggling will begin to diminish before even a minute of all-out battling has elapsed. You cannot afford to lose this physical contest. If you do and you are incapacitated, your weapons are immediately up for grabs. That means your life may quickly be forfeited as well. There is nothing that says you cannot resort to an impact weapon–such as a baton or nightstick–in a battle you are clearly losing. There is also nothing that says you cannot back off until help is on scene, if you can.

Whenever you are faced with a physical threat, make up your mind on a course of action based on what you know at that point. Act on your decision. Be prepared to explain it if you are asked to do so later. All the while, keep one thing in mind: If you lose the battle, there's a good chance you may not be around to explain your course of action later. Act in your own best interests and act decisively when you do. Fight to WIN. If someone *has* to get hurt, make sure it's the misguided soul who attacked you.

Firearms Use and Retention

First things first: If you don't retain custody of your firearm, it won't be there when you need it. Firearms retention is something else you will need to practice under supervision with a training partner. Nonetheless, there is plenty you can learn about it right here.

Keep your sidearm snapped down snugly in a good quality safety holster until you need to draw it for possible use. Unsnapping it as you approach a call or contact won't make your draw appreciably quicker, but it will increase your chances of losing the weapon with or without "help" from an unfriendly party.

When you do level your weapon at someone, keep it well out of his effective reach. Never put your gun barrel against a subject's body. Not only might you experience an accidental discharge during a struggle, you are much easier for a bad guy to disarm when you are up close. If you have the job of approaching, handcuffing, and searching a known-dangerous subject, holster your sidearm as you approach (from his rear) to within arm's reach. Stay out of your cover officer's line of fire. It is up to your covering partner to have his firearm leveled and at the ready; keep yours secured against loss in a sudden grab or struggle.

As noted previously, stay 5 to 6 feet away from a subject you are contacting. Keep your gun side turned away from him. If your weapon is grabbed from in front of, beside, or behind you, quickly lock your attacker's hand in place atop the weapon and holster with your own gun hand. Use every ounce of strength at your disposal as you are fighting for your life here. Simultaneously, distract his attention from your weapon by attacking–hard– with a blow to the eyes, nose, or face with your other hand. A knee to the groin may work well, too, if you are positioned to deliver one. Disengage from his grasp by pulling away from him as you are attacking. As you pull free of your assailant's grasp, step beyond his arm's reach and draw your weapon. Be ready for a renewed assault.

Whatever else you may be thinking about, do not worry about whether you might hurt your attacker with your countermeasures. Whatever discomfort you may have inflicted on him will be minor and temporary compared to what you likely would feel if he were allowed to gain control of your weapon. You can bet that he is fighting to win. You cannot afford to do less.

If you *do* lose control of your weapon, you are in truly desperate straits. Physical tactics instructors teach disarming techniques, and you should learn them. Those same instructors–the really good ones–also will tell you this: A gun takeaway is a last-ditch, desperate measure. Try it only when you are convinced you are going to be killed if you do not recover your weapon. To pull off a takeaway successfully, you have to be very close to your assailant and able to move extremely fast. You have to go all out. You can have no mercy for your opponent–he's already demonstrated he has none for you.

Practice your instructor's disarming techniques for just what they are: an eleventh-hour attempt at saving your own life. Also practice an even more valuable (and significantly more reliable) lifesaving concept: Keep your weapons well out of an opponent's grasp in the first place. That's the best "disarming" advice of all.

YOUR FIREARMS CAN SAVE YOU

Most everything else you need to know about firearms, their use and abuse, you should learn in the classroom and on the range with an expert firearms instructor. Nonetheless, you can make your task a bit easier *there* by familiarizing yourself *here* with some basics of survival-conscious firearms use and doctrine. Some basics like:

- Be on intimate terms with the laws governing use of deadly force in your jurisdiction. Knowing how to shoot is half the battle; knowing when to shoot is the other.
- Be equally familiar with your agency's policies, procedures, rules, and regulations covering the use of firearms and the application of deadly force. Don't forget to read up on your procedural obligations *following* a firearms discharge incident. It takes a little of the satisfaction out of winning a shooting scrape if your own department "dings" you afterward. Do it by the book.
- Be competent with all the firearms of your job. Regardless of how often your agency *requires* you to qualify with your sidearm, try to do it often. That holds true even if you must go to a private target range at your own expense. Be sure to practice with your police shotgun and/or rifle at least twice a year, too.
- Warning shots are a bad idea from another era of law enforcement. Do not use them. They may or may not stop the flight of a fleeing suspect (they probably *won't*). They most certainly *will* pose a danger to you and innocent others. Do not fire warning shots unless you are ready, willing, and able to put some lawyer's kids through Harvard.
- Shooting from a static, standing position at bull's eye or even silhouette targets is great for weapon familiarization. But try to mix that kind of shooting practice with more usefully realistic training, such as low-light shooting, multiple target confrontations, and shoot–don't shoot scenarios. Your range shooting should approximate as closely as possible the real shooting situations you may encounter on the streets. All of your training, whether involving firearms, barricaded gunman response, handling domestic disputes, or whatever else, should be as realistic and meaningful as safety and resources permit.
- Remember that the majority of on-the-street shooting incidents involve firing at a target that is within 5 feet of the officer involved. Hone your combat shooting skills to be proficient at close-in distances.
- If an offender has his gun out and ready and you still have to draw yours, you are already at a disadvantage. As a result, you might con-

sider having your hand on or near your weapon any time you are approaching an unknown-risk encounter. If things look even more suspicious to you, yet you feel you don't have quite enough to go into high-risk vehicle stop or felony suspect procedures, consider drawing your weapon and holding it with your arm extended downward just behind your leg (don't point it at your foot or anything else you don't want to shoot!). Thusly concealed, it is unlikely to draw protests from, say, an "innocent, law-abiding motorist," yet it is available for quick use if the situation dictates. If you then determine that you won't need your weapon immediately, you can re-holster it without fanfare.

- In most shooting situations, you will stand a better chance of getting the maximum number of rounds on target if you utilize a two-handed grip on your firearm. Although wounds or other special circumstances may on occasion dictate a one-handed grip, normally you will do better with both hands on the weapon.

- At short distances–perhaps 15 feet or less–instinct shooting should give you an excellent chance of hitting your target quickly and accurately. Here you merely point your weapon at the spot where you want your rounds to go, much as you would point your finger. You do not waste time by closing an eye and struggling to get a very precise sight picture of the target before you shoot.

- When you must shoot, shoot at your opponent's center mass. That is, shoot for his mid-chest area. It generally presents the largest target for you and contains organs that, if seriously damaged, should cause immediate incapacitation and the cessation of any further hostile acts. Shift your gunfire to the head or pelvic area only if you are convinced that your subject is wearing body armor and your rounds are having no effect.

- Don't be surprised if one hit from your sidearm fails to drop or even significantly slow your opponent, particularly if he is flying on drugs, such as the highly dangerous PCP. In the 1986 FBI shootout in Miami, one killer managed to pursue a firefight and kill two agents in spite of the fact that he had already received two potentially fatal gunshot wounds. Many firearms instructors now teach the "double tap" shooting technique: place two rounds center mass, quickly observe for effect, then fire two more if the subject does not appear incapacitated. Other instructors simply tell students to keep shooting until your adversary ceases to be a threat, period. Yet other competent teachers advocate two shots to center mass and a third to the head. In any case, keep firing until your armed and threatening adversary ceases to be a threat. Be ready to reload quickly behind cover.

- It's just good, common sense: If you are facing multiple armed and threatening adversaries, direct your gunfire to the most dangerous target first. Then shoot the second most dangerous to you, and so on. Practically endless combinations of scenarios are possible here. If a gun-holder and a knife-wielder are threatening you from an equal distance, fire on the gunman first. If you are faced by a man with a gun 5 feet away and another gunman 20 feet distant, take out the closest threat first. If you are confronted by one man with a pistol and another with a shotgun, direct your fire on the scattergun shooter first.

- Don't pass up the psychological as well as firepower advantages of having a police shotgun in your car. It should be mounted in a locked rack where it will be quickly accessible in an emergency. Ideally it should be equipped with an extended magazine. A 12-gauge is right for your needs. A shotgun, after all, can be menacingly effective when you are apt to face some serious bad guys. An example of the shotgun's psychological effectiveness can be seen in the experience of a South Texas police detective. During the search of a residence for a dangerous felon known to be hiding inside, the officer and suspect found themselves locked in a standoff of sorts across the width of a clothes closet. Each was pointing a gun at the other. After several long seconds, the outlaw gave up his pistol and surrendered meekly. He had been staring into the muzzle of the officer's 12-gauge. Variations of this anecdote are encountered from time to time. The message: Do not give up the psychological value of a shotgun. Keep in mind, however, that a patrol rifle can be at least as handy as a shotgun. Train on and carry one of these if it is an option at your agency.

One more "special consideration" of police firearms use deserves your closest attention. It involves your survival in the courtroom as well as on the streets. Law enforcement agencies have, for the most part over the years, taught their members to "shoot to kill or don't shoot at all." This logic recognized the fact that once gunfire was directed at a living target, it was virtually impossible to ensure that the targeted individual could only be "winged" in a nonfatal area. It also recognized the fact that wounded suspects could and sometimes did proceed to kill a police officer *after* being wounded.

But "shoot to kill" upsets some of the civil libertarians and lawyers who seek to make a living from police actions, improper and proper alike. As a result, some agencies as a matter of policy are now directing their officers to "shoot for center mass" or "shoot to stop the threat" instead of "shoot to kill," although the results admittedly will be about the same. If you are questioned further on the witness stand about what you were attempting to bring about by shooting at an armed adversary's chest area, your answers are equally honest and direct: "I was shooting to stop his attack." That's all. If the suspect's death was the consequence of the shooting, it was he, after all, who had brought the fatal gunfire upon himself via his own unlawful, threatening actions.

Granted, words are what you are dealing with here. But words are the stuff of which litigation is fashioned. It just might be worth your while to select yours with care when you are preparing your written accounts of a shooting incident or testifying about one in a court of law.

PRISONER CONTROL IS VITAL

Handcuffing Techniques

Handcuffs are at best a temporary and partial restraint. Use them but don't bet your life on them. They can be defeated too easily. They do nothing at all to restrain your prisoner's biting and kicking equipment.

When in doubt about whether to handcuff an arrestee, take the safest route for you: handcuff. It is hard to be wrong for handcuffing a legally arrested subject, regardless of age, sex, charges, or any other factor. It is easy to be wrong if you do not snap on the cuffs and something goes awry. Use your handcuffs–it's safer all around.

The particulars for properly applying handcuffs under a variety of circumstances are covered elsewhere in this book. Please read them very carefully. Then do it again. It's that important to your safety.

Body Search Techniques

What goes for handcuffing goes for searching, too. If in any doubt at all, go ahead and search a subject for anything he might hurt you with, regardless as to whether he is in custody. It's the only survival-smart way to operate.

Naturally, there is case law as well as, in most cases, departmental policy regarding who you can and cannot search and *when* you can and cannot do it. Your *organizational* survival requires that you be aware of what you can and cannot do. But your *street* survival mandates that you do *at minimum* a careful pat-down search of any person with whom you are in contact in a potentially high-risk situation. That includes drunks you are taking to the Detox Center, juvenile runaways you are putting in your car, and three-piece suit types you are hauling in to dispose of multiple traffic ticket warrants.

By searching and re-searching the people you arrest, you help ensure that you will stay safe from that surprise weapon–the hidden knife, the belt buckle derringer pistol, the concealed razor blade. Check out the rest of what this text has to say about searches and apply it to your own, on-the-street contacts.

Use of Impact Weapons

"The only reason I carry a nightstick," said one academy baton instructor, "is because I can't get a telephone pole out of the ground." The sentiment is well understood by the veteran street cop.

When you are out there "among 'em," it is nice to have something besides your hands to deal with that extra big, extra nasty, two-legged monster. Whether it is the traditional straight stick or a side-handle variety, the police baton or nightstick is most likely what you are looking for when you go up against that unarmed but dangerously assaultive giant. But there is more to it than grabbing your stick and whacking away at any and every attacker. A lot more.

First of all, get in the habit of carrying your baton with you whenever you are on patrol duty, whether you are on vehicular or foot patrol. If you patrol in a car, be sure you have your stick in your baton ring every time you exit your vehicle. Carry it with you as a deeply ingrained habit, even if you are just alighting for a cup of coffee or a bathroom break. The punks you may encounter probably won't care a whole lot that you consider yourself in an "out-of-service" mode. A routine, report-taking call could turn suddenly violent, too. Be prepared for the worst. You (hopefully) wouldn't think of leaving your sidearm in the car. Do not abandon your impact weapon, either.

If you walk a beat, you definitely will need your stick at your side. You won't want to twirl it or bounce it off the pavement as your 1930s predecessor may have done. But you will want to have it quickly accessible in case it's needed in a hurry. A situation requiring you to at least draw and make ready with your impact weapon can arise without warning.

Your stick is useful for plenty besides poking, jabbing, or striking. It has a lot of other uses, too. You can use it to prop a door open during a structure search. You can break a window with it to gain access to a building or vehicle. You can fend off a vicious dog with it. You can push a door open with your stick when you had just as soon not stand in front yourself. You can do a lot of things with a baton to make your job a little easier—and safer.

A good defensive tactics instructor can show you how to use your impact weapon to gain compliance from an attacking individual by jabbing a pressure point or directing a controlled blow to a spot where nerves run atop bone near the skin's surface. (Parts of the arm or leg are susceptible to such maneuvers.) Once you know what to do, it is up to you to practice regularly, preferably with a partner.

Perhaps because of what they have seen on television and in the movies about modern-day cops and robbers, Americans seem to accept batons or nightsticks as police weapons with a legitimate purpose. They tend not to look as kindly upon the saps, beavertails, blackjacks, and slappers still carried by some police officers in some places. In all honesty, these striking instruments most likely belong to a law enforcement era that has passed. They have no place in your assemblage of "tools of the trade" for modern police work. They can lead to bloody scalps and hefty emergency room bills for your employer. Just as bad from your point of view, they can sometimes seriously *irritate* the recipients of their blows.

It will be to your advantage to stick to the carrying and application of a baton or nightstick, short or long, as your impact weapon of choice. When you have been trained well in its use, you can defend yourself quite adequately on the street as well as in the courtroom, if need be, later on.

PUT SOME LIGHT ON THE SUBJECT

Use of Lighting

Light—the stuff that issues from the end of your flashlight or emanates from that big yellow globe in the sky—can be your good ally or your deadly enemy in a hostile confrontation. What it turns out to be for you depends largely on how you learn to use it to your advantage.

The headlights, spotlights, and, if you have them, takedown lights of your patrol car can make the difference between a safe vehicle or pedestrian stop at night and one that goes bloodily awry. Aim your spotlight at your subject's rear view mirror if you are making a vehicle contact. This effort alone will make it more difficult for him to see what you are up to. Use all the candlepower at your disposal during a nighttime stop. If it turns out that you do not want or need some of it, you can always shut it off as the contact continues. When you combine the proper use of your vehicle's lights with good tactics—such as a careful approach to the subject's car—you become a potent force to be reckoned with.

Your flashlight is another valuable component of your artificial light inventory. Surely your life is worth a hundred bucks or so to you. If it is, invest in one of the rechargeable, halogen bulb lights that puts out a 20,000 or 30,000 candlepower beam of light. The advantages this light presents over the more traditional flashlights are considerable.

Carry your flashlight on patrol with you even when you are assigned to a 100 percent daylight shift. You never know when your duties may include the search of a darkened structure or crawl space. Some officers carry a second, smaller backup light on their equipment belt. It's a good idea.

Practice holding your light and your sidearm at the same time, as for a search of a burglarized building. You should hold the light in your non-gun hand extended well away from your body. This will deny an opponent the center mass target he would have if you held your light right in front of your torso. Be sure you stay to the rear of your light. Otherwise, the reflected light will partially illuminate you. You're going to get some of that reflected illumination anyway from walls and the like, so make good use of the best available cover as you advance and search.

Because light—artificial or otherwise—can be your enemy as well as your friend, you must avoid placing yourself in any position where you will be illuminated while your adversary remains concealed by darkness. There are a number of things you can do to avoid bathing yourself in the spotlight of attention, so to speak. You will be able to think of some others, but here are just a few light-survival tips for starters:

- At night, do not park your patrol unit under a streetlight or other bright light source when arriving at a high-risk or unknown-risk assignment.
- Stay out of the light when approaching on foot to a nighttime assignment of known or possible high risk.
- If possible, loosen the light bulbs from nearby, outside light fixtures such as porch lights when you are deploying outside the address of a nighttime disturbance or in-progress crime call. Restore the lights when you are done.
- Don't pause in a doorway or window of a structure you are entering to search for an offender. Move quickly away from a position that backlights you with outside light and makes you an ideal target for anyone inside. Once you are inside, be conscious of standing in front of any light source that sets you up as a target.
- If you and your assisting officers have a large building to search at night, consider turning on the ceiling lights rather than searching the whole place by flashlight. At least now everyone is on even terms in the light department, and you will have better illumination of your target if you have to direct gunfire in his direction. You also will be less likely to be injured accidentally by falls or unseen obstacles. In addition, your peers will be less likely to shoot you in a case of mistaken identity in the dark.
- Whether you are inside or outdoors at night, you can use the beam of your heavy-duty flashlight to temporarily blind or dazzle a potential opponent at close quarters. You can even make it appear accidental as you pass your 20,000 candlepower beam across a subject's eyes as you

approach his position, seated in his car or elsewhere. You always can apologize for the "inconvenience" afterward. The split-second distraction your light provides you may be just enough time for you to determine your party's intent and take protective action if you read him as dangerous.

- Remember, nothing says you have to leave your flashlight "on" the whole time you are searching a building's interior or tracking a fleeing suspect through back alleys or woods. By using the thumb button for short bursts of light, you are less likely to telegraph your exact location to a potential attacker. Move before you activate your light again.

SEARCH IN SAFETY

Because you generally have no way of knowing exactly what awaits you, because many advantages rest with the "defender" of the premises, a building or structure search must be ranked as a high-risk assignment. Fortunately, however, there is much you can do to reduce the danger posed by an otherwise risky undertaking.

Building searches, whether related to an in-progress burglary or some other crime, are central enough to your crime fighting duties to merit a whole chapter of discussion elsewhere in this book. Read carefully for a detailed accounting of the techniques and procedures required for a safe and successful structure-clearing operation.

Approach to a Downed Subject

Don't do it. Not right away, anyhow. Take your time. Go slow and be careful.

The preceding can be taken as sound advice for approaching a man down on the street in an "unknown trouble" call or one sprawled at the end of a dimly lit hallway following a shootout with police. Take it easy. Keep your eyes open. Wait to see what develops and don't rush in.

A subject who is discovered down from unknown causes should be considered as at least *potentially* dangerous until you have convinced yourself otherwise. About the only reliable way to convince yourself of this is to approach carefully and then control his hands while you conduct a pat-down of his clothing and person. He may be an intoxicated or stoned individual who will go for a weapon or come up fighting with his imagined tormentor as soon as you touch him, so be careful and get him into cuffs right away if it looks like a custody situation. Have a backup with you throughout the contact if at all possible. Press firemen or paramedics into service as some added muscle if they are the only help you have available. Gawking bystanders can be directed to help, too. (If nothing else, ordering them to assist you may quickly clear the area of an unwanted crowd!)

Look for indications of what caused the individual to be down in the first place. The presence of booze containers, medical alert bracelets, medical wallet cards, and so on can tip you off about what you may be handling. Stay alert during this preliminary investigation. He may exit his semi-comatose state by attacking you. When in doubt, *handcuff*, even if it does irritate a nonappreciative crowd or an idealistic medical first responder. After all, it's *your* tail that's at risk here. You can remove the restraints if you determine that the individual is not a threat.

If you are faced with a downed subject who apparently has been hit in a gun battle with you or someone else, assume until proven wrong that no matter how bad off he looks he is still capable of functioning to the extent of being able to shoot again—very possibly at you. Stay behind cover. Verbally order the subject to move away from any visible weapon. Wait for a response. Don't be lulled into leaving cover by his apparent nonresponsiveness. Wait and see what happens next. More than *his* life may be at stake here. *Yours* may be, too.

Don't engage in a shouted dialogue with an apparently wounded, downed subject. He may be attempting to distract you. It's hard, after all, for you to talk and shoot accurately at the same time. Stay behind cover and order him to move toward your position, even if he has to drag himself to get there.

If your wounded subject is totally unresponsive after several minutes of having instructions shouted to him, it will become necessary for the officer closest to the individual to advance with weapon drawn and pointed toward the downed individual. This officer uses available cover and is likewise covered by his backup(s) as he makes a slow and observant approach. He stops his advance and seeks cover if at any point the downed individual shows any activity toward presenting or obtaining a weapon. More verbal attempts can be made at getting the downed subject to present empty, visible hands for inspection. He is instructed to look away from the direction that the control officer will be approaching from.

When you do decide that the time is right to move to close quarters with a downed offender, be sure you are out of your backup's line of fire. Also be sure that he is, in fact, still covering you before you move in. Holster your own sidearm before you get within arms' reach of your downed party and take immediate custody of any weapons you can see. Stick them in your gunbelt after ascertaining that they are not cocked or otherwise ready to discharge. Render them safe, if need be.

Place your downed subject into handcuffs even if he seems to be dead or nearly so. This can prevent nasty surprises if he turns out to be not as seriously wounded as was thought. Then complete a detailed search of his clothing and person for additional weapons. Assuming the area has been cleared of other potential offenders, medical personnel can now be summoned to your side to check your subject out. But remain alert and keep the restraints in place. A "miraculous" healing could still take place. It would not be the first time that dangerous people have feigned serious injury in order to launch an escape assault at an opportune moment.

COVER AND COMMUNICATE

Role of the Cover Officer

Cover. It's what you provide for your fellow officer and he provides for you when the chips are down and the danger factor is up. Some officers do a better job of providing cover than others. Given the choice, these are the people you want to work with whenever you can have them along. At the same time, you want to be known among your peers as someone who can be counted on to cover a buddy like a blanket and respond immediately and effectively to any sudden threat. That, too, is what cover means.

Just as some officers cover better than others, some methods of providing cover are superior to others. Perhaps one of the best cover concepts presently in use in American law enforcement has been developed over a period of years by such agencies as the San Diego, California Police Department. It is called "contact and cover," and it applies to all law enforcement contact activities involving two or more officers and one or more unsecured subjects. The concept is applied, when necessary, to field interview contacts, disturbance calls, arrest situations, criminal investigations with suspects present, and traffic contacts.

Agencies utilizing the concept make sure that personnel understand the difference between the "contact officer" and the "cover officer." To apply the commonsense concept to your own activities you will need to understand these two, key definitions, too.

The Contact Officer usually will be the officer who initiated the contact or stop. He or she is responsible for conducting the primary business of the contact. This officer records needed suspect or incident information, performs pat downs and searches, arrests suspects, recovers evidence, writes summonses, and handles radio traffic. In addition, the contact officer ensures the thoroughness of the investigation and guarantees the integrity of the chain of custody of any evidence seized.

The Cover Officer is responsible for surveillance of all suspects to eliminate the possibility of attack, escape, or destruction of evidence. The cover officer frees up the contact officer to perform a more thorough investigation or search. The job of the cover officer, simply put, is to protect the contact officer by remaining ever alert and watchful to all potential sources of danger. The cover officer serves as a lifeguard.

Using San Diego's version of the contact and cover plan, as the contact officer it is your job to brief your cover officer on what is going on just as soon as he arrives. Tell him what you plan to do and what you already know about the subject(s) you have contacted: prior record, weapons seen, reason for the contact, and so on. You also must be sure that your cover officer understands his or her role as cover.

On the other hand, if you are summoned as the cover officer you also have a briefing responsibility. You must tell the contact officer anything you know about the subject, incident, or location he is dealing with, as well as any observations you have made since arriving on the scene. Confirm your role as cover officer.

As cover, you must not be distracted by what your contact officer is doing. You do not recover evidence, engage in conversation with subjects or officers, or handcuff or search prisoners. You are there to watch and protect, and that's it. You'll only want to speak up if you see a threat to your colleague: a weapon, a hostile move, a hidden offender, or whatever. Then you must shout a warning and move to neutralize the threat. Also speak up if you see that more officers are needed to handle contact or cover duties properly. If a number of subjects, particularly hostile ones, are present, more than one officer will need to be involved in both contact and cover duties. Do not work short. It's too dangerous.

If you are the cover officer in any given incident, you must take a position that provides you with your own covering protection, as well as an unobstructed view of the contact officer, the subject(s), and the surrounding area from which trouble could appear. You don't have to stand there with your hand on your gun and drill hostile stares at the subject you are watching. Just stay businesslike, quiet, and alert. If the subject asks what you are doing, avoid discussions. Just say, "I'm here to protect this officer." That's it. End of conversation. From then on just concentrate on your cover duties.

As cover officer, you need to keep your line of fire to the subject(s) open. The contact officer should know this and stay out of your way. Alert him orally if he should block your line of fire or view. If a struggle develops between the contact officer and a subject, stay out of the fight and continue covering any other subjects present, as well as any vehicle that has not yet been cleared of unseen offenders. You enter the fray only if called to do so by the contact officer or if you see he is about to be overcome.

On a vehicle contact, your best position as cover officer probably will be behind the driver's door of your patrol car parked to the left of the contact officer's vehicle, assuming you and he are working one-officer cars. If traffic or other factors do not permit this positioning of vehicles, park behind the contact officer's car and move up behind his driver's or passenger's door to do your covering. Don't light up your partner from behind, however.

If you are working a two-officer car, the two of you should decide in advance who will be contact and who will furnish cover on your stops and contacts requiring this approach. Most of the time the driver will be the contact officer and the passenger will take the cover role, but your own arrangement is entirely up to you and your partner. Spell it out ahead of time.

In a contact occurring away from the police vehicle, the contact officer still takes the lead and handles the subjects involved while the cover officer maintains vigilance from a point slightly to the rear and out of arms' reach to the side of the subject's position. (Be careful not to set up a crossfire situation!) The cover officer's duties remain the same as in a vehicle contact: maintain a surveillance of the subject(s) and area and intervene physically only if requested to do so by the contact officer or if the contact officer is clearly endangered.

Handcuffing and searching a suspect or suspects, potentially the most hazardous part of a street encounter, is carried out by the contact officer under the watchful eyes of the covering partner. If you are the contact officer and get into more resistance than you can handle alone, sing out loud and clear for your cover to assist you. It has just become his task to defend the both of you. If you lose your weapon in a struggle, dive for cover as you yell a warning that you have been disarmed. Now it will be your covering partner's job to defend you both with gunfire, if necessary, so don't make his job any harder by getting in the way.

If you and your agency implement a version of the contact and cover concept, it does not mean that every time you call for aid the contact and cover plan is automatically put into action. You can still merely ask for an assist unit to help you write tickets or field interview cards or whatever. The key is for you to specify clearly what it is you require: cover or assistance. Make sure that everyone you work with understands the difference in terms and what each calls for on everyone's part.

Remember that an encounter that begins as an "assist only" incident can turn into a contact and cover assignment within seconds as the people or situation change. It can change in the other direction, too, as things calm down and deescalate. It is vital for the contact officer to keep his cover advised of any change in circumstances. Whichever role you fill in the contact and cover plan, stay alert and stay in close touch with the other police participants on scene.

Communication on Scene

Whether you are involved in a contact and cover situation or another of the unique activities police officers find themselves caught up in, it is vital that each officer in the lineup know his role in the game, so to speak. It's the best way for everyone to stay safe and effective when things heat up.

You can begin your planning with your fellow officers even before you arrive at the crime or incident scene. That's what that expensive two-way radio is for. You can (and must) use it to plan deployment, position personnel and vehicles, and exchange information about the people and incident you are dealing with. You also can use your radio to pass along warnings about safety hazards known or suspected to be present, particularly the two-legged kind.

Your communicative efforts must continue on-scene. The more risky the call, the more vital it is that each and every officer involved knows where he is supposed to go, what he's supposed to do, and how he's expected to get it done. Limitations on what he is permitted to do need to be made known, too. Limitations like: You will not enter the building alone. Limitations like: You will fire only if the suspect threatens your life or someone else's. On the crisis scene, fast and effective communication can prevent errors that can be very costly in both human and material resources. You can ill afford *not* to stay in close touch with your peers and supervisory personnel.

Your communications with your fellow officers must be secure enough to be used in the presence of offenders. One way this can be accomplished is through the use of spoken codes that all members of the agency know the meaning of. That way, when you tell your backup that you are going to "37" the drunk you are in contact with, the assist officer and not the drunk knows you are planning a custody move. Your partner can get ready to assist you without either of you giving away the plan to the prospective arrestee. Whatever works for you is fine, but you definitely should have some coded means of exchanging information with a peer without other people present knowing what is happening or about to happen. By keeping your suspect largely in the dark, you help bolster your own safety margin.

Hand signals also can aid your communicative efforts on the street. But again it is necessary that everyone you work with be able to recognize the signals, give them, and respond properly to the message contained without telegraphing information to the subject or offender.

If your agency does not already have a system of hand signals for on the street communication among officers, you and your peers should get to work on devising one. It does not need to be elaborate. Hand codes might include the following signals and meanings, just for starters:

- Four fingers of the hand held up and spread apart in a "Code 4" configuration means "Everything is under control; no more help needed; you can leave the scene."
- Closed fist held straight up over your head means "Call more help, quick; subject or situation looks very dangerous; watch yourself and provide cover for me."
- Arm held straight out from the shoulder with fist closed and thumb pointed down means, "I need cover; approach carefully."
- Arm held straight out from the shoulder with fist closed and thumb pointed up means, "I need an assist here; come to me and I will advise further."

You can, of course, add any number of other hand signals and meanings or simply modify these samples to suit your own purposes. What's important is that you are still able to communicate freely and securely with your peers, even in the presence of unfriendly ears. Whatever signal system you devise to serve you, use it consistently and conscientiously, and it will help you stay informed and safe on high-risk patrol.

By reading, reviewing, and rereading this chapter, you will have made a good start toward mastering the skills and tactics required to survive. Of course, there is more to it than that. There are a lot of other chapters in this volume that will spell out for you the tricks and techniques you will need to overcome any number of specific, high-risk threats. In addition, there are vital physical skills and abilities to be learned that you can only accomplish via hands-on practice with competent teachers.

It does not end there, either. There are a lot more sources of field survival knowledge out there. There are good texts now available and more to come. There are plenty of professional journals and magazines with pertinent officer safety tips. And there is always that vast store of experience–your own and that of your fellow officers–to teach you, too.

Be critical of what you see, hear, and read. Not every tactic and technique you become aware of will be a good one. The fact that it worked once for someone else doesn't necessarily mean it will work for you in the here and now. Then again, it might. Consider it in the light of your own common sense and good field survival judgment. Modify it where you will, dump it where you must. But do not stop looking, listening, and learning–ever. Stay current on what is going on in your field and on your beat. As crooks, their tactics and their weapons change, so will your responses to the dangers they pose. You cannot afford to fall behind where a lack of knowledge and ability can translate into a lack of safety for you.

As you advance through a career in law enforcement, you will pick up many additional safety tactics and techniques to add to your survival toolbox. Many of these you will develop and refine based on your continuing training, life experience, and on-the-job lessons, some of which may have been learned the hard way. As your experience grows, you also will find ways to improve or at least personalize for your own needs some of the safety guidelines discussed in this book. That's fine, too.

A major source of officer survival knowledge you should not overlook is the combined street smarts and experience-based wisdom of your peers and supervisors. You should never pass up the opportunity to discuss safety in general or the handling of a specific assignment or call with your fellow professionals.

Because life experiences and on-the-job exposures will vary widely even on the same department, these people almost certainly will have had some adventures you have not—at least not yet. Carefully evaluate what they have to say. Realize that they may have made some serious survival errors on the way to a "successful" conclusion. Also realize that you may hear of "tricks" that are ill advised and are not ones that you would want to try. Then, decide for yourself which practices you may want to file away for possible application later. Talking with and listening to cautious, street-wise veteran officers may bring you the following tips.

Take your car keys with you anytime you are going to be out of sight of your police vehicle during a stop or contact. This is especially true if you are about to engage in a foot pursuit. You don't want to join the ranks of officers who have ended up chasing their own car—on foot. Save yourself some major embarrassment. Take an extra second or two and collect your keys.

Always carry an extra, hidden handcuff key on your person. It'll come in handy if you lose or break your primary key. More important, it may offer you an added chance at survival should you ever be taken hostage and secured with your own cuffs. Consider hiding places than you can access fairly easily, such as taped under your gun belt or some other item of leather gear. A deep, rear pants pocket might work, too. Do a little experimenting to see what works well for you.

When you are on duty, always know where you are, at least as best you can. If you need help in a hurry, your dispatcher will need to know instantly where to send it. "The corner of fire hydrant and big tree" won't help much.

Portable radios give officers a great deal of freedom and help free them from the tyranny of the in-car radio. But wandering too widely without letting your dispatcher know what you are up to can spell disaster. Don't exit your car to make a contact without letting someone know where you are and what you are doing.

Reduce the size of a target you present to a potential shooter. Do not leave something exposed that you want to keep. The idea is to make yourself really small insofar as your opponent's sight picture is concerned.

Shout "Police!" or whatever is appropriate for your agency anytime you confront someone and give a verbal command. It both asserts control and clearly identifies who you are to both the subject of your attention and any nearby witnesses. If the offender chooses to resist or attack you, it will be much harder for him to claim later that he thought he was being set upon by thugs or space aliens. The advice is sound even if you are in uniform and driving a marked police vehicle.

Do coordinate your movements with your partner or backup, but don't stay so close together that a single shot could take you both out. Maintain several feet of space between you.

Whether you are working on foot or in a vehicle, try to avoid developing easy-to-predict patterns in your patrol behavior. Don't eat at the same spot or visit the same convenience store at exactly the same time each shift. Don't do your building checks in exactly the same order or approach these structures from the same direction each time. Don't sit in the very same location to work traffic or do reports every watch. The more of a routine you develop, the easier you make it for an attacker to ambush you. Vary your schedule as much as you realistically can.

Keep your gun hand empty during a contact. You don't want to be slowed in getting your handgun by having to first stick that expensive flashlight or radio someplace when it's time to draw your weapon. At least put nothing in your gun hand that you are not willing to drop instantly if the need arises.

If you have a car partner, set an unbreakable rule for the two of you. Both of you will be out of the car and involved in a contact or cover or assist role on each assignment. No one should be lounging in the vehicle until it's his or her "turn" to write a ticket or catch a report. The value of a backup is far too great to be thrown away through laziness.

Do not allow someone you are checking out to monitor your radio or laptop computer messages. If he is not totally secured, he does not have to know your radio codes to realize that "your subject is Code 6" is probably not good news for him. That little piece of information just might cause him to flee—or attack.

Keep your radio's volume turned down and keep him far enough distant that he cannot monitor spoken messages. Consider using a radio earpiece. Even when he *is* secured, he doesn't need to be given a crash course in your radio or computer operations. Keep your communications secure and keep him guessing.

While your patrol car is in motion, do not allow another vehicle to linger in the blind spot that exists just over your left shoulder. Alter your speed, if necessary, to remove that uncertainty. You do not want the other driver's actions, unintentional or otherwise, to endanger you. If you are curious about what he is doing, pull out of traffic and look him over as he passes.

In other words, stay sharp in all ways. Keep an open mind. Remain attentive to what is happening in your jurisdiction and your profession. A positive, winning attitude that arises from such preparation will contribute mightily to your survival.

A RISK REDUCTION CHECKLIST FOR YOUR PERSONAL PREPARATIONS

1. Put together your complete survival package of tactics and techniques.
2. Learn the basic survival skills.
3. Realize the importance of good cover.
4. Realize your approach, positioning, and how you make contact are critical.
5. Know how to use verbal commands properly.
6. Practice your weaponless defense and control tactics.
7. Remember that firearms use and retention are both important to your survival.
8. Learn proper handcuffing and searching techniques.
9. Train well in the use of impact weapons.
10. Gain an appreciation of how lighting can be used for and against you.
11. Become skilled in building search techniques.
13. Learn how to approach a downed subject in safety.
14. Learn and practice the concept of contact and cover.
15. Strive to perfect your on-scene communication with your peers.
16. Pay attention and learn from the sound officer survival tips you can pick up from your peers.

A county sheriff, age 47, was killed doing a prisoner transport at about 3:45 p.m. The sheriff, who had 26 years of law enforcement experience, was transporting an 18-year-old murderer to allow the subject to show him the location of the murder weapon. While en route, the suspect, who had been handcuffed in front of his body, got control of the sheriff's .357-magnum handgun and shot him in the neck and chest. The prisoner had been in the back seat. It is believed possible that the officer's weapon was accessible under the front seat armrest.

* * * * *

At approximately 9:45 p.m., a patrolman, age 24, and the chief, age 40, of a small town police department were shot fatally. The patrolman

stopped a juvenile male on a stolen motorcycle and radioed for assistance. A struggle ensued upon the chief's arrival, and the juvenile obtained the chief's .357-magnum handgun and shot both officers. The patrolman died instantly from a chest wound; the chief died from a wound to the abdomen after arriving at a hospital. The chief had two years of law enforcement service, the patrolman had four months.

* * * * *

A patrol officer stopped a vehicle for a traffic violation and learned that the operator was a 16-year-old unlicensed driver. The officer took the juvenile to a nearby apartment complex where he said he lived. Upon arriving there, the officer learned that the youth had lied and attempted to take him into physical custody. A struggle began, and the 16-year-old took the officer's .40-caliber handgun and shot him in the head with it. The officer died from the wound.

Chapter 3

VEHICLE STOPS AND CONTACTS

Traffic stops. Suspicious vehicle contacts. Parking violation enforcement. Drunk driver interdiction. Radar surveillance. It has been said that motor vehicles and their occupants are the bread and butter of the uniformed officer's existence. If that's true, the bread and butter can and does turn painfully poisonous for far too many law enforcement officers far too often.

As virtually every police rookie does or should know, vehicle-related contacts can be hazardous in the extreme for the unwary officer. Nonetheless, there is nothing about police-vehicle interactions that requires them to be necessarily, unavoidably dangerous. With as many officer-motorist contacts as occur every day, it is to be expected that a few will go sour. That's to be expected. Fortunately, however, there are a number of positive steps that the survival conscious officer–you–can do to protect yourself. Some of those steps require you to memorize a few very specific safety details. Others require only that you call upon your own good, common sense when faced with a vehicle-related problem. For simplicity's sake, all of these safety steps can be divided into two categories of vehicle stops and contacts:

Unknown-risk stops and contacts
High-risk stops and contacts

The former used to be referred to as "routine stops," but they all involve, of course, unknown risks. Today's police field survival instructors have granted recognition to the reality that not any stop–routine or otherwise–is ever really routine. No street-savvy cop would ever treat it so. The change in terms also recognizes that known-dangerous vehicle contacts may not always involve felons or felony crimes. In many jurisdictions, a drunk in possession of a firearm has not committed a felony offense. But few officers would doubt that encountering him in a vehicle would constitute a high-risk vehicle contact. Thus, the changes in terminology should prove helpful in reminding officers that all vehicle contacts are at least *potentially* hazardous. They require the utmost attention to heads-up officer safety measures. Those measures will be looked at separately here.

UNKNOWN-RISK STOPS AND CONTACTS

There is no such thing as a "routine" traffic stop or vehicle contact. As a result, the only thing routine in the way you respond to these assignments is the officer safety routine you follow in every instance. The fact is that every vehicle contact you make contains within it the potential for sudden injury or death. To put it another way: Bad things can happen to you every time you approach a vehicle of just about any sort under virtually any circumstances.

What can you do to reduce the danger to you under these risky circumstances? You *could* resolve never to stop or approach another motor vehicle as long as you live. But being the curious, aggressive professional you are, you are not likely to do that. That leaves you just one, real option: conducting every vehicle contact you make as if your life depended on it because it very well could. Utilizing that kind of caution in your vehicle contacts will require you to commit to memory and convert to everyday use some basic officer survival concepts and plain old street sense practices. You can begin right here.

Now that you have decided to stop that car with the missing taillight or check out that parked truck with a suspicious occupant, you have an important question to ask of yourself. Namely: What don't I know about this situation that could hurt me? Even while asking the question, you must start looking for any signs that may tell you things are not quite what they appear. Signs that you may be in more danger than you initially thought. Signs like:

- Furtive movements from any of the vehicle's occupants.
- License plates that do not belong on the car.
- Occupants suddenly appearing or dropping from sight in the vehicle.
- Obvious and unexplained nervousness on the part of the driver or occupant.
- Attempts by occupants to flee or elude you.
- A trunk lid not quite secure.
- Weapons, contraband, or possible stolen property in view.

There could, of course, be plenty of other indications to you that things are not right. Your own experience and good, common sense will help you identify them. The point to keep in mind is that you never know for certain exactly what you are getting into at the outset. That's why everything you do from here on in must be carefully thought out and even more carefully done.

Take your time in setting up your unknown-risk vehicle contact. If you can, run the vehicle's plates before you make contact. That act alone could change your unknown-risk stop into a high-risk one with a corresponding change in tactics on your part. Try to pick a spot that will be to your advantage in effecting the stop. You won't always find exactly what you are looking for, but a straight stretch of wide roadway with a parking lot or shoulder to the right would be ideal for your purposes in most cases. You're also looking for a location with minimal vehicular as well as pedestrian traffic if you can find such a spot handily. The absence of a hostile neighborhood such as found around some bar parking lots would be helpful, too. At night, seek an area with good lighting when you can dictate the location of the contact.

Do not make a vehicle contact without first notifying your dispatcher of what you are doing, the license plate or description of the vehicle you are stopping, and where you expect to be when the stop is made. It is not too early to ask for a backup car right now if you do not like what you see: numerous occupants, visibly intoxicated or agitated people, the presence of a second, related vehicle, and so on. Get back on the radio right away if the situation starts to change on you at any time throughout the contact. You can't be too careful. (Note: it is a good idea to summon a backup anytime the vehicle you are stopping pulls into a residential drive. Not only will some drivers become extra aggressive now that they feel they are "home free," a lot of nasty surprises can come out of that residence, too.)

Ideally, your dispatcher should check up on you if you are not heard from within the first three or four minutes after making the stop. If the communications center gets no response, a backup car is automatically sent. Naturally, with such a safety-check system, it is up to you to keep your dispatcher advised of your status. If your agency does not already have a procedure like this in place, you should consider starting the necessary wheels in motion to establish one agency-wide. It is that important to good officer survival practices.

Now that you have selected an intended spot for the stop, looked things over, and radioed your intentions, you can begin the contact itself. Activate all your emergency lights. At night, activate your takedown lights (if you have them) and fix your spotlight on the vehicle's interior. Aim your spot for the inside, rear-view mirror of the vehicle. To draw the driver's attention, first try tapping your horn. If that doesn't work, nudge the siren a bit. Keep trying with more of the siren if the first sound doesn't cause him to yield, but be aware that you might be about to encounter a complication. Perhaps it is just a driver whose mind and ears are elsewhere. Or maybe a pursuit is about to start. Stay alert. Be ready for anything.

When your target does start to pull over, remain alert for surprises. Drivers have been known to slam their vehicle into a panic stop at the sound of a siren behind them, so do not get too close. When your subject does stop, halt your own vehicle with its front bumper about 15 to 20 feet from the rear of the stopped vehicle. Offset the left side of your car about three feet to the left of the left side of the subject's car to give yourself a safety zone within which to approach the subject's car while enjoying at least some protection from traffic. Never walk or stand between the two cars, however. That's a good way to earn a pair of shattered legs–or worse–if your squad car is rear-ended.

Do not be in too big a hurry to get to the driver you want to talk with. Keep looking around. It is not too late to call a backup if things don't seem right to you. Look quickly to your rear as you exit your own car. Then approach on foot, walking as closely to the left sides of the vehicles as possible. Keep watching all occupants of the subject vehicle. Check the trunk lid for any indication that it is not secure and may be concealing someone. Stop just before passing the subject's back seat and check it for concealed occupants. Retreat and draw your sidearm if you see something threatening, like a hiding, possibly armed individual. Seek cover at your own car and call for help. Keep your weapon at the ready and order your potential opponents to freeze as they are. Stay behind cover whether you get a response or not. Don't get rash and take on multiple adversaries alone when you have a choice. If they decide to speed away, at least you are still alive to direct their pursuit and capture.

If you are the officer riding shotgun in a two-person patrol car, your responsibility is to cover your partner as he advances on the stopped vehicle. Unless he has directed you elsewhere for cause, you cover your partner most effectively by remaining behind the passenger door of the police vehicle with all your attention focused on the occupants of the target vehicle and the immediate, surrounding area. It will be your job to shout a quick warning if you spot a weapon or an aggressive move or action. It also will be up to you to furnish accurate, suppressing gunfire if your partner is attacked with deadly weapons.

As you, the driver, approach the vehicle you wish to contact, keep your gun hand free of a flashlight, clipboard, or anything else. You want to be able to draw your weapon quickly if the need arises. Cease your approach again just before you reach the opening edge of the driver's door. By your positioning, you will force the driver to turn slightly to look over his left shoulder while he converses with you. That way it will be harder for him to assault or shoot at you without telegraphing his intentions somewhat and giving you time to respond with some moves of your own.

Keep looking for anything amiss–like a damaged ignition, no key, an empty holster, or shells lying on the seat or console. Stay sharp; you are in a danger zone of sorts when you are this close to your subject(s). Ask for his keys if you are extra suspicious or think he may try to flee in the vehicle, but don't reach in to get them (sticking your arm in his car is a good way to get dragged alongside a speeding vehicle).

Leave the driver in his car for now. While seated and at least somewhat contained, he has much less opportunity of assaulting you and doing real harm. Remain conscious of your position in relation to his car door and don't get beside it so that you could be knocked down or into traffic if he suddenly and forcefully opened it. Address your subject in a polite, firm, matter-of-fact manner. Never berate or belittle him. That is just asking for trouble that you don't need.

Throughout the contact, keep your eyes working for sudden traffic threats or other subjects approaching on foot. Your subject may have companions who were out of the car when you arrived. Watch their hands and watch for weapons. Don't let them surround or crowd you. Call for help early if indicated. As a general rule, it is not possible for you alone to keep close track of more than a couple of people in a vehicle. There are simply too many things to remain alert to that will divide your attention as you go about the business of the contact. Call a cover officer to help with the watching duties.

If the vehicle you are contacting contains back seat occupants you are unsure of, do not walk past them on your way to contact the driver. Stop your approach just before you reach the opening edge of the back door, assuming there is one, or just short of the back seat side window if you are dealing with a two-door model. If you are at all uncomfortable after looking over the characters in the back seat, consider advancing no farther and instead call the driver out to meet you at the front of your car. But don't stand *between* the two cars, and don't permit him to stand there, either. By watching out for his safety, you are also protecting yourself from hungry lawyers.

Meanwhile, keep the vehicle's other occupants in their car and under the surveillance of your peripheral vision. More than one or two officers have been murdered by passengers of drivers they had contacted. Even more have been feloniously assaulted. Watch those riders. One of them may be a potential shooter.

Incidentally, whether you are working with a vehicle occupied once or seven times, consider the value of an approach on foot alongside the right side of their car instead of the "traditional" route. Exit your driver's door and walk around the back of your vehicle, watching your subjects all the while. As you proceed cautiously along the right sides of the two cars, you may be able to surprise someone who has been planning a surprise for *you*. The right-side approach is also a good one when heavy traffic makes a left-side walk very dangerous for you. In any case, make your contact via the right front passenger's window.

Watch out for distractions of any kind when you are dealing with the occupants of a vehicle. The drunk who is needling you from the back seat may be a threat, but perhaps no more so than the big-breasted vixen in the right-front seat who is inching her skirt up a bit as she sweet-talks you. Either of these people could be purposely distracting you to set up an attack by a companion. Stay alert and keep your street survival senses focused on *all* occupants of the vehicle as you call for assistance. You cannot afford to focus so much on one problem that you ignore other potential threats.

As your traffic stop or contact progresses, stay ready to react to any perceived threat to your safety. Keep your gun hand free of anything you would not want to drop quickly, if necessary. A driver's license may be all right in your gun hand; a radio or flashlight would not be. Stay ready.

Get whatever documents you need from the driver and complete your summons or field interview card back in your own car. It removes you from harm's way just a little and also lessens the chances you will get involved in a distracting argument with the subject(s) of your attention. You might try holding your clipboard or ticket book against the upper part of your steering wheel so to better keep the vehicle and its occupants within the range of your peripheral vision. The subject or suspect stays out of your car unless he's handcuffed, searched, and in custody. NEVER put him in your car, unsecured, to write summonses or take other enforcement action against him.

You may want to get your subject away from his companions while you ask him a few questions or complete your summons or field interview form. If so, consider placing him at the left front corner of your hood (not between the cars) while you remain on the left side near the spotlight position. If you are left-handed, you may want to switch sides of the patrol car for your subject because you want to keep your non-gun side toward the subject while you use your car's hood as a writing support. At any rate, keep your subject more than an arm's length away from you. Use your peripheral vision to help you avoid traffic and other threats as you concentrate on the potential risk near you. If he has got to sign something for you, push the book across to him rather than let him get next to you and your sidearm.

Do not enter a still-occupied vehicle to search it or for any other purpose. Get a cover officer or two on scene and then get the occupants out and under close scrutiny away from their vehicle before you go in. This is assuming, of course, that you have legal grounds to be inside the vehicle in the first place.

Do not lean into a vehicle to extract a resistant subject or for any other reason. You're just too vulnerable in that position. Instead, wait for covering help and then do what you must. Physical tactics instructors teach several approaches for removing "difficult" persons from vehicles, even the ones who have their fingers wrapped around the steering wheel like an eagle on a limb. A quick feint or flick of your hand toward his eyes is one trick that should cause your subject to release his grip long enough for you to get a wrist lock on a handy wrist. But move quickly or you will find yourself in a tug-of-war that doesn't look too good to a citizen audience unschooled in the difficulties of your job.

Remember that each and every time you approach during the same vehicle stop, you must treat the contact as the first one. Do not drop your guard on subsequent trips to his vehicle. A weapon may have appeared where none was in evidence before. Attitudes may have deteriorated. He may realize that you are about to find that there is a warrant out for his arrest. Always treat every approach as your first. That way you can be reasonably certain that it won't be your last.

The contact is not over until your subject has been secured or has left the area or you have departed yourself. As the contact terminates, keep your defenses up. Back up toward your car, if necessary, as you disengage from him. You do not have to be paranoid here. You DO have to be very careful.

HIGH-RISK STOPS AND CONTACTS

These used to be called felony stops. There are probably as many ways of conducting them as there are police officers and police agencies in the nation. Each sworn professional may have his or her own, unique twists to the high-risk stop procedure. You, no doubt, have your own, special tricks of the trade for getting a potentially dangerous job done as safely as possible. Nonetheless, for the sake of officer survival as well as operational effectiveness, some guidelines for high-risk vehicle contacts can help ensure that all officers involved know what to expect from their peers. *Safety through consistency* is the primary purpose of the street survival guidelines contained in these pages.

Before beginning any high-risk vehicle contact, you must endeavor to answer as completely as possible a number of key, officer survival questions. Questions such as:

1. What crime is believed to be involved?
2. How many potential offenders are in the vehicle I am about to contact?
3. What weapons are believed to be involved? (Look for others, too, of course.)
4. How much help will I need? (Better too much than too little.)
5. Where can I best make the stop with the greatest degree of safety? (Avoid bar parking lots, areas congested with vehicles or pedestrians, and known hostile neighborhoods.)

6. What special hazards may exist? (Look out for vicious dogs, hostages, and all sorts of other surprises.)
7. Is everything and everyone on my side ready for the stop? Are the odds stacked heavily in my favor? (They should be.)

With as many answers as possible in hand, you are almost ready to initiate the high-risk stop or contact. Even as you make final preparations, there are a few more considerations to run through your mind. For instance: There is at least one absolute to be remembered in conducting high-risk vehicle contacts. You never do them alone. Backups are absolutely mandatory.

Another absolute: All police participants in the contact must understand the role each is to play and the position he is to take *before* the contact is made. The police radio is utilized to make sure everyone is on the same page.

In addition, only one officer (generally, the one in the first unit) gives commands to participating officers and sets up the stop or contact. This officer normally will be the one to issue verbal commands to the suspects, too.

Do not attempt a high-risk vehicle stop unless you have sufficient help on hand to do the job safely, even if that means you must allow the suspects to remain free for the time being. There will always be another time to get them. Assuming, that is, that you are still alive for a later crack at them. Before you attempt any high-risk vehicle stop without adequate assistance in place, ask yourself one question: *Is this worth dying for?* Then, go where your common sense leads you.

Keep assessing a high-risk vehicle contact as it progresses. What seemed to be an adequate number of police personnel on scene when the thing started may change as more facts (hostile subjects, the presence of weapons, etc.) come to light. Call all the help you need. Borrow it from an adjoining jurisdiction if you must, but *get it.*

Never pull your police vehicle in front of or alongside a vehicle you are attempting to stop. Good, experienced cops have been killed doing just that. Leave the ramming and bumping scenes for the TV cops, too. Stay *behind* the suspect vehicle and commence your contact procedures only when you have adequate assistance on hand.

As you begin the stop itself, remember that survival-savvy officers never walk up to an occupied vehicle on a high-risk contact. Operate from cover and bring the suspect(s) into *your* area of control. Meanwhile, avoid straying into theirs.

Traffic and other factors may bring about some necessary changes in tactics for a high-risk vehicle stop or contact. You will need to retain flexibility in your planning as well as in your training and practice to allow for such variables. Nonetheless, every officer participant in the operation needs to understand his responsibilities as the contact unfolds. This is no time for everyone to do his own thing.

Now it's time to *do* the stop. When all backups are ready, the primary officer gives the radio order to begin the stop and advises dispatch of the location. If you are that primary officer, activate your emergency lights, spotlights, and takedowns. Tap your siren to get the driver's attention. Make the stop.

Position your car's front bumper about 30 feet off the rear of the subject's car. The first backup unit should park to your left with about six feet between the police cars. The next backup, if available, goes to your right, again leaving about six feet between the police units.

Depending on the situation and whether you have additional help available, these extra patrol cars should flank out to the sides of the stop, approximately even with the primary police unit. From these positions, the officers can bring additional firepower to bear if a gunfight begins. They also can assist with any foot pursuit that might develop. If available, an additional unit can stop with emergency lights activated 150 feet or so to the rear of the contact site. From that rear-guard position, this backup can provide traffic control and watch for "follow-up" cars with more bad guys. If you are the primary officer directing the stop, you should be advised by your helpers as to where they are and any developments they have noted. If you are a backup, remember that you owe the primary officer a quick and accurate report on your whereabouts and actions.

A special note on police working dog applications to high-risk vehicle contacts: Some agencies instruct their K-9 handlers to position themselves on the right flank of a high-risk stop. From that position the dog can be deployed if occupants flee from the stopped car. Naturally, it is the dog handler's responsibility to let you as the primary officer know that he is in place. If the dog is released, it will behoove you and your peers to remain motionless and in place to avoid distracting the animal and becoming a bite casualty. (The K-9 may key on any moving figure.)

Positioning of the police vehicles is important. At night, all police units are positioned straight ahead to throw maximum illumination into the stopped vehicle. Officers remain under cover behind their car doors and door posts. In the daytime, police vehicles should be parked angled slightly to the left to provide additional wheel and engine block cover for the officers behind them. Here your best position is probably behind your car's left front fender, with the engine between you and any hostile gunfire. The same goes for your first backup officer. The officer in the second backup unit (the one to your right) may want to remain behind his door and door post instead of his left front fender simply because of his relative angle to the bad guys' vehicle. Be flexible, but also be sure you're covered. You get good at it by practicing regularly with your peers.

When all vehicles have come to a stop and officers are positioned behind cover, the primary officer issues the following commands to the suspect(s), always from behind cover and with sidearm or shotgun pointed at the suspect vehicle:

"Police! Everyone put your hands on your head! Don't move again unless you are told to!"

Remember: Real fear or confusion may prevent your subject from complying immediately with your directions. There may be a language barrier. He may not be resistive; he simply may have not heard you clearly over the traffic noise. Remain alert and repeat your instructions if necessary. As you gain compliance, continue with your directions:

"Driver! Remove your keys and drop them out the window! Now put your hands back on your head! Don't move again!"

Now it is time to start clearing out the suspect vehicle. Be sure your cover officers know what's to be done next. Then proceed with your clearing operation, one subject at a time:

"Driver! Reach outside and open your door! Step out facing away from us! Hands up! Leave the door all the way open! Step away from the car! Turn slowly, all the way around! Keep turning! Stop while you are facing away from us! Don't move again!"

Naturally, the whole turning maneuver has been for the purpose of helping you spot obvious weapons.

Now, with your backups covering any additional vehicle occupants, you can start bringing suspects back one at a time. You begin with the driver, already out of the car:

"Driver! Walk slowly backward toward the sound of my voice! Move! Everyone else keep looking straight ahead!"

Keep watching everyone's hands. That's what they will try to hurt you with if things go bad. Stay alert. Now, the driver is guided by your verbal directions to a point just in front of and between your car and that of your first backup. Here you issue another order:

"Go down on your knees! Keep looking straight ahead! Cross your ankles! Leave your hands on your head! Don't move again!"

You become the covering officer now as your first backup leaves cover to come up behind the kneeling subject. Keep watching the car and the other occupants, too. (Remember: There may be someone in there hiding out of sight.) Your first backup holsters his weapon just before he gets within arms' reach of the subject. Being careful to stay out of your line of sight and fire, he handcuffs and searches suspect number one. He walks him back to a patrol car, searches him again, belts him in securely, and locks the car door.

The whole process is repeated with each additional occupant of the suspect vehicle. Only one is dealt with at a time. Others stay seated with hands on heads. You go through the "exit, turn around all the way, back up to the sound of my voice, kneel down, cross your ankles" number with each subject.

If at any time during the procedure *any* officer spots a gun anywhere on a subject's person, he must alert his peers quickly:

"He's got a gun. It's in his waistband in back."

If you are the primary officer on the contact, you address the armed subject:

"We see the gun. If you touch it, you will be shot."

The instructions and warning are necessarily harsh. They may, in fact, help save the life of a misguided crook.

Once spotted, the suspect's weapon is allowed to remain in place (assuming it's not in his hand!) under extra close surveillance until seized by the backup officer who eventually approaches and controls the suspect. This is done in preference to telling the suspect to remove or "drop" it or lay it aside. The risk in allowing the offender to ever get the weapon in hand is simply too great.

If at any time during the high-risk vehicle contact a deadly weapon is seen in the hands of an offender who is pointing it at you or your peers, you must take defensive action, including gunfire targeted upon his center mass, to protect your life and the lives of your fellow officers. Again, that sounds harsh. But it was, after all, the suspect who placed his own life at risk by threatening yours with a weapon. Don't forget that.

Whenever circumstances permit, it is a very good idea to have more than one backup officer on hand to help with a high-risk vehicle contact. For one thing, the extra officer or officers can provide additional cover and observation capabilities. For another, they can furnish extra firepower if the situation really deteriorates. Finally, the extra officer or officers can take over the covering duties if the primary officer must leave cover to help his first backup subdue a resisting subject. (Offenders have been known to "sacrifice" the first of their number out of the vehicle to allow the others to escape or attack during the ensuing, planned altercation.)

Once all known occupants have been removed from the suspect vehicle, you as the primary officer should issue a bluff challenge:

"You! Hiding in the car–sit up with your hands on your head! Do it quick!"

If you receive no response, the first backup officer quietly moves up on the left side of the suspect vehicle using available cover. When he has visually cleared the car's interior, he so advises his peers on scene.

Finally, the first backup officer assumes a position at the left side of the trunk of the suspect vehicle. You as the primary officer then retrieve the vehicle's keys, approach carefully, and take up a position at the right side of the trunk. Get down on your knees, reach up and unlock the trunk while staying low beneath the rear bumper, and then move back to the right side. Have your sidearm out and ready. Stay out of your partner's line of fire as the trunk lid opens. (Naturally, you can use the car's trunk release button on the dash or key chain if the car has this device.)

Remember: No vehicle from which high-risk suspects have been removed should be towed or impounded until the trunk and all other hiding places have been searched for hidden offenders. Some very dangerous people have been known to conceal themselves and their weapons in some pretty peculiar places.

SPECIAL VEHICLES, SPECIAL THREATS

Vehicle stops and contacts may become complicated when you are dealing with something besides your average, four-door passenger car. Things can get more complex, for instance, when you are stopping a big tractor-trailer rig. Here you may want to assign a second backup car to the right rear of the stopped rig to watch out for an attack from the right side or underside of the vehicle. These areas are hard to watch for the primary officer alone.

Another problem: If you are contacting a van with rear doors, it will be up to the first backup officer to cover these added hazard spots from which an offender might emerge or fire. If you are confronting offenders in a van with a right-side cargo door, you will need your backup (or a second backup) to park to the right rear of the van to cover the cargo door area against a possible attack.

A vehicle with very heavily tinted windows also may present special problems. If you cannot see who is inside, you may want to order the driver alone out while you stay at your vehicle. Then, from a position of cover, you can direct him to open the vehicle's other, left-side doors and leave them standing open. After you get the driver secured or out of the way, you can order the other occupants out one at a time. Finally, you can visually check the vehicle's interior by approaching with available cover. It also won't hurt to ask the people you have extracted about who else might be in there, so long as you don't put too much faith in what they tell you.

Finally, motorcycles ridden by a group of outlaw bikers can furnish a special test for you. You will want to keep in mind that the bikes themselves may prove a threat because some thugs like to hide their various weapons there. Shotgun shells fitted into handlebars, knives fashioned onto the underside of gas tank caps, and saddlebags full of explosives and other nasty devices are among the surprises that have been discovered on and around motorcycles by alert officers. Stay watchful and don't, of course, overlook the threats presented by the bikers themselves. Realize that their female companions, if present, may be "holding" their boyfriends' weapons. Remain cautious and make good use of your cover as well as your backups. As with any other high-risk vehicle contact, watch their hands and assume they are dangerous until proven otherwise. Also, assume that they may be video or audio recording your every act and utterance.

There are yet other risks involving vehicles and their occupants. For example: A simple vehicle stop or contact can be transformed into something very different in no time at all. Whether at the end of a pursuit or when occupants simply refuse to exit a contacted vehicle, a high-risk vehicle stop can turn into a barricade situation in short order. In that case, all vehicle occupants who refuse to exit in compliance with police orders are assumed to be armed until proven otherwise. You and other police personnel present must remain behind good cover at your vehicles or close by. No one approaches the suspect vehicle. Inner and outer perimeters are established. Traffic and pedestrians are kept away. A supervisor is called to the scene, and a decision may be made to summon a police negotiator and the SWAT unit.

You as the primary officer on-scene may find yourself temporarily in the role of negotiator. In your discussions with the offenders, always carried out from behind cover, you may wish to allude to the fact that the application of specialized weapons and the introduction of chemical agents into the vehicle are distinct possibilities if the impasse is not resolved quickly. Meanwhile, stay behind cover and negotiate from a position of advantage in manpower and weapons. Take your time. The clock generally will be on your side.

The tactics and procedures suggested in this chapter for use in all kinds of vehicle stops and contacts represent a starting point only for the survival-conscious police professional. You as the officer on-scene retain the flexibility to alter tactics for handling the exceptional or unusual situation based on your training, experience, common sense, and analysis of the specific problem at hand. This flexibility remains coupled with the requirement that all of the assisting police personnel are adequately briefed as to the game plan and each officer's role in it before the stop or contact is attempted. This kind of approach will help ensure both officer safety and certainty of apprehension of potentially dangerous offenders.

That's what officer safety on vehicle stops and contacts is all about. Those contacts are a big part of your work life if you are anything like the average police officer. Don't allow a personal focus on commonsense safety precautions to be any less a part of your professional life. The emphasis here is on the word LIFE.

There is no such thing as a routine vehicle contact. Whether it is an unknown-risk or a high-risk interaction, each one will require that you bring into play everything you have learned about staying safe on the street. In order to survive a lot of vehicle contacts over a lot of years, you will have to call on all your powers of observation to help you identify dangers and react promptly and effectively to them. You will have to remain alert, get your facts together, stay in close communication with your dispatcher and fellow officers, and watch your approach and positioning. You will need to get plenty of help when you need it and constantly assess for situational changes.

Additionally, making a vehicle contact in safety will require that you utilize cover wisely, follow contact and cover procedures with your helpers and handle prisoners carefully. Finally, surviving a career filled with vehicle contacts will necessitate that you never treat a vehicle containing unknown threats as just a traffic stop.

A RISK REDUCTION CHECKLIST FOR
VEHICLE STOPS AND CONTACTS

1. Know as much as you possibly can about who and what you are contacting before you make the stop.
2. Don't start or continue any vehicle stop or contact without sufficient police personnel on-scene.
3. Watch for any indication that you are dealing with something different than you first believed.
4. Make good use of cover and cover officers in any questionable or high-risk vehicle contact.
5. Watch your body positioning in approaching and contacting vehicle occupants. You can't afford to get sloppy where your life is concerned.
6. Top-notch communications among you, your dispatcher, and all officers involved in a vehicle contact are a must. Everyone needs to know the plan.

7. Remember that vehicle stops and contacts are made much safer by the proper use of all of the tools—radio, spotlight, take-down lights, emergency lights—that you have been provided.

A five-year state trooper, age 28, was killed after stopping a weaving vehicle at 2:30 a.m. As the officer approached the stopped car, he was shot in the head and left arm with a .357-magnum handgun and in the left shoulder with a blast from a 12-gauge shotgun. Assailants ages 34 and 23 fled the scene, killed a resident of a nearby house, took a woman hostage, and fled in a commandeered van from the police. Officers saw the van swerve and crash. Investigation revealed the hostage had been killed, and both male suspects committed suicide.

* * * * *

A 49-year-old sheriff's deputy was killed at about 12:30 p.m. The deputy was attempting to arrest a 32-year-old drunk driver when a struggle took place. The man got control of the deputy's 9-millimeter handgun and shot the officer once in the head.

Chapter 4

DEFUSING DISTURBANCES

A lot of American law enforcement officers are injured, some seriously, while handling disturbance calls of one kind or another each year. Most years, a number are killed. The figures back up the assumption voiced by a lot of experienced cops that disturbances spell danger for those sent to defuse them.

Many of these disturbance call assignments telegraph their potential for danger. They sound and look as dangerous as they are. Occasionally, however, danger can lurk in situations that at first glance do not appear that hazardous. In one such case, a 29-year-old patrol officer responded to a 4:30 a.m. call of a man causing a noise disturbance *while feeding birds*. The officer, who was wearing body armor, confronted the 48-year-old male in an alley behind the man's home. Shortly thereafter, the officer radioed that he had been shot. When backup officers arrived, they found the two-year patrolman dead from nine 9-mm bullet wounds, two in the head. The killer was eventually wounded and arrested following a barricade situation. Indeed, even a disturbance assignment that sounds harmless enough can end in tragedy.

As veteran officers know, so-called civil disputes also can turn deadly. Hardened criminals and crazies get into disputes with landlords, tow truck drivers, and business managers, too. When they do, the results sometimes can include violence. If you are smart, you will realize that what started over an unpaid bill or vehicle repossession could have turned into a violent episode involving weapons by the time you arrive. You will tailor your response, arrival, and tactics accordingly to protect yourself from the unexpected.

Civil situations clearly can be hazardous to you. Consider this example of an initially noncriminal disagreement gone awry. A veteran patrol officer and his partner responded to a rent dispute call. As he was getting out of the patrol car, the officer was struck fatally in the head with a .30-06 rifle round. The 57-year-old male killer then barricaded himself with a hostage before surrendering three days later. It was subsequently learned that the man had killed his landlord following an argument over rent just before police arrived.

If disturbances are potentially risky affairs, what makes them so? Actually, several factors may come together to increase your risks while you are striving to restore calm to the situation. Perhaps first among the factors increasing the danger for you are the powerful emotions felt by the disturbance's participants, whether they are barroom brawlers or gang members having a falling out. They likely already have had their "fight or flight" mechanism activated, with a resulting adrenaline dump fueling them for action. While you are there only to try and calm things down, your potential opponents are emotionally and physically ready to do battle. They may have engaged in a physical altercation before you arrived. Now, you represent only one more target. If you are not careful, you have been set up to be a victim before you even have gotten involved.

A second element of danger for you at the site of a disturbance call may be found in the frequent presence of weapons, actual or improvised. The chronic Hell-raiser who knows he is likely to get involved in an altercation may have equipped himself in advance in order to have an advantage. That may have caused him to stash a pistol in his vehicle or stick one in his pants. Or he may have concealed a knife in his boot or a club under his car seat. Whatever the weapons of choice for the disturbance's actors, all remain dangers for you, the peacekeeper sent to fix things.

There is another factor often found at the scene of a disturbance that makes handling the incident in safety a critical challenge for you. It amounts to under the influence behavior by one or more of the participants. It is not unusual for a veteran night shift officer to have a hard time recalling the last time he answered a disturbance call that did not involve drunk, drinking, or drugged disputants.

As you know, the presence of alcohol or drugs in any call or contact you handle increases the danger factor for you. When lowered inhibitions and weakened judgment come into play, the normally compliant individual may decide to take you on. Add to that lack of self-control the escalating feelings often present at a disturbance, and you have a situation ready to go critical. That's assuming, of course, that you do not respond promptly and effectively to prevent an explosion of violence. You can and must do that. Following are some guidelines for doing so in safety.

REDUCING THE DANGER

The basic survival practices that help keep you safe on many other high-risk assignments can protect you on a disturbance call, too. Certain kinds of disturbances, such as bar fights, call for specific strategies. But a set of general survival guidelines should serve you well in virtually every disturbance scenario. These steps for safely managing a disturbance scene include the following:

Plan Ahead

Your planning should begin well before you arrive and continue through your departure from the disturbance scene. Think about your safest route of approach to keep the element of surprise on your side. If you have been there before, where are the known hazards and potential ambush sites? Who are you likely to find there? Gang members? Outlaw bikers? Plan your actions and arrange for all the help you will need. Start planning your tactics based on what you know or suspect so far. Stay flexible, however. Your handling of the situation could change drastically depending on what you discover on-scene.

Only Fools Rush In

Do not be in too much of a hurry to charge into the midst of mayhem. Seldom will you have to act immediately upon arrival in order to save a life. Generally you will have at least a moment to catch your breath, observe and plan what you are going to do next. If you can arrive quietly and observe, unnoticed for a bit (don't park right in front!), you may be able to learn things that will help you solve the problem in safety. Your ears might tell you, for instance, how many people are involved, who the aggressor is, whether there are weapons involved, and the demeanor of the people present. Thus informed, you and your backup(s) should be able to handle the call with greater effectiveness and safety. One pair of officers, listening outside the door of a residence where a domestic argument was in progress, made a quick change in plans after hearing the male party say, "I'm going to get my gun." They forced a fast entry and controlled the subject before anything worse could happen. There are plenty of true accounts of officers who bided their time, observed carefully, and then acted in safety on what they had just learned.

Watch Your Approach and Positioning

Note the location of good, solid cover in case gunfire should erupt as you approach a disturbance call. Park away from the reported location of the problem and move in on foot along the neighboring structures. Try to avoid taking the most obvious route of approach in case a disturbance participant, alerted to your arrival, has set up an ambush for you. Do not stand directly in front of a door you are knocking at. Rather, stand to the side and against a wall. Once you have announced your presence, maintain a generous reactionary gap of several feet between yourself and any persons present. Keep your gun side turned away from them and keep your firearm covered by your elbow or arm to the extent possible. Be aware of anyone who attempts to get close to you, as he may be planning an attack and weapon takeaway attempt. Tell him where you want him to stand or sit. As courteously as the situation permits, tell him to stay put until directed otherwise.

Control Your Surroundings

Control the environment and the people present as opposed to allowing either to control you. Do not allow people to move out of your sight. Watch their hands. Don't let anyone maneuver to a position behind you. Be aware of what is happening in this tense environment at all times.

The cover officer on-scene is responsible for watching the primary officer carefully as he or she goes about gathering information and then acting to resolve the dispute. You also must clear the area of any uninvolved people who might decide to take sides and intervene. In a crowded establishment such as a bar, it will generally be better if you guide the main actors outside so you can continue your investigation in an atmosphere that may be a little less volatile. It is to your advantage to stay out of a crowd when you are attempting to handle a disturbance of any kind.

Get Sufficient Help

You will hear that mandate repeatedly throughout this book. It applies here, too. It is that vital to your survival. Do not attempt to handle any sort of disturbance without adequate resources on-scene to help you. A disturbance call ranks near the top of the list of assignments never to be handled by a lone officer. Call as much help as your best judgment says you will need if your dispatcher has not already provided you with adequate cover. Then, wait for it to get there before you enter the fray unless someone's life is clearly at immediate risk. Do not join the roster of officers who had help on the way but failed to wait for its arrival before committing to action. Too many of these courageous but unwise officers have been found dead or dying when their help did get there.

Let Them Talk, But Control the Discussion

It is up to you and your backup to stay safe while you gather enough information to determine what you are going to do to solve the problem at hand.

It is important to learn as much as possible by permitting the free flow of information. You need to learn the facts that you eventually will act on. Be prepared for all of those present to want to enlighten you with their particular version of events and tell you what you should do next. Separate the participants so that the primary or contact officer can interview each without interruption. While you should seek to position each actor beyond the hearing of the others, you nonetheless also should take care to remain close enough to your fellow officer so that the two of you can watch out for each other's safety.

As you gather information, listen more than you talk. Take your time. Handle it the first time so that you do not have to return later. Let your speakers vent, but steer them back to the present issue when they want to tell you about everything the opposition has done wrong for the last two weeks— or two years. Try to remain patient. Find out everything relevant to help you in the coming "action" phase of handling the call.

Stay Alert for Big Changes

Disturbances can get worse rather than better, even after you arrive. Watch for the individual who appears to be getting more agitated as your contact proceeds and it becomes evident to him that he may be headed for jail. Keep watching for new threats, like weapons or additional people, to appear without warning. Call more help at any point that it appears it may be needed. Modify your approach, if necessary, even if it means employing delaying tactics until more help can arrive.

Take Appropriate Action

Act decisively on the observations you have made and the information you have gathered. If a full-custody arrest is your decision, all officers present should be alerted to what you are going to do next. Be fair but firm. If the suspect believes that you are unsure of yourself, he may attempt to take advantage of you. Realize that if you cannot or will not make a decision, you turn the decision making over to someone who is not your friend. Say what you mean and mean what you say. Quell the disturbance by taking whatever lawful action is required to return some degree of normalcy to the scene. Act with authority and act in safety.

Follow Careful Prisoner Handling Practices

Remember the officers killed and assaulted statistics the next time you respond to a disturbance call. They will remind you that some of the people you meet on disturbance assignments are dangerous. Some of them have injured police personnel even *after* they were in custody. Resolve now never to be hurt by a disturbance call prisoner.

While working with an alert cover officer, properly handcuff your subject from his rear while he remains off-balance and cannot watch you easily. Search him carefully, as many times as you feel you must, to be sure he has nothing with which he could hurt you or someone else. Stay alert for a surprise assault from even a previously compliant prisoner. His attitude and intentions could change without warning.

Keep your weapons secure and well out of his reach. More than a few officers have in the past lost their firearms—and their lives—to handcuffed prisoners. Remember that your prisoner represents a serious threat to you until he is finally behind bars or is otherwise totally removed from your presence. Don't forget that virtually anyone on-scene could attack you. Relaxing too soon could have fatal repercussions for you, so do not do it.

Is It Really Over?

Make your break from the disturbance site quickly and cleanly. Do not remain in the immediate vicinity unnecessarily to complete paperwork or discuss the call with another officer. Go someplace else to write or talk, just in case a participant in the disturbance or one of his pals decides to track you down to renew the altercation. Even when you have left the area, keep an eye out for "tails" you may have picked up at the scene. It is a good idea to stay both observant and cautious.

Get Better for the Next One

Experience is of no value unless you learn from it. Once the disturbance assignment is over, think about how you handled it. What worked well and what didn't? Be your own toughest critic in reviewing and, where necessary, revising your tactics in order to do even better next time. Add some tools to your growing tool box based on what you experienced and learned. One of them may be just what you need to save your own life the next time a disturbance call is your assignment.

BAR BRAWLS

The bar.

You know which one it is. There are probably several in your jurisdiction where the patrons remind you of nothing so much as the inhabitants of the cantina scene in *Star Wars*. When a fight or disturbance takes place in this environment, you *know* it has the potential for real danger for you, the person expected to restore order from chaos.

Bar fights are dangerous for several reasons. First of all, you may be dealing with disputants whose judgment and inhibitions have been dimmed by alcohol. These people may be capable of just about anything. They are unpredictable. And they just might decide to take you on.

Second, bars can be dangerous due to the weapons to be found there. The regular patron of a sleazy establishment knows that there are others of a like character there. He knows that they may be violent. He's not about to be caught dead without a weapon of some kind at hand. If he is drunk or agitated enough when you confront him, he just may be willing to use it on you.

Third, the bar environment may help set up an attack on you if you are not careful. Attacks can develop without warning from dark, hard-to-see places. Attackers can hide and escape in the tumultuous crowd and confusion. There also are plenty of obstacles to fall over in the semi-darkness if you get into a struggle.

In addition, bars can be risky places because you and authority figures in general may be seen as outsiders there. The anti-law enforcement attitude that prevails in some of these joints can make it psychologically easier for someone to attack you, perhaps with help from his fellow barflies.

You must offset these hazards with safety tactics of your own that will help protect you when duty takes you into these establishments. Whether you are responding to a bar fight in progress or doing a liquor law compliance inspection, some bar survival guidelines should help you stay safe. Consider the following advice.

Know What You Are Facing

It is important that you know as much as possible about the challenges on your beat, bars included. Learn the safest routes in and out of "your" bars. Pay special attention to back doors and potential hiding places. Practice approaching these establishments undetected. Then, when trouble does bring you there, do not use the most obvious entry point where an ambush may be waiting. Try to determine in advance where special hazards, such as the bartender's hidden weapon, might be located. Try to discover where hidden rooms and similar areas from which an offender might launch an attack are situated.

Don't Pass Up a Problem

Realize that with the built-in delay involved in the call to 911 and the dispatching procedures that follow you may encounter the suspect from a bar crime a good distance from the establishment. Do not overrun danger. Know that a bar fighter who knows you are coming may have plenty of time to hide in the parking lot or elsewhere to elude or attack you. It has happened before. Stay alert and keep looking for danger.

Stop, Look, and Listen

Pause outside a bar where a problem is reported to be occurring until your backup(s) can catch up to you. As you wait, use your senses to gather as much information on what is happening as possible. If you can hear raised voices, how many are there? What can you see from outside, if anything? What is going on at the moment? Use what you learn to plan a safe approach and intervention. What you find out may cause you to alter your response. It could, for example, result in your calling for additional help.

Wait for Help and Use It Wisely

A bar problem calls for *at least* two officers. It could require several more. Unless there is a life-threatening event occurring in front of you, stand by for your help to arrive before you get involved. Everyone is safer that way. Once your help is present, employ careful contact and cover tactics. That concept is valid regardless of how many officers and subjects are involved.

Covering officers should maintain their watchfulness from a position where it would be difficult for anyone to get behind them. The cover officer does not participate in the call other than to be a lifeguard, provide a very visible deterrent, shout a warning, and instantly intervene with threat-appropriate force if a contact officer is endangered.

Get as much help as you need to the scene promptly. Keep it there until you are absolutely certain that it is no longer needed.

Stay Alert for Danger

Don't lower your guard for even an instant when you are in a bar. Danger can emerge quickly. Watch the hands of everyone in the vicinity. Keep an eye out for new "players" and new threats to appear. Look out for weapons, actual or makeshift. Know that previously uninvolved drunks may jump on your back, go for your weapon, try and whip up the crowd, or otherwise insert themselves into the action. Practice excellent weapon retention.

Get Out Quickly and Safely

It will be safer for everyone if you move the subjects of your attention outside of the bar as soon as possible. You are still at risk outside, of course, but you likely have reduced a bit the danger from friends, allies, and enemies of the person or persons you are now taking into custody.

Getting a recalcitrant offender out of a bar can be a task in itself. If feasible, consider waiting until you get him outside to handcuff him. It may be less emotional and thereby safer there. But do a pat-down search for weapons immediately upon contacting the subject. Do so under the observation of your cover officer and keep him advised of what you plan to do next.

Following your weapons search, advise your subject that you need to talk with him outside. Don't try to control or shepherd multiple drunks—that's why you may require more than a single back-up officer to help you. Guide your subject ahead of you to help clear a path as you point him toward the exit. Your cover officer should walk behind you to watch your blind side. Ideally, one officer should be present to handle each individual to be removed from the bar. The cover officer bringing up the rear of the procession should continue his or her watch for danger once you are all outside the bar. More problems still could develop.

Make Your Break

Do not hang around the bar once you have finished your business there. The establishment's parking lot is not a great place to loiter and do your report, either, especially if you have a prisoner aboard. You or your passenger just might draw the attention of someone with ill intent. A prisoner rescue attempt also remains a possibility if you hang out in the neighborhood. Make a clean break but still keep an eye out for trouble that could have followed you from the cantina scene.

LARGE-SCALE DISTURBANCES

Large-scale disturbances are sometimes seen as nothing short of a full-blown riot or mass civil disorder requiring huge numbers of officers or even the National Guard to suppress them. Those kinds of problems do occur, however infrequently. When they do, everything you have learned about surviving on the street will be required to keep you safe. At the same time, much more likely to occur in most jurisdictions is the big, out-of-control party turned nasty, the sporting event crowd turned destructive or the clash between two groups of gangsters, families, protestors, or other zealots convinced that their way is the only way. Even domestic disputes can escalate into a huge battle involving the whole building or the entire neighborhood as the partisans from each side get involved.

Even worse, the number of disturbance participants can grow vastly even after you arrive on-scene and attempt to take action not to the liking of the principals and their allies. What started out as an argument can get out of hand as various friends, relatives, and other supporters of the battling parties get involved. Change the setting for the dispute to a rowdy bar or a drunken, after-wedding reception or similar event and you have all the makings for a full-scale donnybrook. It is just this sort of scenario that results in officers injured far too often.

The dangers for you at a large-scale disturbance scene are multiplied because of the increased number of participants present. There are more human threats to deal with and many more directions from which that danger can come from. Unless you are cautious, a roiling mass of humanity will make it easier for someone to go for your gun or slip a blade in your back. A large crowd can separate you from your backups and virtually carry you along, thereby setting you up for being beaten, disarmed, and worse. You are even at risk of being knocked down and trampled by the throng. Finally, there is the added factor of anonymity, which, combined with mob psychology and the perceived safety of numbers, may cause someone to attack you when he or she would not even think about it while facing you one on one.

The same basic officer safety tactics and techniques that will shield you from other disturbance call dangers will serve you equally well when the number of potential attackers is much greater. In addition, some additional disturbance-handling techniques may come in handy.

Know What You Are Facing

Collect information, where possible, before the trouble starts. Good intelligence is the key. Keep the lines of communication open to your informants in the community. What you learn may help you prevent a problem from occurring or respond to it more effectively if it does happen. By keeping your intelligence-gathering feelers out there, you may be able to learn who's mad at whom about what, who the actors are, and otherwise feel the pulse of the street. But you will not learn any of this unless you get out of your car, ask questions, and listen carefully to the answers. By staying tuned in, you help keep yourself and your peers a little safer.

Make Some Plans

This advice applies to your whole law enforcement agency as well as to you, the individual officer. Plan ahead for any big disturbance scenario that your imagination can dream up. Determine in advance how quickly you could obtain additional personnel resources, and from where. When should your plans include a temporary tactical withdrawal until more help arrives? Are formalized, preexisting mutual aid agreements or understandings in place? Who is to be in command of a multi-agency operation? Are there plans and facilities for handling large numbers of prisoners? Exactly how is it to be accomplished? Good contingency planning is a must for responding safely and effectively to a large-scale disturbance.

Get Help

It has been said before, but merits repeating. Get your help on the way early before the situation you are dealing with gets out of hand. When adequate assistance does assemble, try to commit your people as an organized unit as opposed to dribbling them in piecemeal where their impact will be diluted. When you commit your forces, do so with a plan in mind concerning what you intend to accomplish (arrest the ringleaders, disperse the crowd, etc.). Then be sure each officer knows the plan and his or her part in it.

There is much evidence that a show of force in the early stages of a budding mass disturbance can help achieve a quick resolution of the problem. Many of the participants may decide that they aren't really as committed as they initially thought, now that it has become evident that the law means business and arrest is a real possibility. Form up your forces within view of your opponents and let them see for themselves that you are serious about restoring order.

Never Go It Alone

Controlling a large-scale disturbance is not accomplished via cowboy tactics. Teamwork backed by adequate resources is the only way to get the job done in relative safety. Wait for your help to get there, even if a rowdy crowd is already committing law violations in your presence. You help no one, particularly yourself, if you charge into a hostile crowd alone and get attacked and disarmed in the process. Pause until sufficient help is on-scene to do it right. Use the intervening time span to gather information through your observations and then formulate a plan of attack.

Assess a Crowd for Danger

Monitor the crowd at a disturbance scene for indications that it is getting drunker, braver, or more threatening. Are threats of violence toward law enforcement being voiced? Have bottles, rocks, or other missiles been hurled? Has the group begun to engage in vandalism or fire-setting? Can you determine by watching and listening who the obvious ringleaders or agitators are? You may want to identify them as well as possible (video is nice) for removal later when you have adequate help on hand. Report what you observe to the supervisor running the crowd control operation.

Avoid the Mob

Neither you nor any other officer should charge into a potentially hostile crowd in pursuit of a rock-thrower, epithet-shouter or some other offender. Doing so is an almost certain shortcut to the local emergency room. Instead, note who you want and go after him with a plan and a solid wedge of officers once you have plenty of assistance on hand, assuming you still consider getting him worth the effort. If you know who he is you also have the option of arresting him later when he is not part of the crowd. It may be the safest choice.

Weapon Retention is Vital

Any time you enter a crowd at a disturbance scene, all of your weapons and other equipment must be securely snapped or strapped. Cover your sidearm with your arm or elbow to the extent that your other duties permits. Be alert for someone to grab for your weapon. Instantly meet such an assault by holding your weapon down in its holster with at least one hand while you launch a no-holds-barred counterattack on the would-be weapon thief. Practice your weapon retention skills ahead of time, of course. They may one day save your life on the scene of a large-scale disturbance.

Apply Contact and Cover

There is nothing that says contact and cover involves only two officers. Contact and cover guidelines are absolutely appropriate for large-scale trouble. Adjust the numbers as the situation dictates. A large-scale disturbance may call for six contact officers and two covers, for instance. But the principle remains unchanged. The contact officers write tickets, make arrests, remove prisoners, and disperse crowds. The cover officers watch out for the safety of the contacts and get involved only to protect them from attack. A really large-scale disturbance in a big city might call for 200 contact officers and 20 covers, and so on up the scale.

Avoid Entrapment Attacks

Beware of surprise assaults at or near the scene of a large-scale disturbance. Do not get suckered into a location where you are badly outnumbered and are likely to be overwhelmed. Work closely with your partners and covering officers and remain with them.

Realize that following the dispersal of a disturbance crowd, some of the still-hyped participants may set a trap for you elsewhere, perhaps with the intent of getting even. Be wary of odd calls to out-of-the-way places at such times. Decline to meet an alleged informant at such a location. Consider varying your patrol routes to frustrate those who may be laying a trap for you.

Maintain Your Self-Control

The survival-smart officer will smile, say little, and maintain his professional demeanor at the scene of a large-scale disturbance. When you must use force, you will ensure that it is the minimum amount required to do the job of overcoming unlawful resistance safely and no more. You realize that engaging in arguments or shouting matches with your tormentors is a waste of energy and brain cells, so you will do neither. By keeping control of yourself and your emotions, you thereby deprive some unfriendly elements in the news media of the graphic images of "brutal, out of control cops" that they desire. By making sure that you do not overreact, you also avoid inflaming an already overheated crowd that may be looking for an excuse to escalate the violence against law enforcement.

Most important of all, you will know that by maintaining personal discipline and steady self-control, you have done the right thing.

Have the Right Equipment

Every officer responding to a large-scale disturbance should be properly equipped for the threats he may face there. For you, that equipment includes, at minimum, gloves, baton, aerosol defense spray, body armor, helmet, an adequate number of prisoner restraint devices, and a quality safety holster that keeps your sidearm safely in your possession. Remember that all of your equipment must be kept secure against a quick grab by a member of the unruly crowd.

At a large-scale disturbance turned violent, the decision may be made to deploy chemical munitions such as pepper gas to disperse the crowd. If chemicals are deployed, personnel trained in their proper application must be involved. If chemicals *are* deployed, it first will be necessary for all law enforcement personnel on-scene to be equipped with adequate gas masks and the knowledge of how to use them properly.

The decision to use gas at a disturbance scene is not one to be taken lightly. In most departments, it requires supervisory assessment and authorization.

Tell Them to Leave and Let Them Go

There may be a select few you want to grab, but generally speaking your best bet at the scene of a large-scale disturbance is to allow the crowd members ample opportunity to leave. Tell them to go and advise them that they are subject to arrest if they do not. Repeat the order several times, loud enough that it can be heard clearly. Give them time to obey your instructions. Meantime, you can be assembling your forces to make good on your promise if you have to do so. Many of the individuals present want to be where the action is but have no desire to go to jail. By giving them repeated directions to disperse and allowing them the means to leave (a clear escape route), you also legitimize any reasonable force you may eventually have to use to deal with the hard-core troublemakers who remain.

Never block a big crowd's exit from a disturbance scene. A cornered group of rowdies may feel obliged to fight you. This may be a good time to ignore minor law violations, such as an open alcohol containers, so that you can get these people away from the problem site. Save your law enforcement resources to handle the real problem people.

Target the Agitators

It's another basic principle of crowd control. Assuming you have adequate resources to do it and that your agitator targets have committed clear violations of the law for which they can be charged, a wedge of several officers (the exact number depending on the size of the remaining crowd) can quickly move into the throng and arrest and remove the violators. These arrestees must then be immediately handcuffed, searched, and transported out of the area before their pals can attempt to rescue them. Once removed to a secure area, such as your police station, they should be photographed and fingerprinted for later, positive identification.

If existing conditions make it impossible or unwise from a tactical standpoint to arrest the primary troublemakers, seek to identify them to be charged at a later (and safer) time. Digital photos are a great means for doing so.

Protect Your Equipment and Facilities

To avoid having your transportation vandalized and immobilized, leave officers to guard your police vehicles parked away from the large-scale disturbance. Try to group your vehicles in one spot to make the task of maintaining security easier.

Realize that a disorderly crowd may follow you to a police station or jail to advocate for or bail out their compatriots. Security should be heightened at your facilities with officers visible in strength to deter vandalism or violence. Stay alert for a new, large disturbance to erupt inside or outside your building. Be prepared to deal effectively with it. Just as in the original disorder, properly applied chemical munitions may be required for dispersal of a violent or destructive crowd. Do not relax before the danger has dissipated.

BRINGING IT ALL TOGETHER

Unless handled with all the care and caution you can bring to bear from your training, experience, and officer safety awareness, a disturbance could result in your violent death. All of the emotions, willingness to do violence, and (oftentimes) drug- or alcohol-induced complications that can accompany a disturbance call have stacked the deck against you unless you are ready for the challenge in every way.

To be ready as well as safety-smart, you must plan your response and arrival to surprise your potential adversaries as opposed to getting surprised yourself. You must secure sufficient help to aid you in safely defusing the crisis, and you must wait for that help to get there before you go into action. You must continuously assess who and what you are dealing with and remain sensitive to situational changes, like a subject or crowd escalating in belligerence. You have to control the scene to the extent practical and keep track of all the participants involved, as well as any players on the periphery who are not yet involved but may want to become so.

You absolutely must stay sharp and expect the unexpected. To remain safe, you must determine the action appropriate for the handling of the incident, act decisively, and then disentangle yourself from a less-than-happy environment as quickly as possible. Any prisoners you take into custody must be properly secured, searched, and watched closely every second that they are in your presence.

Disturbance calls and the violence that attends them can spell serious injury or death for the unwary, careless, or lazy law enforcement officer sent to handle these critical assignments. You cannot afford to fall into one or more categories of these misguided and endangered officers. No matter what kind of disturbance you are confronting, by adding the officer safety tactics and practices you have learned in these pages to your own, good common sense and decision-making abilities, you can bring order from chaos and restore peace from violence. You can do all of this without sacrificing your own well-being in the process. In pulling it off, you will be more than a safety-wise professional. You also will be a winner in the biggest contest of all: the daily struggle to survive the rigors of the street.

A RISK REDUCTION CHECKLIST FOR DEFUSING DISTURBANCES

1. Do some careful planning and information gathering before you arrive.
2. Approach the disturbance site inconspicuously and try to remain unnoticed while you collect additional observations.
3. Get enough help to the scene before you intervene in a disturbance. Don't leap in over your head.
4. Control the scene and the discussion once you commit to action. Stay alert for situational changes and surprise dangers.
5. Watch your positioning and that of your weapons around others. Follow excellent weapon retention practices.
6. Act decisively, take whatever enforcement action is indicated, and make a clean break from the scene. Do not hang out nearby afterwards.
7. Realize that a "civil situation" dispute can prove just as dangerous for you as any other kind of disturbance call.
8. While handling a bar brawl, keep an eye out for weapons and other dangers to appear from dark corners and surprise directions.
9. Know that you are at increased risk inside a bar. Disengage as quickly as possible and watch your back as you do.
10. At a large-scale disturbance, never enter a volatile crowd alone. Make your plans and get plenty of help before you attempt enforcement or crowd dispersal.
11. Leave a crowd an escape route.
12. Apply good contact and cover tactics while handling any kind of disturbance.
13. Implement a temporary tactical withdrawal at a disturbance scene if it is clear that the odds are stacked heavily against you and you are short of the resources required to regain immediate control in safety.
14. Maintain your professionalism and self-control on a disturbance-solving assignment. Do not respond to taunting or baiting behavior.

Two officers responded to a disturbance call at a motel where a man had allegedly fired shots in the parking lot. A witness directed the officers to the second floor of the motel, where they encountered a man who was standing in the doorway of a room. His hands were empty. One officer attempted to handcuff the subject, who then produced a handgun and shot both policemen. A fatal round struck one officer in the chest above his body armor. Return fire from the officers killed the

subject, who was determined to be under the influence of alcohol and to have a prior record for assault on police.

* * * * *

A police sergeant was slain at the scene of a large-scale disturbance. At about 2 a.m., several fights were reported in the parking lot of a night club. The sergeant arrived to find a crowd of more than 200 people gathered outside the club. The sergeant had just left his car when shots were fired at him from a 9 mm handgun. One round struck the sergeant in the jaw and traveled downward, where it ruptured an artery. The arrested killer was found to have a criminal record and was under the influence of alcohol at the time of the murder.

* * * * *

A 30-year-old patrolman was shot and killed after responding to a disturbance call at about 2 a.m. The officer and a backup approached two men who were fighting in front of a home. One man produced a handgun and shot the victim officer in the face. In the following gunfight, the other officer shot and killed the 26-year-old offender. The subject was found to be intoxicated at the time he murdered the officer.

Chapter 5

DOMESTIC VIOLENCE

Domestic disturbances, family fights, d.v. violence. Whatever they are called in your area, they may be one of your least favorite calls to handle. It has been estimated that half of American marriages will experience an incident of physical assault at one time or another during the life of the relationship. Most of the time, the woman will be the primary victim of the violence. During the average year, more than two thousand American women will die at the hands of their domestic partners. This is domestic violence.

All of this violence is dangerous to you, too, because it establishes a general atmosphere of mayhem where an assault upon you, the authority figure, is a natural outgrowth of already-violent behavior. Every year in the United States, police officers are murdered at the scene of domestic violence. The "officers killed" anecdotes accompanying this chapter detail recent tragedies. For every officer killed, many more are assaulted and injured answering these dangerous calls. The message for you here is a clear one: Working domestic violence calls can be hazardous to your health.

BE AWARE OF THE CYCLE

Before getting down to the specifics of risk reduction, it is worth noting that the violence of a domestic relationship follows a fairly predictable pattern. In a battering relationship, the tension begins to build as the batterer verbally and psychologically abuses his partner over real or imagined grievances. Eventually a crisis—again either real or created—occurs, and the assault is committed, perhaps with serious injuries as the result. Afterward the offender may express sorrow and present apologies and gifts in an attempt to make up. The victim tries to convince herself that the danger is over. If she can just keep from doing again whatever it was that she did "wrong" last time, everything will be alright. Then the whole cycle begins all over as the batterer works up to another attack. The violence almost certainly will occur unless effective intervention takes place. YOU may be that intervention.

In an environment where homegrown violence prevails, children can become the targets of angry assaults, too. Other relatives present in the home, particularly elderly parents, also can be attacked by an unrestrained aggressor. So can a nosy, interfering cop. A cop like you. It is the nature of your job that you MUST interfere. You MUST be professionally nosy for your own good and that of innocent others. The question for you is how to interfere in relative safety.

In recent years, many law enforcement agencies have adopted a long-overdue, enforcement-oriented approach to domestic violence incidents. The conclusion that warnings and requests that one party leave to cool down for awhile just were not getting the job done (or stopping the violence) is based on a great deal of often painful experience on the part of a lot of street cops. Now, cops are asked to be law enforcement officers and not social workers. In many cases, deserved arrests are replacing counseling as the favored approach to stopping domestic violence.

As law enforcement's stance on domestic violence toughens, many of the violent abusers are catching on to the rules of the game. They now know they are very likely going to jail if the police are called to the scene of a domestic assault. That knowledge may make them more likely to attack you. But the danger factor can become unacceptably high only if you let it.

STEPS FOR INTERVENTION

There are specific officer safety steps to be followed in answering the domestic disturbance call. They include the following guidelines.

1. Respond as Inconspicuously as You Can

In other words, arrive as quietly as possible. You want the element of surprise on your side whenever possible, and that means no screaming sirens or flashing lights within blocks of the domestic's location. Park your patrol car several houses away. Don't drive past the address, park in front of it, or turn into the driveway. If it is nighttime, douse your headlights and cut off your brake lights as you arrive.

Approach the address on foot by using the front yards of neighboring houses or other buildings. That way you avoid making an easy target of yourself. Stay out of the street and off of the sidewalk approaches as much as possible. Try and be as unpredictable as you reasonably can be in your approach to the problem address.

In an apartment building or similar structure, stick close to the hallway's walls as you move. Stay alert. If you are suddenly confronted by an armed offender, the recesses of doorways can offer some cover even with the door closed. Remain conscious of your nearest available cover in case things get really nasty. Walk softly and quietly by silencing any noisy, jangling equipment. Turn down the volume on your portable radio but do not turn it off—you may need it in a hurry. Consider the use of a radio earpiece.

2. Keep Your Dispatcher Informed

Let your communications center know when you arrive at the scene of a domestic violence call. Also let the dispatcher know if anything seriously wrong is immediately apparent—like a person down or somebody being attacked right in front of you. It is not too early to call for more help in addition to the absolutely mandatory *minimum* of one backup officer, if the situation dictates. Also notify dispatch of any other special needs you may have, such as paramedics.

3. Stop, Look and Listen

Unless someone is obviously being murdered in your presence, don't announce your presence at a domestic scene right away. Size things up before you commit. Listen for the sounds of a struggle or agitated voices. Just listening often will tell you who the aggressor is and just how cranked up he or she may be. It also may tell you if weapons are about to become a factor ("You call the cops and I'll blow their heads off!"). You may even be able to see what's happening through a partially open window or curtain. Be careful not to expose enough of yourself to become a gunfire target for someone inside. Don't rush in, particularly if you have expended a lot of energy (and air) climbing stairs or running. If at all possible, give your heart and your nerves time to settle down just a bit. Wait for your backup to get into place, too. You may need him any moment now.

4. Be Cautious in Your Approach and Assessment

Stand quietly beside, not in front of, a door or window while you assess the goings on inside. Force your way in only if no one will admit you and you are convinced by your observations that someone inside is in immediate danger of death or serious injury. Continue your assessment. How many people are present? Where are they? What are they doing? What is their condition, especially insofar as injuries and sobriety are concerned?

When you're ready, announce yourself as "the Police." Be authoritative but don't act as if you are spoiling for a fight. Speak in a firm but steady voice. Remain alert to everything going on around you. You may have to defend yourself, take immediate enforcement action, or even beat a tactical retreat with little or no warning, so stay ready.

5. Check for Weapons and Injuries Immediately

Do a quick visual survey of everyone in sight for any obvious weapons, firearms, or otherwise. Eyeball their hands as well as their clothing, including rear waistband areas. If you are talking with an apparent victim of a domestic assault, ask an initial question or two right away: Did he (or she) have a weapon? What kind? Your initial, visual once-over should include a quick check for obvious injuries. Don't lose sight of the most likely aggressor during all of this, however. He (or she) remains your major threat. You also can pose another simple query to everyone present: Is anyone hurt? Where? Not only does an answer tell you whether or not you may have a crime on your hands, it also gives you an idea about the potential danger of at least one of the participants. There's one more benefit to this line of questioning: It indicates to the disputants that you just might really be interested in their welfare. That just might give you an edge if push comes to shove later. Naturally, if what you see or hear shows a need for medical assistance, you can call for paramedics.

6. Obtain Necessary Assistance

You do not want to go to a domestic violence call without a backup officer. What you see and hear upon your arrival (number, attitude, size, weapons, and sobriety of potential combatants) may dictate that you call for additional officers before you get embroiled deeply in a domestic beef. Never hesitate to call in more help. It is much easier to send away surplus aid than get quick assistance later when there is no one close by to help. It is not *unmacho* to call for assistance; it is *stupid* to fail to obtain it when it is indicated by good, common sense.

A final note on necessary assistance: Don't wave off your backup unless you are absolutely *positive* you won't need it. In one incident in the South, a young officer waved off backup cars on two separate occasions during a potentially hazardous contact. The patrolman was slain with his own weapon not long after the last backup drove away. To repeat: *Do not send away help you may soon need.*

7. Attempt to Remove Uninvolved Parties

Arguments can draw a crowd very quickly. The members of the audience, particularly when related to one or both participants in the squabble, tend to take sides in the contest. If an outsider (like YOU!) intervenes, they are apt to get downright nasty. If at all possible, it is beneficial to get brothers, sisters, friends, and others away from the domestic scene while you try to defuse the actors. Send them down the street, next door, or whatever else you can manage. Try and rely on persuasion here. You really have little authority to start ordering people around when they are not involved in the problem itself.

By reducing the number of persons present you proportionately cut the number of potential attackers you have to worry about if you must take physical custody of a domestic batterer. If you cannot reduce the size of the gathering on-scene, at least get additional help to stand by with you in case things go downhill in a hurry. Further, your backups should be very clear on their responsibilities ("You watch the girlfriend and Uncle Harry, you watch the drunk sisters," etc.).

8. Separate the Combatants

Remove the opponents beyond arms' reach of each other, preferably into different rooms. Stay away from potential weapons and out of the kitchen and bathroom entirely. The former contains too many good weapons and the latter offers an oversupply of suicide-by-drugs opportunities.

You should remain with one disputant while your backup listens to the other side's story. If possible, position the individuals so that each faces away from the other but so that you and your partner can see each other. Try to keep the combatants physically separated until you have taken whatever action is indicated and are ready to leave.

Watch your back during your departure from the area. As every veteran police officer knows, domestic violence victims can turn quickly into attackers of their rescuer when their tormentor is arrested or otherwise "mistreated." Remember that everyone present is a potential threat to you.

9. Find Out What Happened

Before you can decide on a course of effective intervention, you will need to know what you are dealing with. Has a crime been committed? How serious? By whom? You get the information you need by asking questions and listening carefully to the replies. Take your time and get the facts you need for sound decision making. Try to spend more time listening than talking, but do not lower your defenses while you are taking in the conflicting accounts and mulling over your best response.

10. Be Sensitive to Situational Changes

Keep your senses attuned for attitude changes from anyone on scene. A previously docile offender may plan to launch an assault on you if he concludes that your investigation is moving toward an arrest–his. Watch for the physical indicators of pending trouble: tightening facial muscles, pacing back and forth, exaggerated arm movements, stiffening arm muscles, clenched fists, a vacant stare.

Remain aware of your physical surroundings and where the disputants and others are located at all times. Watch out for weapons and potential weapons, such as fireplace tools and cooking pots. Admittedly, it can be a bit difficult to do when you are in someone else's home, but it is vital to your survival that you do not allow domestic disturbance participants to wander around at will, out of your sight and immediate control. They can reappear suddenly with all sorts of deadly surprises in hand.

Two officers in the southwestern part of the United States encountered the "keep 'em always in sight" rule the hard way when they allowed the male half of a domestic fight to enter his bathroom while toting a small briefcase they permitted him to remove from his bedroom. When one officer eventually entered the bathroom to check on the subject, he was killed by a pistol shot to the heart.

Sadly, this same, tragic domestic scene has been repeated time after time in America. Too many officers have perished over the years in variations of the same, basic officer survival error. Remember always: When you lose control of your immediate surroundings, you lose control of the odds of surviving. Don't let it happen. You control *them;* never let them control *you.*

11. Check "Records and Wants"

Your department most likely has access to some lifesaving, precautionary information on the people you are dealing with. But you will never know about it if you don't ask. While covered by your backup, run radio checks on those present at the scene of the domestic battle. Be sure they are not in a position to overhear the replies you receive. You may learn that you are dealing with more than you expected, and you can then take necessary countermeasures–like getting more help. More than a few domestic calls have been "solved," at least for awhile, by the discovery of an outstanding arrest warrant for one of the subjects involved.

12. Decide on a Course of Action and Act Decisively

Assess, plan, and make a decision. Then, *do* something. The attacker at a domestic disturbance is more likely to take you on if you communicate via words or body language that you really don't know what you are doing or what you should do next. That does not mean that you should jump to rash conclusions and take hasty action before you know the story. It *does* mean that once you have a handle on law violations and a plan for doing something about them, it's time to *act*. Inform your backup of what you are going to do and his role in it. His job is primarily one of cover officer unless you direct him otherwise.

When you do decide what you are going to do, give any necessary orders in a manner that is firm without being obnoxious or challenging. Don't make threats. Just let everyone know in a matter-of-fact manner what is going to take place and then carry out your plans. Naturally, you do not want to commit yourself to actions you do not have the resources to carry out ("I'm hauling all ten of you to jail!"). But do carry out what you've said you will do or you'll have a hard time dealing with these same parties the next time. Your credibility is one of your biggest allies in taking care of business at the scene of a "hot" domestic. Don't damage it.

13. Make Your Departure Quick and Clean

Do not stick around waiting for applause when you have finished handling a domestic violence call. It is very unlikely there is going to be any. It is much more likely that by hanging around you will catch more grief and possibly some physical interference from the allies of whomever you removed or otherwise took enforcement action against. If the friends and relatives of the offender don't come after you, there is always the possibility that the "victim" you just helped will undergo a sudden change of heart and go on the warpath against you now that you have removed her (or his) financial support or sometimes-lover from the picture.

If you have paperwork to do on the case, it is safest to go somewhere else to do it. There is some officer survival truth in the old "out of sight, out of mind" maxim. Even then, stay alert for fallout from the call you have just handled. Offenders from domestics as well as their buddies have been known to track down and attack the "offending" officer even hours and miles removed from the disturbance scene. Stay alert and stay alive. Remember that you've got enemies out there.

14. Don't Expect to Achieve Miracles

A final piece of violence-handling advice is aimed as much at your *mental* well-being and survival as it is your physical safety. The advice is simply this: Do your best, but do not expect to solve permanently in 15 minutes a crisis that has been building for 15 months–or 15 years.

There certainly may be more assaults involving these same players later on. There may be injuries. There may even be a tragic death. It is possible that police officers may be hurt (or worse) dealing with these same people. None of this is your fault as long as you have handled your call to the best of your ability. Don't agonize over past calls.

The cycle of domestic violence and abuse is a complex one. As long as you have interceded to end the ongoing violence where you can and taken enforcement action whenever appropriate, you have carried out your obligations to your department, your peers, and the victim of the domestic mayhem. When you carry out these duties with proper attention to the basics of good officer safety practices, too, you have fulfilled your obligations to yourself and those who care about you.

Although they may never be your favorite kind of call to handle, you should expect to respond on a lot of domestic violence intervention assignments during your tenure as a law enforcement officer. You also should anticipate that, because of the dynamics involved, these calls will remain among the most potentially hazardous you will encounter. By preparing yourself mentally and physically to handle them in safety and carefully planning your response ahead of time, you can reduce the danger to a manageable level.

By using a tactically sound approach, getting sufficient help, and gathering in everything that your senses can tell you, the assignment can be made much safer. By remaining constantly alert, positioning yourself carefully, and using careful scene control as well as safe arrest and prisoner handling techniques, you can defuse the danger that these encounters with violent offenders can bring.

In safely mastering the dangers of domestic violence intervention, you serve the needs of the victim and the community while you shield yourself from harm. That is officer safety with a community-involved twist!

A RISK REDUCTION CHECKLIST FOR
DOMESTIC VIOLENCE

1. Respond as inconspicuously as you can.
2. Keep dispatch aware of your whereabouts and activities.
3. Stop, look, and listen before you announce yourself.

4. Use caution on your approach and initial assessment.
5. Check for weapons and injuries immediately.
6. Obtain necessary assistance—always!
7. Attempt to remove uninvolved parties.
8. Separate the persons involved.
9. Find out what has happened by being a good listener.
10. Be sensitive to situational changes and watch your back.
11. Check "records and wants" on those present.
12. Decide on a course of action and act decisively.
13. Make your departure cleanly and keep watching your back.
14. Don't expect to achieve miracles. Just do your best.

A 71-year-old police officer with more than 30 years of law enforcement experience was killed responding as a backup to a domestic violence call at a diner. In the establishment's parking lot, the officer was interviewing a woman when her male companion went to a vehicle and obtained a .38-caliber handgun. He fired rounds at the three officers on-scene, striking the victim officer in the left shoulder area. The two other officers wounded the assailant, who was arrested. The victim officer died from wound complications 13 days later.

* * * * *

A domestic disturbance call received at about 4 p.m. resulted in the death of a 43-year-old sheriff's deputy. The officer, who had 9 years of law enforcement experience, arrived at the address ahead of his back-up, parked in front of the residence, and had just exited his car when he was hit in the chest with a rifle round fired from the front door of the dwelling. A 58-year-old man fled the scene in a vehicle and was later apprehended in the killing.

* * * * *

Three patrol officers were killed in an ambush around 6:30 p.m. while answering a domestic violence call. All three were veteran officers. Each was wearing body armor. The first officer arrived and spoke with a woman who said she had been assaulted by her husband, who she indicated was intoxicated. She said there were firearms in a vehicle in the home's garage. After failing to contact the suspect at the front door, the first officer went to the back of the house and entered through the rear door. He was hit in the jaw with a shotgun blast. He returned fire and staggered out of the residence, fatally wounded. A second officer took cover against the side of the rear of the house, but the subject leaned out a window and shot him fatally. As additional officers arrived, the male subject fired again from a window and struck a third officer fatally in the face. After a 4-hour standoff, a 58-year-old suspect with a history of violent crime and weapons offenses was taken into custody.

Chapter 6

UNDER THE INFLUENCE PEOPLE

Intoxicated people are unpredictable. Because they are unpredictable, they are potentially dangerous to you. If you remember nothing else of what this chapter has to say about dealing with intoxicated people, know that fact for a virtual certainty. Alcohol abuse and its resultant effects on those who abuse it pose major threats to the safety of every law enforcement officer.

How great is the threat? Statistics can tell part of the story. It has been estimated that there are at least nine million "problem drinkers" in the United States. It is likewise stated that the country amasses more than 25,000 alcohol-related traffic fatalities and 15,000 alcohol-involved homicides and suicides annually. Stir in another 20,000 or so deaths each year from diseases brought on or aggravated by alcohol's effects, and you begin to get the true picture of alcohol's influence on the American scene.

Alcohol intoxication has a very definite, pronounced impact on crime in this country. Research has clearly established, for example, that 40 percent of all victims of homicide are intoxicated at the time of their deaths, as are 50 percent of their attackers. Alcohol's connection to other serious crimes is also well established, including a significant alcohol intoxication contribution to arson, child abuse, domestic violence, and sexual assault. It should come as no surprise that intoxicated offenders also assault and, sometimes, murder police officers who are attempting to control their unlawful activities.

LOOK FOR THE SIGNS

If it can be taken as a given that intoxicated people are dangerous to police officers, it is obviously important for you to be able to recognize the tell-tale signs of alcohol intoxication in those you meet on the street. A "drunk recognition" primer might list the following indicators of intoxication:

1. Watery, bloodshot eyes
2. Clothing disarranged or disheveled
3. Smell of alcoholic beverages on the breath and person
4. Slurred speech
5. Confused attitude or mannerisms
6. Display of emotional extremes, such as crying or giggling for no apparent reason
7. Weaving or stumbling while walking
8. Swaying while standing; unsteady on feet
9. Leaning or holding onto objects or people for support
10. Belligerent, combative demeanor displayed with little or no provocation.

It is important to remember that other factors—including some life-threatening medical conditions—also can produce similar symptoms. Likewise, drugs other than alcohol can cause these physical and behavioral signs of diminished control.

But for you, the police officer faced with confronting the potential threats of the drunk or drugged offender, another effect of alcohol intoxication is even more important than the physical and behavioral indicators of intoxication. That very real and dangerous factor comes from the judgment-destroying and commonsense-inhibiting effects of alcohol (or chemical) intoxication.

The mind-numbing effects of intoxication permit an individual who is under the influence to engage in or attempt conduct that better judgment would cause him to refrain from when sober. The middle-aged businessman who wouldn't even argue with a uniformed guardian of the law when sober just might physically assault that same officer when functioning under the influence of alcohol intoxication. The juvenile offender who would provide only verbal abuse when sober could well escalate to the use of a deadly weapon against you when operating under the inhibition-suppressing influence of alcohol. Indeed, the consumption of quantities of alcoholic beverages can produce big changes in human behavior. Unfortunately for you, most often those changes are bad and dangerous ones.

Unpredictability remains one of the most sinister changes that alcohol intoxication inflicts upon its victim. For you, unpredictability means danger. Intoxication means that the drunk driver who is cooperative and polite one moment may turn suddenly hostile and assaultive the next. It means that the down-and-out drunk whom you scooped off the downtown sidewalk last week with no trouble at all may produce a knife and attack you the next time he sees you coming. And it means that the fellow peace officer whom you thought you knew well may respond quite differently from what you expected when you must "officially" visit his home on a call of a drunken domestic disturbance. Unpredictability is indeed a very dangerous thing for you.

Alcohol intoxication in the people you contact on the job is dangerous for you because of the drastic changes it can bring about in rational thinking and normal, expected responses to life's experiences. That is why the relatively sober thug may surrender when you level your firearm in his direction while his intoxicated companion will dare you to shoot. It is why the young lady who, when sober, would kill nothing larger than a fly may, if given the opportunity while drunk, put a knife blade between your ribs.

By this point, there should be no doubt in your mind that the incoherent wino, the puking-drunk teenager, and the tastefully blitzed society matron all can be hazardous to you, the police officer interfering with their booze-tainted pursuits. If that danger can be as extreme as it is real, what can you do to protect yourself from it while carrying out your sworn responsibilities? Actually, you can do a lot.

DON'T UNDERESTIMATE THE DANGER

You can (and must) resist the temptation to see an intoxicated individual as "just a harmless drunk." There is no way to tell the difference between "just another drunk" and a drunk who will kill you if he or she gets the chance. As a result, every intoxicated person you contact as you go about your duties must be treated with dignity and respect but also with caution and more than a little healthy suspicion. That means you pay attention to your positioning and physical separation as you approach the suspected inebriate. It means you follow good weapon retention practices. And it means you remain alert for *anything* to happen even as you hope that it doesn't.

You must follow safe and proper prisoner handling techniques when contacting, detaining, and transporting an intoxicated person. That means that all intoxicated persons taken into custody must be handcuffed properly. Simply put, "properly" translates into hands behind the back with the cuffs double-locked and checked to see that they are snug yet not circulation-stopping tight. A kicking, violently resisting drunk also should have his ankles secured together with a nylon rope "hobble" or flexible, plastic ties prior to his being transported in a police vehicle. If necessary, additional restraints may be required to prevent the car's windows—and your head—from being kicked and damaged.

An intoxicated prisoner must be searched just as carefully as anyone else you take into custody. He can, after all, kill you just as dead as anyone else if you miss a hidden gun or blade. Your search should be a systematic one that starts at the head area and extends down to the footwear. Don't overlook coats and other outer garments as well as belts and hats as possible hiding places for weapons or contraband.

You already know that an intoxicated person can be very unpredictable. As a result, you should expect the unexpected at all times and be prepared to react accordingly. An intoxicated person may have been quietly docile the entire time he has been handcuffed in your backseat and yet become violently uncooperative the instant his restraints are removed. Or an under the influence prisoner who has bluffed and blustered about what he is going to do to you when the cuffs are taken off may in fact ignore you completely when the bracelets are removed–and instead attack another officer he has never seen before.

There appears to be a dangerous belief held by some officers that says a mouthy, threatening drunk will shape up once the cuffs are off and he has an opportunity to make good on his promises. This may or may not prove to be the case. Play it safe. If he claims that he's going to try to hurt you, *believe* him and be ready to respond appropriately.

If at all possible, do not deal with an intoxicated subject without the benefit of having a backup officer present. Even with their inhibitions relaxed and their judgment impaired, most drunks still will recognize and respect the old "strength in numbers" element as being on your side. Many will be less likely to mount a full-scale assault against you when you obviously have the advantage of superior numbers. With a backup present, if he *does* decide foolishly to take you on, you will have valuable help in controlling him without serious injury to anyone, the drunk included.

It is not a good idea to take on more than one intoxicated person by yourself. Now the "strength in numbers" maxim is working against you, and even a thoroughly blitzed opponent can sense his improved position. Do more talking (and even that in a nonthreatening manner) than anything else until adequate help is on the scene. Even then, do not let yourself be outnumbered. Five intoxicated bikers in a nasty mood very likely will require more than you and a single backup for safe handling. Ideally, a couple of officers per drunk is the proper ratio of police to intoxicated subjects for sound officer safety practices.

An intoxicated person can pose problems enough without you aggravating the situation. As a result, you must never belittle or verbally harass even the sloppiest, most out of it drunk. It is amazing what nearly unconscious inebriates sometimes can remember when they sober up and land on Internal Affairs' doorstep. More important, a verbal assault by you may be all that is required to push an already surly drunk into actual physical resistance. As more than one surprised police officer has discovered to his chagrin, a thoroughly blitzed prisoner still can turn out to be a very effective battler. Fighting with drunks is a dirty proposition. The application of sound tactics and carefully chosen control words can reduce the number of battles you have to fight.

Also, keep in mind that alcohol is not the only drug that can pose serious dangers for you via the relaxed inhibitions and logic-weakening effects that can overcome those who fall under the influence. Whether an individual zonked out on PCP is technically intoxicated or not may be a question for the experts to decide. Whatever the case, anyone operating under the influence of *any* drug is a potential menace to you, the emergency service responder who must deal with him or her in spite of the distracting effects of mind and behavior altering substances.

An individual operating with a big load of cocaine or methamphetamine on board may not feel the pain of your comealong hold and thereby become an extra handful to control. A subject strung out on PCP may display incredible physical strength and be virtually impossible for one officer to handle without resorting to deadly force. The message for you in all of this is a straightforward one: Intoxication, whatever its source, in the individuals you must deal with means potential danger for you. Act with great caution. Have help on hand.

SOME SAFETY GUIDELINES

In addition to the larger considerations and bigger issues, there are a number of little things you can do to protect yourself when working with persons whose reasoning abilities have been weakened by excessive consumption of alcohol. Added together, they will help you remain safe while you stay effective in your handling of an alcohol-involved crisis. Some may at first glance appear very basic and somewhat self-obvious. That's alright. Ignoring or forgetting ANY of them can have consequences in injured or murdered police officers. These quick guidelines include the following:

1. Don't permit an intoxicated motorist you have removed from his vehicle to return to the car "to get my cigarettes" or for any other reason. He may return with more than smokes in hand.

2. Along the same line, do not allow an intoxicated subject you are dealing with to leave your field of vision to "get my coat," or anything else. You are in particularly perilous straits when encountering an intoxicated person on his own premises. He knows where the weapons are, you don't. Watch your subject closely and be positioned to get to him or her quickly if things start to deteriorate. Remain alert to the location of cover possibilities, too.

3. Remember that an intoxicated person you take into custody may get even drunker as well as more unpredictable and unruly after he has been in your care awhile. If he was drinking heavily just before you busted him it may

take awhile for all of the booze to affect him. He could even become quite ill or go unconscious. Watch him carefully for your own welfare as well as his.

4. Protect yourself from civil liability by obtaining medical assistance for the sick, unconscious, or extremely intoxicated individual. Never put an unconscious person into the lockup. And don't forget that some life-threatening medical problems—such as head injuries and stroke—can mimic the symptoms of alcohol intoxication. Don't allow a verbally abusive or physically resistive drunk to derail you from obtaining the medical attention he should have. You are protecting *yourself* by seeing to his medical needs.

5. Drunks can be particularly skillful at identifying what will "get your goat" and then harassing you mercilessly. Many are equally talented at obscene taunts and insults. Don't lose your cool and overreact by responding in kind or taking physical action against your tormentor. When you resort to force unnecessarily, the drunk wins. And when you go too far you may help him win big in civil court as well. Don't do it. That's part of officer survival, too.

6. If you intervene in an altercation between two or more inebriates, remain aware that the victim or complaining party may turn on you without warning if it appears you are about to take action against his former opponent. It probably has something to do with the fact that today's combatants may have been drinking buddies yesterday and will be again tomorrow. You are the outsider and enemy, so do not turn your back on anybody.

7. Be mindful that a thoroughly intoxicated individual may have his senses dulled enough to be slow in understanding what it is you want him to do, such as put down a weapon or get into a search position. Stay alert but patient; repeat and simplify your instructions to him if it looks like you are not getting through. But don't be lulled into leaving cover or getting in too close before you are ready.

8. Alcohol's numbing effects may also raise an individual's pain threshold to the point that a normally effective comealong or control hold does not work for you. Be prepared to switch to something else if your first attempt at control is clearly not working. At the same time, use care not to escalate the force you put into a hold to the point that you injure the subject.

9. Collect all of an intoxicated individual's personal effects before you place him in a cell or other holding facility. Depressed and disturbed inebriates have been known to kill themselves by self-hanging with a belt. They also have suffocated in fires that they started with matches or a lighter that an officer failed to seize. For that matter, some of these people have attacked and injured officers with uncollected items ranging from a rat-tail comb to a high-heel shoe. Search and collect before incarcerating drunks.

10. Be patient yet firm in working with an intoxicated man or woman. Twice is certainly not too many times to have to repeat your instructions; a

dozen times certainly is. By drawing on your own common sense and patience, you will have to decide for yourself when action initiated by you is needed to overcome inaction by your drunken contact. Talk when talk will get the job done. Act when talk will not work alone.

11. When that suspected drunk you have just pulled over reaches out of sight and rummages around under the car seat, don't automatically assume that he's just hiding his beer. He may pop up with a gun in his hand. When you pick up on furtive movements like this, seek cover and be prepared to defend your life with gunfire if it becomes necessary. On the street and elsewhere, be suspicious of the drunk who reaches inside his clothing at your approach. He may be hiding a bottle, but he also might be after a weapon. For that matter, a bottle itself can be turned into a dangerous weapon. If you are close enough, grab and freeze his hand in place even as you orally challenge him: "Don't move! Freeze!" Then do what's reasonable to bring the subject safely under control.

12. For your own safety, do not accept an intoxicated person's word that he will or won't do or refrain from doing anything. His diminished mental capacity brought about by alcohol intoxication will make any promises he makes to you easily forgotten—and practically worthless. As a result, his statement that he won't drive if you'll just release him or his "word before God" that he'll behave if you'll just skip the handcuffing is worse than worthless to you. It is just plain dangerous. Don't bite. Stay healthy.

The peace officer determined to survive encounters with infinite numbers of intoxicated people over a lengthy career in policing can afford to assume little about the persons and situations he deals with. He can, however, safely take for granted the fact that each and every meeting with an intoxicated human being is full of uncertainties and potentially hazardous possibilities. The drunk he encounters today will not be exactly the same individual he met the last time the same subject was "under the weather." He will not even be the same person he was 20 minutes or two beers earlier.

Personal pressures, emotional feelings, physiological conditions, amount of alcohol consumed, and yet other factors will all intervene to prevent any two encounters between police officer and drunken subject from ever being *exactly* the same. What worked in controlling this intoxicated party last time may be less effective (or more so) today. Because there is so much that cannot be known in advance with certainty, the prudent police practitioner (that's you!) must proceed with caution and be prepared for any eventuality. When it comes to working with intoxicated persons, that's what being survival smart is all about.

The safe and humane handling of under-the-influence people can prove a challenge for the most experienced, skilled, compassionate, and safety-conscious law enforcement officer. In a society that presents a steady flow of these sometimes sad, always unpredictable, and sometimes dangerous under the influence people, as a first responder you are destined to face that challenge on a regular basis whether you work in an environment that is urban, rural, or somewhere in between. Get sloppy in your tactics or apathetic in your demeanor, and you could become a casualty.

Whether they have alcohol, other drugs, or a combination of mind- and behavior-altering substances on board, under the influence people present a threat to themselves and others. Those endangered "others" include you when you must deal with often irresponsible and sometimes violent behavior. Through constant vigilance and regular application of basic officer safety practices, you can drastically reduce the threat. That's how to survive a career full of under the influence people.

A RISK REDUCTION CHECKLIST FOR
UNDER THE INFLUENCE PEOPLE

1. Learn to recognize the symptoms of intoxication from alcohol or other drugs.
2. Remember that all intoxicated persons are unpredictable and thereby potentially dangerous.
3. Obtain necessary assistance in dealing with intoxicated persons.
4. Handcuff and search all intoxicated persons you take into custody.
5. Believe a drunk who says he will hurt you if he gets a chance. Don't give him that chance.
6. Don't belittle or otherwise antagonize an intoxicated person, and never underestimate his or her ability to harm you.
7. Expect the unexpected when dealing with an intoxicated person. Don't lower your guard for even a moment.
8. Remember that certain injuries and medical conditions can mimic the symptoms of intoxication. Get medical help for these people.

A seven-year patrolman made a traffic stop at about 11:30 p.m. and took a female adult driver and her adult male passenger into custody for intoxication. He placed the female in the front seat and the male in the back seat of the police unit. En route to the jail, the male produced a knife and stabbed the officer at least three times in the throat. The prisoners escaped the vehicle, and the officer drove himself to a hospital where he died an hour later. A 22-year-old male was later arrested for the murder of the 30-year-old officer.

* * * * *

A 21-year-old patrolman was shot to death at 11:35 p.m. by a 60-year-old male. The male had been arrested for drunk driving by another officer and released on bond. The arrestee's spouse called police to warn that the subject, still drunk, had gone looking for the arresting officer. When the subject was seen driving past the police station, the victim officer and a second officer (the original arresting officer) pursued him in separate cars. The victim policeman, who had one year of experience, stopped the subject, who partially exited his vehicle firing a 12-gauge shotgun. The victim officer was struck in the chest and head. The assailant, wounded five times by return fire from both officers, was captured.

Chapter 7

SUSPICIOUS PERSONS AND INCIDENTS

Your radio assignment: "Check out a suspicious person at First and Tremont. White male; early thirties, blue coat, and brown pants." That's it. That's all you know going in. Somebody has seen something that he or she thought didn't look right. The police were called. Either because the caller did not know any more or because the communications clerk just didn't ask, you have no further information on exactly why somebody thought this individual was spooky enough to merit a call to the cops.

The suspicious person contact could begin another way, of course. It could begin because you spotted somebody you did not like the looks of as you covered the byways of your beat or sector. Maybe he just didn't fit in with his surroundings. Perhaps he was entirely too nervous when you looked his way. Or maybe it was something more elusive that you could not quite put your finger on. Your gut told you something wasn't right and deserved a bit more investigation. However it started, you had by now brought yourself to the start of a suspicious person investigation.

Most suspicious person investigations conducted by police officers—and there are literally thousands of them carried out in this country every day—begin and end without injury or serious incident. A subject is checked out, perhaps F.I.ed, and then sent on his way. Or a party is taken into custody as a result of an alert observation by a patrolling peace officer.

But all too many suspicious person contacts do not end that way. The "Officers Killed" accounts that accompany this chapter relate situations that did not end as planned for the police officers involved. Perhaps they got careless. Perhaps they were surprised. Maybe they were the victims of their own poor tactics or procedures. Whatever the cause or combination of causes, these officers died while investigating suspicious persons. Undoubtedly, more officers will die doing the same thing this year. And the next.

Despite what prior experience has shown, it is not inevitable that police officers must continue to perish while conducting suspicious person investigations. These extremely commonplace police tasks CAN be carried out in a manner that satisfies law enforcement's objectives without exposing the officers involved to heightened risks of death or injury. There ARE some practical things you can do to reduce your risks even as you effectively carry out your sworn duties. Many of them will be reviewed here.

START WITH A PLAN

As in just about every other sort of street encounter you involve yourself in, you will need to do some planning before you get deeply involved in a suspicious person contact. Whether you are in a car or on foot, try to keep your subject(s) under observation for a bit before committing yourself to the actual contact. Answer as many of your own questions about the individual and his actions as you reasonably can. Is he committing a crime as you watch him? Do you know who he is or anything about his background that tells you right away that he's dangerous? Is he accompanied by other subjects? Is he visibly agitated? Armed? Intoxicated or high?

What you learn about your suspicious person from your early observations should help you decide whether you want to get a backup on scene and perhaps implement contact and cover tactics at the outset. If in any doubt at all, get help before you attempt to make contact. Start planning the location for your stop if the subject is moving. Your options may be fewer if he is stationary, such as leaning or sitting in a doorway, and appears likely to stay put for awhile.

If you have a choice in the location of your contact with a party or parties on foot, look for an area with good lighting and limited avenues of escape for your subject. You are looking for something of a compromise as far as other people nearby are concerned. If you have a choice, you don't want an area so isolated that an offender has no worry about witnesses if he decides to try to kill you. At the same time, you need to avoid densely crowded areas such as shopping malls or playgrounds where stray rounds are likely to hit innocents if gunplay ensues. In reality, you probably never will have as much choice in your contact location as you would like. Do the best you can with what you have at hand.

A final consideration before you commit yourself to a suspicious person stop: Take a second to review your reason for stopping the subject or subjects in the first place and be sure you can articulate your reasoning if you are ever asked to do so, either by the subject at the time or later after the stop turns into a fight or a shootout. You also need to know in advance how much force you have a legal right to use when he answers your request to stop with a one-fingered salute. Do you have reasonable grounds to believe he has committed a crime? Do you thereby have a right to detain him by force for further inquiry? Or do you have something less solid that will require you to rely on talk and persuasion to get him to yield to you? Try to determine the limits on your actions up front. It is too late to worry about it after someone gets hurt in a confrontation that did not have a legal basis for occurring in the first place.

Don't let your ego get you into trouble. Before you go after a subject who has ignored a request to talk with you, be sure you have the grounds to detain him against his will. If you decide you don't have enough, just chalk it up to experience and swallow your pride. Don't make matters worse by forcing an illegal arrest. Let him pass until you can develop something more solid, however long (minutes, hours, days) that may take. It's the smart way to go.

MAKING CONTACT

Now that you are making the contact, tell your dispatcher what you are doing and where you are doing it BEFORE you start the process. Keep dispatch advised of your location or the status of the contact changes. You also will use your communications net to run EVERY suspicious person you contact for "wants," locally and nationally. Do this radio check as early as possible in the contact. If he's wanted, you want to know NOW before he works up the courage or finds an opening to attack you. If you do find that there's an arrest warrant out for your subject, get him handcuffed and searched right away, even before the warrant is confirmed, if need be. Do it with a cover officer present, if possible. The less time he has to get nervous and plan an assault or escape attempt, the better off you are. You always can uncuff him and apologize if the warrant turns out to be invalid for some reason, or if further inquiry shows he is not the wanted party. Your safety is always more important than possible inconvenience or embarrassment to your subject. Make amends afterward.

Where possible, approach your target from the rear. Keep watching his hands. Can you see them continuously? Take special care if you cannot. Be conscious of the cover that is quickly available to you if your subject pulls a gun when challenged. If you are approaching in your vehicle, get out before you direct an oral challenge to your party but try to keep the car between you and him until you can be reasonably certain he is not going to produce a weapon. Don't get rushed; take your time and stay observant.

When you get out of your vehicle to speak with a suspicious person, take your portable radio with you if you have one available. Otherwise drape the microphone to your car's two-way out the driver's door. You may need to call for help in a hurry.

What about communicating with the subject himself? What do you say? Try starting out all of your suspicious person contacts with "Police officer!" in a firm, clear voice. This settles any question of your identity and will be a big point in your favor if resistance develops and your party tries to claim later that he thought he was being set upon by gangsters. Consider activating your vehicle's emergency lights for the same reason as well as to keep yourself from being rear-ended by traffic if you are on or near the roadway. Both the oral and visual "announcements" are particularly important if you are working in plainclothes or out of an unmarked car. Don't omit either of them.

What you say next depends a lot on the circumstances of the contact. "Sir, I need to talk to you a minute" may be a good start for the individual whom you do not suspect of serious lawbreaking. "Stop! Don't move your hands!" might be just as appropriate if you have reason to believe your subject has committed a serious or violent crime and/or may be packing a weapon. There are, of course, a great many more word options falling somewhere in-between. Choose what your good, street survival sense tells you is appropriate to the situation. Then voice it firmly, clearly, and authoritatively. Don't bluff and bluster; do make it clear verbally that you mean what you say.

Watch your positioning during any suspicious person contact. This holds true whether the meeting occurs on the street, in a hallway, on a tenement roof, or anyplace else. Keep your subject five to six feet distant. Don't stand between two subjects. Keep your back, where possible, to something solid. Keep your gun side turned away from the subject(s) you are contacting. Don't stand in a spot where the location alone could disable you if trouble starts: stairways, in the midst of clutter that could trip you. Don't stand on the roadway with your heels backed up to a curb where you would fall easily if pushed backward.

Don't totally abandon your visual surveillance of a suspicious person in order to run "wants" checks, fill out field interview cards, or do anything else. Use your peripheral vision to watch for movement, particularly by your party's hands. Realize that you cannot reasonably expect to keep track of more than a couple of people by yourself. Get a backup to cover you if you are dealing with more suspicious subjects than that. It's not cowardly; it just makes good field survival sense.

CHECKING FOR WEAPONS

How about a weapons search of your suspicious person? You bet, but with a condition attached. That condition is legalistic in nature and requires that you have *reasonable grounds* to believe that the person you are planning to check for weapons may be armed with a harmful device of some sort which he is capable of using against you. Your reasonable grounds for this belief can be based on a lot of things, including the following factors or indicators:

1. Bulges in a subject's clothing indicating the possible presence of a weapon.
2. A portion of something that could be a weapon showing to open view. Example: the handle of a knife or club.
3. Furtive movements by the subject upon the approach of police.
4. Statements by victims, witnesses, or informants that the subject is carrying a weapon.
5. Past history of violent crimes involving weapons by this known subject.
6. Past history of weapons violations by this person.
7. Misleading or elusive subject replies to questioning about weapons.
8. Subject's presence in a high-crime area in which subjects contacted by police often turn out to be armed.

According to the U.S. Supreme Court in *Terry v. Ohio,* you may conduct a pat down search for weapons (and *only* for weapons) if you can state your reasoning for believing the subject constitutes an armed threat to you. A valid stop does not automatically justify a search for weapons. For a weapons frisk to be valid and lawful, there must have been some reason for you to have stopped the individual in the first place. (That's called reasonable suspicion!) Something in the total circumstances of the contact, including the subject's reaction to it, must give you good reason to believe he may be armed and thereby dangerous. But remember: In order for the search to be lawful, it must be limited at that point to a check for weapons and not be a general search for evidence or contraband. (That can come next—*after* your legal arrest for carrying a concealed or prohibited weapon!)

If you have reason to suspect that your suspicious person is armed, you will need to check out that potential threat ahead of anything else you might be planning to do with the individual. Get behind cover. If you see a weapon or have strong grounds to believe he is armed, draw your own firearm and level it at him, meanwhile addressing him orally: "Police! Don't move! Stand just as you are!" Or words to that effect. Never lose sight of his hands. Be prepared to fire if a hand does dive beneath clothing and produce a weapon. Stay alert. Keep him covered and wait for a backup officer before you do a weapons search, if at all possible. Do the search as a contact and cover operation, most likely using yourself as the contact officer.

If you do not immediately sight a weapon or know for sure that your party is "packing" but nonetheless suspect that he is armed, consider verbally challenging him while you remain behind cover: "Police! Don't move! Keep facing away from me until you're told otherwise." Or similar words to that effect. Proceed with great care, particularly if you are searching without benefit of a backup. When you do search, never do so from the front. Have him face away, place his hands on his head, and spread his legs widely apart. Do a pat down of his clothing and person from top to bottom, starting with his headgear and finishing with socks and footwear tops. All the while you must remain alert to the real possibility of a sudden attack or escape attempt. Keep him off balance.

Before you get busy with searching an individual, talk to your subject firmly but quietly. *Ask* him if he's carrying a weapon and where it is. If he reveals that he has one, instruct him not to touch it. *You* will take custody of any weapons encountered. Meanwhile, be sure you keep your own sidearm out of the subject's reach.

Remember: Pat down and squeeze clothing from the subject's rear, not his front, where he could more easily assault you, with a weapon or otherwise. Be meticulous in your search; there's no big rush. It is your safety that is at stake here. Remain conscious of the location of the nearest good cover in case things deteriorate rapidly.

Don't overreach or otherwise lose your balance while checking a suspicious person for weapons. Be prepared to shove him away, disengage contact, and draw your own weapon if the situation warrants. Naturally, if you have established probable cause to arrest the suspicious subject before this point, you should always handcuff first and search second.

Very early in the contact you will want to separate your suspicious party from any sacks, boxes, backpacks, or other containers he might be carrying until you have a chance to check these items for weapons. (Check him first; then worry about the things he is toting.) *Ask* him what's inside those closed containers. He may even tell you there is a weapon there. You lose nothing by asking as long as you do not accept at face value his statement that there are no weapons inside.

If you decide to give your party a ride for any reason (out of gas, juvenile out late, etc.), separate him from any carry on baggage, such as satchels or knapsacks, just in case you missed something while checking for weapons. Explain to your passenger what you are doing and why. If he is truly on the level, a real objection from him is unlikely.

And speaking of objections. There should seldom be any loud ones from the individuals you detain briefly for inquiry if you do a decent job of explaining *why* you have stopped these people in the first place. A simple, polite explanation is in order here: "I stopped you because you fit the description of a wanted party believed to be around here." Or: "I was afraid that bulge there was a gun." Or: "A guy was just beaten up down the street and since you were coming from that way I thought you might have seen something." Or whatever else appears appropriate to the situation.

If it is appropriate, and very often it will be, offer an apology to go with your explanation. Apologies are cheap and can save you trouble in the long run. They make it less likely that you will be assaulted at the end of your suspicious person contact. They may reduce the likelihood that you or another officer will be attacked by a still-resentful subject the next time he meets up with law enforcement. Explanations and apologies are also parts of a comprehensive officer survival package. Do not hesitate to take advantage of what they have to offer you.

Because of the lack of solid information that you may experience at the outset, suspicious persons and suspicious situations are potentially risky affairs. Your best bet for your continued safety is to utilize sound tactics designed to offset the initial information disadvantage. Gather as much information as you can prior to the contact. Stay sharp and continue collecting observations as the contact proceeds. Position yourself carefully. Do not let your subject or subjects get too close. Get assistance quickly if anything looks or sounds funny. Stay suspicious and survive!

A RISK REDUCTION CHECKLIST FOR SUSPICIOUS PERSONS AND INCIDENTS

1. Don't rush into a suspicious person contact. Learn as much as you can about the subject(s) you are contacting before you commit yourself.
2. Try and contact your subject at a location that is to your advantage.
3. Watch his hands. Never stop looking for a weapon—or another one.
4. Be conscious of your positioning and cover options during a suspicious person contact.
5. When the situation indicates, conduct a thorough weapons search of a suspicious person.
6. Stay firm, fair, and alert throughout the investigation. Disengage cautiously.

At approximately 1:20 a.m., a ten-year veteran patrolman was slain after being flagged down by some bar patrons and told there was a suspicious male at the rear of the establishment. Getting out to investigate on foot, the officer was then warned by the patrons that the subject was behind him. The officer shined his flashlight on the 26-year-old subject and was immediately felled by a shotgun blast to the chest from six to nine feet away. The killer of the 36-year-old patrolman later shot himself to death.

* * * * *

Two uniformed patrolmen were killed when they stopped to question three males whom they suspected were involved in a drug deal. At approximately 9:30 a.m., the officers were searching the males when one subject drew a .25-caliber handgun and shot each officer once in the chest. One officer, a 16-year veteran, managed to fire shots, which missed the fleeing subjects. The second officer killed had 18 years of police experience. One officer was 48 years old; the other was 39.

* * * * *

A 24-year-old patrolwoman was shot and killed with her own handgun while investigating a suspicious man seated on a curb at 10 a.m. A struggle began when she reached for the man and both fell to the ground. The officer attempted to call for backup, but her radio was set at the wrong frequency. The man took control of the officer's baton and struck her in the head. He then seized her .40-caliber handgun and shot her 15 times. The killer remained at the scene and surrendered to other officers.

Chapter 8

BURGLARIES AND STRUCTURE SEARCHES

It was approximately 1 a.m. when the 44-year-old deputy sheriff arrived at a hardware store in a small West Texas town where a burglar alarm had been activated. As a second officer covered the back door, the deputy entered alone. The officer was subsequently shot fatally in the back with a 12-gauge shotgun by a 40-year-old male who had entered via the roof and was in the process of stealing guns when interrupted. The killer was himself slain by other officers.

Burglaries in progress and structure searches for interrupted burglars or other criminals have accounted for a host of officer fatalities over the years. Indeed, the cornered burglar or other felon appears more likely to be armed today than even a decade ago. He likewise appears more willing to direct his weapons against responding police officers in order to preserve his freedom.

Improved technology in the realm of alarm systems may also be contributing to more confrontations between police and surprised burglars or other criminals. Silent, central station alarms that notify the police but not the burglar that he has been detected increasingly bring the cops on the run before the crook has made good his escape.

Of course, there are other calls for police assistance in addition to trapped burglars that can result in your having to search a business, residence, or other structure for a hidden and dangerous subject or subjects. Barricaded gunmen and hostage-takers pose a particularly significant threat to you and your fellow officers. In addition, a fleeing armed robber could take refuge in a building that you may end up having to search. So could a wanted subject on the run. So, for that matter, could any other crook whose unlawful activities have just been exposed by responding police units. The various possibilities can be left to the imagination of the survival-savvy police officer.

Tragically, not all police officers approach the building or structure search assignment with equal imagination when it comes to ensuring their continued survival. Too many get careless. Consequently, too many are killed or seriously hurt by suspects waiting to confront them. The mistakes can be many but often include one or more of the following deadly errors:

1. Attempting a building search alone.
2. Searching too large an area with too few officers.
3. Making dangerous assumptions, such as "It's just another false alarm" or "They've already left."
4. Poor coordination and communication among personnel doing a building search.
5. Rushing a building search to a premature completion.
6. Careless or incompetent search of a structure and its surrounding area.
7. Poor entry tactics.
8. Poor use or no use of available cover.
9. Poor officer positioning around and inside the structure.
10. Lack of proper police equipment or misuse of equipment and resources available.

GATHERING INFORMATION

You probably can think of other structure search problems you have witnessed. You may even have contributed to some of them. Nonetheless, there is nothing to be gained by perpetuating past mistakes by repeating them until they become habit. There is everything–including your life–to be lost by such a course of inaction. Although no set of tactics can remove every element of risk from this or any other facet of law enforcement, the dangers you face can be reduced significantly. You really *can* manage your personal risks while doing an effective, efficient job of clearing a building of burglars or other bad guys. As in so many of the assignments you will handle in your law enforcement career, you will be wise to start this one with an intense focus on information gathering.

One good piece of advice for your pre-search information-gathering efforts can be applied to everything you do in a structure search operation: DON'T GET RUSHED. Not because it's time to go home, not because you've got other calls to answer, not because your supervisor is impatient. Not for any reason. Take the time to do it safely and correctly. It is worth it in lives (maybe yours) saved.

There are a number of officer safety questions you will need to answer as you gather data concerning the search operation you are about to launch. Among them:

What has any past experience at this location taught? Perhaps you have searched this structure before. (Burglar alarms, for instance, tend to repeat at the same locations.) What do you remember about it? Any special problem spots that are hard to see or reach? How about other special problems? If you have not been there before, perhaps another officer who is en route or on the air has been. Ask him what he knows about it that could help you. Exchange information freely with your backups or other officers on the street while you are still en route to a potential building search assignment. It can make your searching duties much safer.

If you are responding to an alarm, what kind is it? As you know, there are different kinds of burglar alarms. A perimeter alarm tells you that the security of a door or window may have been compromised. On the other hand, a motion detection or infrared alarm may indicate that there is a good reason to believe someone is currently inside the structure. Or an alarm system's sound detectors may have picked up voices.

Area protection alarms may be in place to guard a specific item or room in the structure, such as a display area or an office. With point protection, things get even more specific. This kind of alarm setup may protect something such as the safe inside an office.

Stay in close touch with your dispatcher to keep updated on what the alarm sensors are reporting. Some larger structures have their detectors reporting in zones or sectors, which should help the operator monitoring them tell you where the intruders are and where they may be moving to. If the sensors are being monitored by an alarm company instead of the police communications center, be sure your dispatcher maintains an open telephone line to the alarm company operator.

There are still other questions to be answered before you plunge into a building search. You can answer many of them once you reach the scene. For instance:

Who has heard or seen what? Get hold of your reporting or complaining party, if one is known, and find out exactly what he or she observed. How many offenders were seen? Exactly where were they last sighted? What did they look like? How about clothing? Any weapons or vehicles noted? What was the entry point? And don't forget: How credible is your reporting party? Does what he has to say make sense? Generally speaking, you will put a lot more stock in the observations of a fellow officer than, say, those of a passing motorist. But no matter where your information comes from, allow room in your planning for incorrect data. It's dangerous for you to assume, for instance, that only one suspect is inside because only one has been seen. Part of being careful is being just a bit cynical.

What is the physical layout of the place to be searched? How many doors and windows will have to be watched from the outside while an interior search is conducted? How many floors or levels are there? How about special problem areas, such as false ceilings, basements, crawl spaces, and roof access? Generally speaking, the bigger and more complex the area to be cleared, the more people and the more time you will need to do it right.

Try to get a manager, employee, or resident of the address in question to come to the scene to provide you with the answers to these and other questions. Other questions include:

Who and what may be inside besides the offender(s)? Should there be a cleanup crew or other employees inside the structure to be searched? Can it be determined exactly where they are? The manager or employee called to the scene by your dispatcher or the alarm company may be able to answer these queries.

Knowing *what* is inside is vital to your safety, too. Whether you are dealing with a burglarized general merchandise outlet or a private residence in which a crook is hiding, it would be more than a little nice to know if any firearms are inside. If so, what kind are they? As a general rule of thumb, long weapons such as rifles will pose a greater threat to you than handguns.

You also need to know in advance, if possible, if any other extra problems such as animals or hazardous materials await you inside. Where, precisely, are they located? The more you know in advance, the better your planning for the search can be.

Can you get keys, particularly those to interior doors? Your search will not be complete nor will you be able to guarantee that there are no suspects hidden inside until you have checked out ALL of the rooms present. You only can arrive at that degree of certainty by obtaining keys to get you into locked offices, storerooms, and whatever else stands between you and a truly complete search. Unsearched rooms are more than an impediment to your "free of suspects" guarantee. Worse, they are a source of real danger from which you could be attacked at any time. Do not leave any area of a suspect building uncleared, even if you have to wait awhile for keys. If you have reason to suspect that there are offenders hidden inside, you will be justified in forcing entry to locked areas if you are absolutely unable to obtain access any other way. But be careful. There is nothing that says an offender has to wait for you to finish your entry to attack you. Be sure someone is covering the officers who are occupied with forcing entry.

What looks out of place or amiss on scene? How did the subject or subjects you are seeking make entry to the place you are about to search? Maybe they walked through an open door, and maybe not. Look for ladders, ropes, boxes stacked under windows, merchandise or other loot piled outside an intended point of exit, broken doors and windows, and any other indicators of intruders. Keep an eye out for vehicles, especially trucks and vans, parked close by. Naturally, suspicious persons in the area must be checked out to your satisfaction, as well. Armed robbers are not the only ones who utilize the services of lookouts. Never cease looking for anything that just isn't right. When you find it, trust to your good judgment and common sense and don't stumble ahead into an ambush. It is quite acceptable to take a lot of time in order to be a lot careful. Don't worry about what your more foolhardy peers might have to say. It's *your* life that's at stake.

GROUND RULES FOR A SAFE SEARCH

Although it is in itself a high-risk undertaking to talk about absolutes in the realm of officer survival, there are at least a few ground rules that come very close to making the "always" or "never" categories. In building search operations, these "almost always" or "almost never" basics can go a long distance toward keeping you safe as you ferret out suspects in a carefully executed structure search. These cardinal rules include the following pieces of time-proven, exceptionally good street survival advice.

Don't Enter and Search a Building Alone

It is simply too dangerous. Without a backup to cover you, your back becomes an attractive target for any creep with a deadly weapon. Having a cover officer readily available can be easier said than done on a very busy night in a metropolitan area or any night in an extremely rural jurisdiction. Nonetheless, the wait you might have to put up with before help gets there is worth the inconvenience many times over in officer safety. (Besides, the bad guy may come out to you in the meantime, making your task of apprehension both easier and safer. Stay close to cover so you're ready for him if he does.)

Don't give up the advantage of having a trained backup to cover you just so that you can do the search quicker and be done with it. The trade-off in heightened danger to you is just not worth any time you might save.

Don't Allow Civilians to Enter and Assist With a Search

Building managers and employees have died at the sides of officers they were assisting in a building search for intruders who turned out to be there and armed after all. Do not bring unarmed and untrained people, including police "observers" or "ridealongs," with you while you search an as-yet uncleared building. You have no way of knowing for sure how they will react in a crisis or how an offender will react to them. You will not have time or attention enough to worry about the location and welfare of anyone beyond yourself and your backups. Leave any civilian "assistants" outside, secure in your car, their own vehicles, or in some other safe location. Tell them to stay there. It's safest for everyone concerned.

One Officer Moves at a Time During a Search

You cannot cover your search partner effectively if both of you are advancing at the same time. One of you needs to remain behind cover while the other moves and searches. You then trade off and he covers you while you move with increased safety. You cannot afford to get so caught up in your searching endeavors that you lose track of one another. Watch out for him and expect him to watch out for you. If things aren't happening that way, stop the operation long enough to get your signals straight. It's that important.

If the area to be searched is so large that it requires multiple officers to search it, divide up the area and search in two-officer teams. Again, one officer on each team searches and moves while the other covers, independent of the other teams but with knowledge of where they are and what they are doing. Stay in radio or voice communication with other officers present inside and outside the structure at all times.

If a police working dog is being used in the building search operation, the K-9 handler observes and directs the animal while a backup officer covers the handler. For their own safety, other police personnel do not move ahead of the dog or otherwise freelance on their own. Once again, teamwork is the key to everyone's safety.

Don't Stray From Your Search Partner

A structure search is not the time or place to engage in a little freewheeling, independent police work. Although you cannot afford to bunch up with your partner and other officers, *do* stay close enough to keep each other under observation at all times. It's the only way you can watch out for one another effectively.

Be Conscious of Sounds as You Search

Pause from time to time during your building clearing operation to *listen* for an adversary. Your ears may reveal his careless mistakes and alert you to his whereabouts. At the same time, you must squelch your own noise to avoid telegraphing your location to your opponent. Step quietly and deliberately. Silence any jangling equipment on your belt or in your pockets. Turn your portable radio way down or use an earpiece. Talk softly when you must speak. Otherwise use hand signals to communicate with your search partner.

Peek Before You Move; Move Quick and Low

It's nice to know where you are going and what you'll find there *before* you go, particularly if there may be a bad guy with a gun there waiting for you. "Peeking" does not mean sticking your whole head and upper torso around a corner to catch the view. Peeking means just what it sounds like: *very* briefly exposing one eye and that side of your head in order to get a *very* quick look around cover. You begin moving your head back behind cover just as soon as you sight the lay of the land ahead. If you need a second look, do not peek again from the same level. An alerted offender might have a bullet targeted on that spot this time.

When you decide to change locations, offer an adversary as small a target as possible by moving fast and low. Get to cover again as quickly as you can. Plan your next move. Peek again when you must and move again when required. But no matter what else you do, keep the proverbial "low profile" as you carry out your building search. It's the only smart way to move.

All the preceding advice considered, you cannot carry out a successful building search until you get there. And you cannot get there safely without making a well-planned approach to the scene. Naturally, you will need to arrive in the vicinity quietly and park out of sight of the structure in question. You also will need to determine early the number of officers you will require to secure a perimeter and search the building both safely and effectively. With a single-family residence or small to medium-sized commercial or office structure, an officer apiece at two diagonally opposite corners of the building with two additional officers to enter and search may be enough to get the job done. With a larger or irregularly shaped building with numerous doors and windows as potential escape routes, more officers posted at additional points will be required.

The idea is for no area of the structure's exterior to go unwatched while its interior is searched for offenders. At the same time, police personnel are positioned so that no officer is firing in the direction of a colleague if an offender emerges and threatens with a deadly weapon. Inside, meanwhile, the really large building may call for more than a single two-officer search team. Get the help you need to do it right.

If you are hard-pressed for adequate police personnel to seal off and search the building in question, borrow some people via a mutual aid agreement with a nearby jurisdiction. Your agency can return the favor when the neighboring department needs help. The use of a well-trained and expertly handled police dog also can reduce considerably the number of people you will need to probe the interior of a structure. If your department does not have its own K-9 program, you should look at an arrangement with a nearby police agency that does have police working dogs. These four-footed partners are invaluable in a building search.

Your approach to the building to be searched should include a careful check of the surrounding environs by responding officers for suspicious vehicles and unexplained loiterers or pedestrians. If you have serious doubts about the legitimacy of someone found close by the problem location, do not hesitate to detain him until a crime can be confirmed or disproven and his role in the affair established. You can apologize afterward, if need be. Your primary concern at the moment must be for the safety of yourself and your fellow officers.

Before commencing your structure search, be sure that you have available the equipment you will need to carry out your operation in safety. Obviously you will need a quality flashlight and portable radio for each search participant. You also may need a ladder to gain access to the roof to check that area for suspects or forced entry. Your fire department should be able to assist you here. There are also ten-foot ladders on the market that can be folded up and stored in the trunk of a police vehicle.

You may or may not want to deploy a long gun in carrying out your structure search. If the quarters are tight and there is even a chance that innocents may still be inside, a scatter gun often will not be your weapon of choice. If you decide to search with your sidearm at the ready instead, be sure you keep it close in to your body to foil a hidden adversary's takeaway grab. Don't point your piece in the direction of your feet or your backup's body, however.

There is a small arsenal of building search tools of the trade you may want to have available to simplify and make a bit safer your exploratory mission. A small, hand-held mirror can help you see around corners without exposing your body to an opponent's gunfire. A roll of masking tape can help you mark doors leading to areas you have already checked out if you seal them as you pass with a strip of tape across the opening crack. (Now you'll also know if anyone backtracks behind you through an area you thought was secure.) Carrying a few rubber or wooden door wedges also will allow you to secure doors that are at your back until you can clear them effectively. Lacking these you might also, of course, move a piece of heavy furniture or other obstacle against the questionable door.

SAFETY STEPS FOR SEARCHING

Beyond the general building-clearing principles noted earlier in this chapter, the specific tactics and techniques you will employ in searching a structure are best examined one at a time. In practice, you will then put these skills together into a complete officer survival package for clearing suspect structures. These related yet separate operations include:

Covering the exterior
Making entry
Determining where to start and finish
Room-clearing techniques
Covering your back
Clearing closets
Negotiating stairways
Moving down hallways

Covering the Exterior

Most every year, a police officer is murdered as he approaches or waits outside a structure where a robbery, burglary, or disturbance of some kind is taking place. Officers have been killed by being shot from windows, through closed doors, and by offenders who had exited the building before police arrival and ambushed the responding personnel.

To prevent your adding to the murdered officers statistics, you want to remain behind cover to the extent possible. If you are one of the officers left outside to guard against offenders escaping from the building during an interior search, see to attaining good cover for yourself as your first priority. Unless you are in the middle of a major blizzard or hurricane, it's best to get out of your patrol vehicle and seek cover behind it or seek other, even better cover close by. You will, of course, select a spot with a good view of the area you are supposed to be watching. Keep a sharp lookout for what is going on outside as well as inside the target building. Your initial check of the area may have missed a lookout. Or an additional suspect or getaway driver may have just returned to the vicinity. Stay sharp. Check behind you.

Be prepared to challenge any unidentified subjects exiting the building during the interior search. Do so from cover and with your weapon out and ready. Fire only if clearly menaced by a deadly weapon—the fleeing intruder may turn out to be an innocent party who was not known to be in the building.

Know where your own people are, too. Keep in mind that if a suspect does run from the building, there is a chance he will be followed closely by a pursuing police officer. Use restraint—challenge a fleeing subject from behind cover and stay there for a few seconds to see what else develops before you decide to pursue on foot. There may be additional suspects (or officers) about to exit. If they turn out to be suspects, you don't want them behind you in a pursuit parade. It is also important to stay put if a police dog may be exiting on the tail of a fleeing crook. You cannot afford to have *him* getting confused over moving targets.

Making Entry

The point where a suspect forced entry to a building is oftentimes the worst one you can enter through simply because it is probably the spot the offender is most aware of. He may be more likely to detect you there. If possible, keep a tight perimeter around the structure and wait for keys to arrive so you can enter at some other point. Try not to use a window as your entry point. You are more "clumsy" entering by climbing in and dropping down. You can be attacked while you are at a tactical disadvantage. If you just wait quietly instead of forcing an immediate entry, your quarry may simplify the whole operation by coming out to you, blissfully unaware of your presence.

It's a good idea to create a diversion at some other point on the structure just before you enter. Your diversion can be a slam against a door, a breaking window or whatever else you choose, probably directed against the side of the building opposite your entry point. Timing is important here. Radio your assisting officer to create the diversion just as you start your own entry. Naturally, the diversion-making officer must stay behind cover himself in case his fake entry draws hostile fire.

Your own entry is your primary concern now. You and your partner remain on opposite sides of the exterior door, staying low in case an opponent attempts to shoot through a wall where he thinks you might be. If you are convinced that your adversaries already know the police are on scene, try having your partners at the diversion point issue a call for them to come out. (Don't give away your location by making the announcement at the point you plan to enter.) Have the announcement made at least twice.

There is more than one way to pass through the danger area that surrounds any doorway. (It's a danger area because at this point the suspect can focus all his attention and firepower into a single, small area.) The *wraparound technique* may be the safest and most effective way for you to enter. Here you swing the door open with force, staying low and allowing it to slam hard against the wall, assuming it opens inward. You may turn up a hidden suspect that way. Wait a couple of seconds to see whether your assault draws gunfire. Then you and your partner enter very rapidly, one at a time. Agree in advance who will move first in order to avoid a collision in the doorway. Wrap around the same side of the door you started from. Stay crouched low, keep your back to the wall, and have your weapon at the ready. The first officer through covers his following partner. Scan the area quickly for your opponent and move right away to better cover, such as behind a piece of heavy furniture. If you do not encounter immediate opposition, you are ready to expand your careful search to the rest of the building.

Determining Where to Start and Finish

If you are tackling a multiple-story building, it's best to start at the top and work your way down to the bottom floor or basement. Don't overlook the roof if it has access from the inside of the structure. There is officer safety logic in proceeding this way: An offender trapped on an upper floor may feel he has no option but to stay and fight it out. If you start from above and work down, you may be able to flush him out to waiting perimeter officers. Carefully use the stairs in preference to the elevator, if at all possible. Those little boxes can become death traps.

Remember some searching basics as you go about a probing operation. Be methodical and meticulous in your search. That means every place a human being could possibly hide gets searched. Don't forget to look up during your search, too. Crooks have been known to hide in and among false ceilings, rafters, and storage lofts. If you are searching a darkened area, consider holding your flashlight in your non-gun hand, arm extended to the side, away from your body. If you are moving from a lighted into a darkened area, try to turn off the lighting behind you to avoid being set up as a target. Move quickly and move in coordination with the other members of the search team. Be aware of everyone else's location. Take as much time as you need to do the search right.

If your search results in the apprehension of a subject, stop your operation long enough to secure him and have him removed from the building and turned over to an outside officer. During the escort out, one of you handles the prisoner while the other provides alert cover. Then the search resumes where it left off. There may be more hidden offenders. Remember that virtually anyone encountered inside must be considered suspect and must be secured and searched, at least until proven uninvolved.

Try to mark (remember that roll of tape?) or actually secure doors to each area you have cleared in a big structure. Lock a door behind you, place a piece of furniture against it, or use a door wedge on it. Anyone trying to come out that way should thereby alert you via the noise they make in trying to get through.

Finish your search at the lowest level of the structure a trespasser could gain access to, whether that means the ground floor, basement, or crawl space. Again, take care not to peer into a darkened area with a lot of light behind you. Use your flashlight sparingly and held away from and slightly forward of your body. Do the search all over again, top to bottom, if you suspect you have missed someone who could still be there. If you find no one following subsequent searches, yet you still believe an intruder is present, consider pulling out your people but quietly leave a couple of officers behind and outside to cover diagonally opposite corners of the structure. They just may latch onto a departing suspect who was fooled into thinking he was home free.

Room-Clearing Techniques

Keep in mind that you are searching as part of a two-officer search team. One moves while the other covers. You coordinate your movements utilizing hand as well as voice signals. Do not pass by and leave uncleared any locked closet doors, large pieces of furniture, or anything else an offender could hide in or behind. Whisper if you have to talk to your search partner. Yell only if you've spotted a subject who must be orally challenged right away or if you've sighted an imminent threat to another officer who doesn't see it.

Your room-clearing techniques should require that you look into any spot that could possibly contain a suspect. Some bodies are flexible enough to fit into some incredibly tight places, including cabinets, the center hole of a stack of car tires, the undersides of automobiles, and crawl spaces. If you are searching a known crook's home or place of business, be aware of the possibility that some criminals have prepared hiding spots in floors and walls to avoid probing lawmen. Drug-dealing criminals also sometimes prepare hiding places in their clandestine labs. Sometimes they add a few booby traps in the vicinity, too. Move cautiously on this kind of search and avoid handling suspicious objects. Call in explosives or hazmat specialists if necessary and wait for them to declare an object or area safe for you.

Inside a potentially hostile structure, you may want to use a pocket-size mirror to see around corners. You can hold it in your hand or protect your digits a little better by attaching it to a short handle or extension. However you utilize your mirror, it's worth remembering that looking is always better than *going* until you know what awaits you.

Remember that the "peek quick and low" technique is not limited in its usefulness to the outside of the building. When you have to round an interior corner or cross an open doorway, try to peek before you go. You may see something that changes your mind about going at all. If you need a second look, do not take it from the same height–your opponent may be expecting you this time. And, as mentioned before, don't leave your head out there as a target. Start pulling back the small portion of it that shows as soon as your eye clears cover.

Don't ignore any of your senses when you are searching a room for a hidden offender. You may be able to *smell* a scared, perspiring suspect. Or by staying quiet yourself and listening intently, you might *hear* him step or shift his standing weight on a creaky floorboard. And you always can help your *vision* by turning on the overhead lights in the area you are searching. (Try to be behind cover when you flip on the light switch. Stay there for a bit while you size up the situation. The sudden light may startle your suspect into a rash act.)

Your watch words for the room-clearing operation should remain:

- Coordinate your movements with other officers.
- Search everywhere.
- Look before you go.
- Take your time.
- Utilize good cover and covering tactics.
- Use light to your advantage.

All in all, it's the smart way to clear a building, one room at a time.

Covering Your Back

It's important on the street. It is equally vital inside a building where an opponent may be waiting for an opening to attack you. Whenever possible, you want to have something solid at your back to prevent an attack from behind. A wall or a heavy piece of furniture will do nicely. Naturally, anything you trust enough to put behind you must have first been determined to be clear of an offender.

Carrying out a thorough premises search likely will require that you give up your solid backing sooner or later, however. At that point, you will want something behind you that is just as effective—or more so. That something will be a *someone:* your search partner. When you are advancing from one location of cover to another, he will cover your back. Once you have reached cover, it will be up to you to protect him after the same fashion as *he* moves. Most important of all, whoever is searching at the moment MUST have his back covered by his partner at all times. It is the only safe way to go about your search and apprehend mission.

Clearing Closets

Treat a closet door like any other closed door until it has been cleared. Never stand in front of it. Stay low beside it, on the doorknob side if possible. Fling it open forcefully and wait a bit before you poke a hand mirror around the door frame (if you have one) or do a quick and low peek yourself if you don't. Use your flashlight with care to probe the dark corners within.

Treat a large, walk-in closet as you would a small room, which is exactly what it is. Watch your back, stay low, use cover, and work with a search partner. Don't forget to look up. Check atop shelves or stacked boxes inside.

If you spot an adversary concealed in a closet space, think about backing off and ordering the subject out at gunpoint from behind cover. The limited space available could make it difficult for you to deploy safely or manhandle him out, so give your party an opportunity to surrender before you resort to the use of additional force. If you have access to the use of a police working dog to aid in your search operations, the K-9 can prove quite useful in extracting a recalcitrant offender from tight quarters. It is always better to send in the dog as opposed to committing officers to a retrieval operation.

Negotiating Stairways

As noted previously, try to avoid the use of elevators during a search operation. They are too confining, too predictable, and thereby too dangerous for your purposes. If a brazen adversary decides to go on the offensive and take you on, an elevator may deliver you right into a narrow area he can control—and fire into. If you absolutely must use the elevator—say, you are going up 20 stories and can't afford to be out of breath when you get there—exit the elevator a couple of floors from the floor where you *think* he may be and proceed on foot from that point. But realize that he may no longer be where you think he is.

Although using the stairs in a hostile building environment still could not be described accurately as a safe means of travel, there are some practical steps you can take to reduce the risks to you and your cohorts. A number of different strategies for traversing stairways have been advanced over the years, yet experience has demonstrated that, generally speaking, what is simplest often works the best. This eliminates the need to walk backward while practically intertwined with your partner and similar (and equally impractical) maneuvers.

To negotiate a set of stairs, work with your search partner so that one of you goes up or down stairs while the other covers from behind. The cover officer remains behind good cover during this time. The backup's weapon is out and leveled in the direction of the impending threat, as is the firearm of the advancing officer. As usual, only one officer moves at a time. When the moving officer reaches a logical stopping point, such as the next landing, he becomes the covering officer as his partner moves. Stay in close proximity to one another for as little time as possible. By ganging up, you become a doubly enticing target for a shooter, not to mention an easier one to hit.

As you move on stairs, watch ahead and move your head as necessary to get a peek at what is out there regardless of the direction you are going. Use a hand mirror to aid in this task, if you've got one. It will bolster your safety margin. Be alert to possible hiding places nearby from which a hidden offender could attack you. Work quietly. Walk softly. Don't permit your personal gear to rattle or bang against a nearby wall.

If you elect to navigate the stairs while standing up, don't fail to crouch and stay low as you move. (You'll present a bit smaller target that way.) But there are other options. The idea, of course, is to present an opponent a very poor target.

Use the stairs when you must and stay away from them the rest of the time. Their dangers can be minimized by the application of good tactics but never totally removed.

Moving Down Hallways

These places can be dangerous for you because your cover opportunities are often limited. A long hallway raises the threat level proportionately higher still. Once again, however, you can reduce the hazards to a tolerable level. You start by using cover and a cover officer properly. Use the quick look technique to see what awaits you around a hallway corner. Better still, use a hand mirror poked around the edge to see what's there. Look for the out of the ordinary: a door broken or ajar, loot stacked in the hall, things that are out of place. Let your partner know what you see. He must do the same for you.

As with the stairway, officers move one at a time with the cover officer staying shielded to the extent possible. You probably will elect to be on opposite sides of the hallway as you advance with weapons at the ready. The lead officer should be 6 to 10 feet ahead of his partner.

Listen for noises behind any of the doors that lie ahead of your advance. That doorway could soon present an armed threat to you. If you do hear suspicious sounds, seek whatever cover is available before the suspect door has a chance to open. Do not hesitate to beat a retreat to safer ground if you think you are about to be confronted by a possibly armed adversary in a hallway that offers little or no cover. *Some* cover is available, of course, by flattening yourself out in the recess presented by inward-opening hall doors. If trapped, you can kick one in to take advantage of the better cover offered by the open doorway.

Nonetheless, the best cover available in a long hallway is something less than great. It is far better to look before you go and don't go at all if immediate danger is evident. Seal off the area and put in a call for SWAT. If you *must* proceed, stay alert and avoid getting caught in the open hallway by an armed offender.

But if all else fails and you *are* caught in the open, respond to an armed assault with an all-out, no holds barred counterattack of your own. If you are some distance from your attacker and unable to get to better cover, consider dropping to the floor and returning fire from a prone position. You will present a smaller target that way. It's not an ideal solution to your lack of cover problem, but it is a considerable improvement over standing flat-footed in the open, slugging it out in a hot lead exchange.

Clearing and securing a structure in which you know or believe dangerous suspects are hiding definitely qualifies as a high-risk patrol assignment. By learning, practicing, and applying the commonsense guidelines discussed in this chapter, you can reduce those risks to an acceptable level. In doing so, you will, with increased experience, develop your own special touches, revisions, and additions to the suggestions made here. By adding these personalized procedures to your search operations, you will make them safer even as you increase your efficiency and effectiveness.

As you go about many more building searches over what hopefully will be many more years of police service, never forget the basic concepts of building search survival. You never become complacent or take anything for granted. You do not make risky assumptions. You never really relax in somebody else's home or other building. You never ignore what your common sense or gut reaction is telling you.

As you continue a career of structure clearing assignments, you will recognize each one as a new and potentially hazardous challenge. And by staying sharp, you will be staying alive as well. That, by itself, is the ultimate structure search directive.

Structure searches represent an ultimate challenge to your safety as a survival-smart law enforcement officer. Fortunately, there is much you can do to reduce the danger as you probe the unknown to bring an offender to justice.

You lower the danger quotient by gathering data before you search, by approaching the structure cautiously, by making good use of cover, and by working in cooperation with your partners. You don't declare the building "clean" until it really is. You never stop looking for the next threat, the as-yet-undiscovered hazard.

When you are done with your search, critique yourself, examine your tactics, and start getting ready for the next one. That way you will always be ready when your search for trouble does not come up empty-handed.

A RISK REDUCTION CHECKLIST FOR BURGLARIES AND STRUCTURE SEARCHES

1. Have as much information as possible before you begin the search operation.
2. Never enter or search alone. Have adequate help inside and outside the structure.

3. Take your time and search in detail.
4. Search with a partner officer. Only one searcher moves at a time while the other covers.
5. Make use of available cover during your search.
6. Maintain good communication with all police personnel on scene.
7. Make full use of all the equipment at your disposal: police working dogs, ladders, portable radios, quality flashlights, and so on.

At about 9:30 a.m., a 23-year-old patrolman was killed after responding with a backup to a burglary. Restaurant employees had reported seeing an armed man in the building upon their arrival for work. During a building search, the officers discovered a 24-year-old male standing on a commode seat in a restroom stall. As he attempted to peer into the stall, the officer was shot in the head with a .380-caliber handgun. Return fire from the other officer killed the subject. The slain officer had two years of police experience.

* * * * *

Shortly before 6 a.m., a 39-year-old patrolman was shot fatally when he intervened in a burglary in progress at a clothing store. While backup officers were still en route, the 18-year veteran entered the store and struggled with one offender. The male subject, shot in the hand, disarmed the officer and shot him with his own weapon. Although the officer was wearing a protective vest, the bullet entered through a gap on the right side of the vest and pierced the victim's heart. Two adult males were subsequently arrested.

* * * * *

A deputy with 25 years of law enforcement experience was struck and killed by a vehicle escaping from the scene of a burglary of a convenience store. The adult male suspect, who had a lengthy criminal record including a conviction for murder, drove a stolen pickup truck deliberately at the officer, who was on foot. Her fatal injuries included a broken neck.

Chapter 9

BARRICADES AND HOSTAGE-TAKERS

"Sniper Kills His Two Children, Wounds 14 Cops," said the newspaper headline. By reading the story accompanying the headline, you would have learned that the killer, later mortally wounded by officers, had first injured, among others, one police captain and four lieutenants by firing bird-shot through his apartment door. (The reader of the news item is left to wonder why this assemblage of police brass was in such proximity to the shooting end of a barricaded gunman incident.) The standoff took place in a major metropolitan area.

Another headline reported on a bloody hostage-taking incident in Germany. Before the 54-hour disaster was at an end, the following developments had been reported:

- Two armed men robbed a bank in Germany, took two bank employees hostage, and were permitted by police to leave in a car with their captives.
- The robbers took another hostage the following day in another city.
- They hijacked a bus with more than 20 people aboard.
- Two journalists were allowed to replace the two bank employee hostages.
- The hijackers executed a teenage bus passenger.
- The gunmen and hostages were allowed to enter Holland where their bus was surrounded by police. Another getaway car was then furnished by officers.
- The killers and a female accomplice next took two women bus passengers hostage and sped back into Germany in their police-provided car.
- A police officer was killed in a car accident during the chase.
- Police forced the gunmen's car off the road, hurled stun grenades and opened fire.

111

- The hostage-takers shot and killed one of their female hostages and seriously wounded the other.
- The gunmen were captured alive.

America, of course, has had its share of hostage-takings gone sour. In one small U.S. city, for example, a male gunman fleeing the scene of a domestic disturbance where he had shot a police officer in the arm took 20 hostages in a nearby restaurant. During the ensuing standoff, the 35-year-old subject exited long enough to shoot a second officer in the shoulder. About an hour later, a police sharpshooter shot and wounded the hostage-taker, who in turn shot a female hostage to death before turning his gun fatally on himself. Another hostage who fled after climbing out a restroom window of the building was subsequently shot and killed by an officer on the perimeter.

A lot of things can go wrong in a hostage-taking or barricaded gunman incident. A hostage is shot by a gunman. A hostage is shot mistakenly by a police officer. A police officer is shot by a gunman. And so on. The tragic and often bloody results of a hostage-taking or barricaded gunman episode gone awry are as close as the daily newscasts. Undoubtedly, the all-too-familiar scenario will be repeated again.

Although it is true that specially trained police units ultimately may handle a great many of the hostage-taking and barricaded gunman incidents occurring in this country, it will most often be the uniformed first responder—YOU—who is responsible for police reaction during the vital and especially hazardous first minutes of the confrontation. In some cases and in some jurisdictions, these same patrol officers may handle virtually the entire operation without assistance from specially trained and equipped forces.

A good many texts, professional journal articles, and hands-on training seminars are available to the street officer wanting to know more about the safe handling of hostage-taking or barricaded gunman incidents. Avail yourself of what they have to offer. Meanwhile, consider the commonsense basics provided in this chapter to establish your own, personal foundation of officer survival knowledge for tackling the barricade or hostage-taker.

TYPES OF OFFENDERS

Generally speaking, individuals who take hostages or barricade themselves with weapons can be divided into several categories:

1. The Interrupted Criminal. This may be the barricade or hostage-taker you are most likely to encounter. He may have been trapped when the cops showed up sooner than expected at a burglary or robbery in progress.

Of all the barricaded suspects you are liable to encounter on the street, the interrupted criminal may be the easiest to deal with. Once he has a chance to settle down from the initial, jarring confrontation, he is likely to realize the gravity of his predicament and begin looking for a nonviolent way out. Be patient with this one; time is on your side.

2. The Inmate With a Grievance. You may run into this guy if you work in a jail or correctional facility. He wants attention from the news media and the public to redress real or imagined grievances, and he's willing to take hostages to draw the desired attention.

3. The Mentally Ill. If he is totally out of touch with reality, you will have a tough time bringing him to surrender in a peaceful manner. Because this individual is extremely hard to predict, he is quite dangerous. Use utmost caution in dealing with him. Tolerate his possibly rambling, disjointed speeches in order to keep him talking instead of acting against you.

4. The Intoxicated Subject. You may see a barricade develop from a simple domestic squabble involving a drunk. Or a fight call with an inebriate involved. A standoff might even develop from a pulled-over drunk driver. While intoxicated, the barricade or hostage-taker may be extremely volatile as well as unpredictable. As he sobers up, you may find it easier to bring him around to your way of seeing things. Or he may pass out from the alcohol or drugs and make your entry and approach even easier. Again, time is often your ally here. Don't rush.

5. The Social Protest Extremist. Whether he represents an animal rights group, either side of the emotional abortion issue, or some other social cause, this individual wants the attention of the press and public. He may not really want to harm anyone. He may be relatively easy to defuse once he gets the attention he seeks. Be patient.

6. The Terrorist. This subject is many times more dangerous than his little brother, the social protestor. If he is truly fanatical about his cause, he will be very difficult to convince to surrender peacefully. The worst of these offenders may be willing to die for his cause. But he, too, may be willing to surrender once he has gotten the attention he seeks. Be careful and go slow.

7. The "Suicide by Cop" Subject. This individual thinks he wants to die but is not quite up to doing the deed himself. He wants you to do it for him, and he may menace or kill a police officer to get other officers to shoot him. If he is really serious about dying, he is an extremely dangerous person for you to go up against. Take no chances with him. Use all caution.

Of course, human beings are not quite so easily categorized as these labels might indicate. Any one offender you will face may fall into several of these categories, all at the same time. Or he may fit none of them all that neatly. But having a basic understanding of the sorts of folks you are likely to be confronting should help you prepare yourself mentally for the crucial challenge ahead.

YOUR OPTIONS

When you arrive at the scene of an in-progress barricade or hostage-taking incident, at first glance your options would appear to be several:

1. Do nothing aggressive and wait the subject out.
2. Storm the subject's location immediately.
3. Use chemical agents to drive him out.
4. Call on a police sharpshooter to neutralize the offender.
5. Negotiate for the release of hostages and the surrender of the suspect.

There are, no doubt, instances in which each of the preceding actions could be the appropriate police response. At the same time, the course of action open to you with the best overall chance of success (that means no deaths, no injuries, freed hostages, a captured suspect) may combine several of these optional responses. In other words, you must reserve for yourself the right and ability to use force, including chemical agents, sniper fire, or the storming of the premises, while you work to isolate the offender and establish communication that will get him to do what you want. This formula for the successful resolution of barricade and hostage incidents is often summed up as:

TIME
TALK
TACTICS

The ingredients of the formula are worth examining one at a time.

Time is on your side in most incidents. As time passes, agitated offenders sometimes calm down and act more rationally once they become convinced the cops are not going to immediately kick in the door and kill them. As time passes, a lot of things, most of them good, can happen. Hostages escape. An offender starts to see the hopelessness of his position. The police consolidate their position. Specialists are deployed on scene. A bonding begins to develop (sometimes) that makes it harder for a hostage-taker to kill a hostage.

Generally speaking, you have a lot more time than the offender does. You are not going anywhere. You have access to reinforcements and relief, if needed. You can afford to wait him out. In the meantime, you work to get him out via. . . .

Talk that often will help defuse the situation. These negotiations are intended to free any hostages and result in the eventual, peaceful surrender of the offender. The talk can start and stop, reach emotional highs and lows, and continue for a very long time. But while he is talking, he is probably not acting to hurt anyone. Keep him talking even as you act to isolate and neutralize him through. . . .

Tactics that will result in his capture. Tactics include evacuating the immediate area of innocents, setting up inner and outer perimeters and traffic control points, establishing a command post, and planning an assault. Tactics will dictate just how that attack is to be executed, if necessary. They will cover team movements, weaponry, and entry and arrest techniques.

It is worth noting that neither time, talk, nor tactics will work well absent the other two. You will not have a chance for time and talk to bring your subject to the surrender point, for example, if he can escape with his hostage any time he wants. Tactics in the form of officers on the inner perimeter will prevent that from happening. Remove any of the three legs of the time, talk, and tactics triad and your chances for success in the operation will drop dramatically. By providing yourself with options in addition to the use of force, you greatly increase the chances that you won't have to call on the force option. Remember: If casualties are to occur once the police are on scene, they are statistically most likely to occur during an assault operation.

So much for the principles and guidelines for handling the barricade or hostage-taker. They are, of course, vital to your successful handling of a potentially hazardous challenge. Just as important, however, are the specific officer survival steps you will take as one of the first—perhaps THE first—officers on scene of a barricade or hostage-taking incident. You will want to look at the following steps and considerations as parts of your early evaluate, contain, and neutralize operations.

STEPS TO A SOLUTION

1. Do a Quick Assessment

What are you dealing with here? Based on what you see and hear when you get there as well as on what you find out from your dispatcher, witnesses, and others on scene, make some quick plans for action. Do not overlook the necessity of staying out of harm's way yourself while you are doing this quickie evaluation. Park out of sight. Use cover in your movements. Do not draw attention to yourself or your position. Be prepared for a sudden assault and have your weapon at the ready.

Obviously, you will need to continue to gather new information and assess the situation throughout the duration of the incident. Stay flexible. You may need to change your response quickly as the situation shifts. The information you will gather will help in resolving the confrontation at hand even as it helps you stay safe. That information-gathering can be divided into several categories of questions that you will need to seek answers to. The categories include:

The incident
The location
The barricade or hostage-taker himself
The hostages, if any

Here are a few of the questions you will need to answer in your intelligence-gleaning efforts:

The Incident

1. What caused the incident in the first place (interrupted crime, domestic dispute, etc.)?
2. What is the hostage-taker demanding?
3. What are you willing to give him?
4. Has a crime been committed? What is it and how serious?
5. Are there any time or other constraints on the police response?

The Location

1. What kind of building or location are you working with (residence, office building, occupied structure, etc.)?
2. Can building plans or diagrams be obtained?
3. What are the contents of the structure (explosives, weapons, etc.)?
4. How is the structure constructed?
5. Where are the access points (doors, windows, vents)?
6. Where are controls for the structure's utility services, such as electric and water, located?
7. Is there a telephone inside?
8. Will special equipment be needed to gain entry to the structure (cutting torches, ladders, etc.)?

The Barricade or Hostage Taker Himself

1. Who is he (or they)?
2. What is his physical description (mistaken identities can prove fatal)?
3. How is he dressed?
4. Is he drunk? high? stoned? angry? crazy?
5. Is anything known about his criminal history?
6. How is he armed?

7. What does he want from the police?
8. Can his location in the structure be pinpointed?
9. Is he out of touch with reality or relatively sharp?
10. Does he appear suicidal or intent on becoming a martyr?

The Hostages

1. Who are they?
2. What are their physical descriptions and manner of dress? (Remember: Hostages and hostage-takers may have exchanged clothing.)
3. Where are they confined?
4. Are they injured or ill?
5. What are the hostages' relationship, if any, to the hostage-taker?
6. How well are the hostages guarded? Are they immobilized?
7. Is there any indication that the hostages are cooperating with their captor?
8. What are the hostages' mental condition? Are they likely to attempt a self-rescue on their own?

There is no such thing as too much information. As you progress with your quick assessment, never cease your efforts to learn more about the situation.

2. Get Help

Part of your early assessment will be aimed at determining how many more officers will be needed to seal off the area and solve the problem at hand. If in doubt, call for more assistance than you may need. Include a field supervisor in your request for assistance. If you end up with more help than you need, you or the supervisor can always send the extra people back into service. Don't forget to put in a call for whatever specialized help you'll need to handle a barricade or hostage-taking incident. In many cases, that will mean a request for the SWAT unit.

3. Evacuate or Protect in Place

Determine who will be endangered if the subject continues or begins shooting. Consider the total circumstances. Naturally, you will have to evacuate to a greater distance if you are dealing with someone armed with a rifle as opposed to an offender with a "Saturday night special." Inasmuch as rifle fire can penetrate several residential exterior and interior walls, you may need to empty houses for at least several addresses on every side of a building occupied by an offender.

Move people out only if you and your peers can get to the endangered locations under cover, such as by using back doors and parallel streets and alleyways. If you cannot safely move these people out without exposing them to the subject's gunfire, instruct them to remain where they are. You may be able to get your dispatcher to use a "reverse 911" notification to contact the neighboring addresses and advise the occupants to remain inside, door locked, down and away from the windows.

4. Set Up an Inner Perimeter

Officers must be posted at vantage points on diagonally opposite corners of the suspect's location. They remain behind good cover and do not fire unless fired on, and then only if they have a clear view of their armed target. Portable radios are a must for keeping other police personnel on-scene advised of the offender's actions and movements as detected from these up-front positions. Two officers may be able to maintain an effective inner perimeter on a small building. Additional points will have to be covered and additional officers utilized if you are sealing off a large or irregularly configured structure. The inner perimeter officers are there, of course, to do more than keep the offender under observation. They are positioned to prevent his escape as well as take him into custody if he decides to surrender.

5. Set Up an Outer Perimeter

You will need at least three or four more officers to establish a second, wider perimeter around the barricade or hostage-taker. These people will serve as insurance that the bad guy does not escape if he slips past the inner perimeter officers. They are also present to prevent bystanders or pedestrians from wandering into the threatened area and becoming new hostages or casualties of gunfire. Additionally, the outer perimeter officers will prevent unwanted outsiders, such as media representatives or friends of the offender, from reaching his position and further complicating the affair.

6. Look at Traffic Control

If your ongoing incident is anywhere near a street or highway, as most will be, you will need to cut off vehicular access to the area. That will require still more officers to assist you. As with the other perimeters, your aim with your traffic control points is to keep the public far enough from the action to avoid being hit by stray rounds or getting in the way of your operations.

7. Establish a Command Post

As your assist units, supervisory personnel, and perhaps specialized units arrive to help you resolve the incident, a place to run the whole operation from will be needed. It can be a house, store, or vehicle. But the site chosen for the command post should be close to the scene of the action without being in the line of fire or view.

8. Obtain Needed Specialists and Specialized Equipment

Call for the specialized help you will need to resolve the incident. Depending on the time, location, and nature of your incident, you may require the assistance of SWAT personnel, hostage negotiators, and electronic surveillance experts, among others. Special tools required may include extra lighting, foul weather gear for personnel exposed to the elements for long periods, or equipment for setting up communication with the offender.

9. Establish Contact with the Offender(s)

Face-to-face negotiation with a barricaded criminal is a very bad idea. It's a good way to get yourself shot. But talk with him you must if you are going to get him to end the standoff peacefully. Use a telephone for your negotiating, if possible. Shout over a distance to your subject if that's the only option available, but stay behind cover when you do. Talking from around a corner can work just fine for your purposes. Don't leave cover and expose yourself to your adversary no matter how critical or sensitive the discussion becomes. If he insists on a face-to-face meeting, advise him that you will arrange it once he is in custody. Then, keep your promise to do so.

10. Negotiate with the Offender

Until and unless a trained police negotiator has arrived, you may have to serve in the role of hostage or barricade negotiator. Do not wait for experts to arrive to begin the communication. By engaging in any kind of conversation with a barricade or hostage-taker, you are attempting to talk him into giving up before anyone gets hurt—no more, no less. You are not trying to give away the farm or promise pie in the sky. What you *are* trying to do is make a personal connection with the offender and then bring him around to your way of seeing things. You are trying to convince him that you and your advice are his ticket out of the mess he has created for himself. By talking with you and giving in to your wishes, he can extricate himself alive.

Any talking you do with the offender *must* be done from a place of safety for you. Most often your dialogue will be by telephone. Try to get the subject's first name and use it a lot during your negotiations. It should help in your effort to make a personal connection. Let him rant and rave, if need be, and vent his frustrations and hostilities verbally on you. It may help to settle him down. While he is carrying on thusly, he is unlikely to shoot someone at the same time.

Make it clear to the offender that you expect him to give up peacefully. Ask him to do so. Give him your personal guarantee of safety after he surrenders. At the same time, endeavor to sound sympathetic as you listen to his woes. Agree with him where you can ("Yeah, it sounds like your boss is a jerk!") Find out what you can about his hostages during your conversation, but be careful not to sound a lot more interested in their welfare than his. A hostage negotiation scenario will call for your best abilities as an actor. Pull out all the stops and put on your best performance.

Calming the barricaded offender is your top priority en route to obtaining his surrender. You can accomplish this by talking more softly and slowly than he is. Don't threaten him. It's not necessary to tell him he's going to get killed if he doesn't surrender to you–he most likely expects that much already. Don't talk about trials, jails, and the like. It won't help your cause.

Don't accept any time deadlines set by the offender ("I'll kill a hostage at 5:30 if you don't get me a plane and a million bucks!"). Keep him busy and talking as the deadline approaches and do not acknowledge his demand. At the same time, do not set any deadlines of your own ("We're coming in after you if you don't give up by noon!"). Just keep the conversation going and realize there may be breaks in his desire to talk. The whole process is very likely even more wearing on him than it is on you. Take your time and be patient.

Keep gathering information and continue to analyze your offender as the talk proceeds. Is he becoming more or less agitated? Is he getting sleepy? Could he be about to pass out from booze or drugs? Or is he becoming further removed from reality? All of this intelligence information should be passed on to the incident commander or SWAT supervisor on-scene. It will affect the decision if and when to storm the offender's position. Meanwhile, brainstorm with your peers on-scene as to what might work in your continuing effort to talk him out. Be patient and learn all you can about the party on the other side of the wall or at the other end of the telephone line. You just may pick up a tidbit that will aid in obtaining his peaceful surrender.

There are still more Do and Don't guidelines in the negotiation process. If you find yourself drafted by necessity into the role of negotiator, consider the following additional guidelines:

• Don't let the offender "talk to the boss"–it's important for you to be able to stall and defer decisions about things that he wants to somebody else. As far as the offender is concerned, you are the boss that he gets to talk to.

- Don't routinely use outsiders in your negotiations. Especially avoid spouses or relatives of the offender. If he got along all that great with these people, he probably would not be where he is now. Unknown to you, these individuals may constitute a big part of the offender's problems, at least in his mind. Bringing them in now may only aggravate matters.

* Don't lie to the offender if he has a good chance of discovering the falsehood. Once he finds you out, he will be much harder to deal with.

- Don't make promises that anyone with a smattering of brain matter knows you cannot keep. It would be unwise, for instance, to promise the subject he won't be prosecuted for the two people he just killed!
- Don't furnish the offender booze, drugs, or weapons as part of a trade for hostages or anything else. It's just too risky.
- Don't give him something for nothing. Offer to trade, instead. He can, for instance, have a sandwich and a cold drink for a hostage, and so on. Negotiate!
- Don't allow him to "go mobile" as part of a deal even if he offers to give up a hostage in trade. There's nothing to say he can't seize more elsewhere. You cannot contain him effectively once he starts moving in a vehicle. Keep him isolated where he is.
- Don't encourage his fantasies. Remind him from time to time that the situation will require his surrender. Remind him that you have the means to get him out of his mess safely.
- Don't permit him access to news reporters while the incident is in progress. Consider promising him media access after he surrenders without harming anyone.
- Do keep the conversation going.
- Do wear the offender down by forcing him to make decisions from time to time ("Do you want sugar in that coffee we're sending you? What *kind* of sandwich do you want?").
- Do be prepared to abandon negotiations and begin an assault if the offender begins harming hostages.
- Do continue to assess the offender's willingness to keep talking. Really listen to what he is saying. If he sounds like he is straying further and further from reality, an assault operation may become a more reasonable course of action.
- Do keep in mind that, whatever the outcome of your negotiation efforts, any eventual "bad" results are his fault, not yours. You have no ultimate control over what the bad guy elects to do. If he selects a bloody outcome to the confrontation, it was his choice, not yours.

Don't buy into a guilt trip that rightfully belongs to him and him alone.
- Do be aware of indicators that the offender is being affected favorably by the negotiation process: he's continuing to talk, he's calming down, his demands are lessening, he's allowing the deadlines he has set to pass without incident, he's treating hostages well, and so on.
- Do allow the offender to surrender with some personal dignity intact. (Having him crawl out of the building nude "to be sure he doesn't have a weapon" is a bad idea.) Remember, you may have to deal with him again one day. Memories can be lengthy.
- Do remember that you cannot talk out every offender you make contact with. Some cases have been decided for you long before you arrive. The "suicide by cop" subject, for example, may already have decided on his fate, and nothing anyone can do or say is likely to change his plans. His fatal decision is his, not yours.

11. Consider the Use of Chemical Agents

There may be a better and safer solution to the standoff than going in after a holed-up gunman. It's called bringing him out to you. If you cannot accomplish it with talk, sometimes you can with gas. A gas gun or projector in the hands of a trained officer who knows how and where to put the gas rounds can be a powerful persuader for a barricaded criminal to call it quits.

At the same time, remain mindful that police use of chemical agents in a barricade or hostage situation has some built-in dangers or drawbacks. First of all, certain chemical agent ordinance can start a fire when introduced inside a structure. As a result, the decision to employ it must carry with it the understanding that serious injury or death could result from the application.

Second, the introduction of a chemical agent may cause panic and flight among hostages just as readily as among offenders. This could result in their being shot by the offender or injured during their flight from the gas.

Third, a chemical agent may not incapacitate an offender who has prepared for it (gas mask, wet blanket, etc.) or who is very high on drugs, such as PCP. The chemical agent may further aggravate a wildly insane offender but not otherwise seriously incapacitate him.

Fourth, the application of chemical agents requires that you and your fellow officers are not only well-trained in the use of gas but also equipped to deploy it without falling prey to its effects yourselves. That means, for one thing, that everyone in the immediate area must have quick access to a functioning gas mask.

Nonetheless, chemical agents, properly understood and deployed, can lead to the safe resolution of a barricaded offender crisis. They are most successfully used when offender(s), unaccompanied by hostages or other innocents, are contained in a relatively tight area under police control. Here chemical agents are at their most useful best. If you do elect to go with gas at a barricade incident, consider the following broad guidelines for their application along with whatever other restrictions may apply to your particular situation:

- Chemical agents should only be dispensed by a "gas officer" trained and practiced in their use.
- Your stock of chemical agents should be checked on a regular basis for expiration dates, leaks, and revisions in instructions for use.
- Remember that the object of a chemical agents application is to incapacitate the offender or drive him out to you, not suffocate him. Use restraint. Allow your trained gas specialist to calculate how much gas to apply.
- Follow the accompanying product instructions and cautions for whatever chemical agent you are using. If markings or directions are missing or unclear, don't use it.

Don't automatically assume that a lot of gas put into a given structure has incapacitated your subject. It may not have reached him or he may have taken protective measures against it.

Thoroughly wash with water anytime you get a chemical agent on your own person. Shed any contaminated clothing as quickly as possible. Get into fresh air.

It's worth noting one more time that some chemical agent grenades or projectiles, while fine for outdoor use, have a good chance of starting a fire if set off inside. Know what the instructions and precautions say.

12. Use Safe Entry and Search Techniques

It is best that you isolate the offender, open communication with him if possible, and then stand by for the arrival of a SWAT unit of specialists in handling the barricade or hostage incident. On rare occasions, you can't do it that way, however. You can't wait because the offender is attacking his hostages. Or perhaps he's continuing to fire into a crowded area and the casualties are mounting. Or the specialists are unavailable. YOU are faced with the prospect of taking direct action to neutralize a deadly threat. Now what?

What you know about building entries and searches can take you a long way toward resolving the barricade problem and getting out of it alive. But remember: *Go in only if there is no other way of resolving the crisis.* Going into a structure where an armed subject is barricaded, perhaps with hostages, very often ensures that *someone is going to get hurt.*

If you *must* enter to go after a barricade or hostage-taker, you have two choices in your approach to the operation. You can attempt to sneak in without the offender's knowledge and seek him out very quietly using careful entry and room search techniques. In reality, however, your chances of getting into the same building with a barricaded offender whose senses are already on high alert without his knowing you are there are not as good as you would like. That leaves you with the second option: Assault the structure, complete with a diversion operation, and gain entry by force. Then your room-to-room search can proceed quietly and carefully.

Anytime you elect to enter a hostile area with the intent of either causing the subject's surrender or otherwise neutralizing him as a threat, recall what you already have learned about safe structure searches, including the following tips:

- Be sure everyone on the perimeter and everyone going in knows his role ahead of time. Be sure everybody knows the rules on use of deadly force as applied to the situation at hand.
- Learn everything you can about the structure to be assaulted before you go. Utilize plans, diagrams, and information gained from witnesses and others on-scene.
- Practice your entry outside, when there is time to do so, perhaps using a similar structure in the area. The entry team should practice as a unit.
- Unless you are going to try a furtive entry, create a diversion well away from your actual point of entry.
* In making entry, wrap around the door and then move quickly away from it to cover.
- Keep your movements quick and low. Use the best cover available.
- Only one member of a two-officer entry team moves at a time. The other provides cover. The roles can switch back and forth, as necessary, as the search operation continues.
- Physically secure or put a guard on every floor or area you have searched and declared secure. You don't want to risk attack from an offender who moves back in behind you.
- Take your time and search every possible hiding place available to an offender. Don't overlook such out-of-the-way places as basements, crawl spaces, attics, and utility equipment vaults. Areas that are locked from the inside cannot be declared "clean" until they have been checked out, too.
- Be constantly ready to shoot, but don't forget that innocents may be present, too. Target identification is critical.

- When you have located an offender and taken him out of operation, continue the search with no less caution. There may be other offenders you are not even aware of. Keep looking until the structure is cleared completely and everyone–good guys and bad guys alike–is accounted for.

It is worth stressing one more time that the search of a structure or an area for an armed barricade or hostage-taker is a highly risky affair best left to a skilled SWAT team whose members have repeatedly trained and rehearsed their operations as a single unit. Rarely should a situation require that you do more than isolate a barricade or hostage-taker, gather information, and open communication while awaiting a specialized unit response. Intervene yourself only if hostages or innocent others are being attacked.

Read everything you can about the assault techniques to be employed in a hostage rescue or barricaded gunman operation. Learn about the tactics and procedures you will need to employ to safely and successfully resolve these high-risk problems. Stay abreast of updates and revisions to these operational guidelines. And never forget your obligation to delay an assault pending the arrival of tactical specialists if waiting won't result in harm to innocents.

13. Plan a Safe Surrender

The hostage-taking or barricaded gunman incident is not over until the bad guy can no longer pose a danger to anyone. Even though you have him in your sights, so to speak, he can still pose a danger to you and others until he is handcuffed, thoroughly searched and searched again, and locked up in a secure facility.

Plan for what you will do when the offender gives up. What access point will you have him exit through? (It's vital that all of your people know when and where he's coming out.) What surrender instructions will you give him? ("Leave any weapons inside. Exit by backing out the door with your hands on your head. Freeze on the bottom step and don't move again.") How will you secure him? (One officer advances with his weapon drawn while his partner covers. The officer holsters the weapon just before he reaches the suspect and then handcuffs and searches him.)

Remember that a safe surrender means that you finish clearing the building and any other area that was under the bad guy's control before you consider the incident terminated. In addition to undiscovered offenders, there may be victims and evidence yet to be uncovered. The surprises may not be over, so move carefully.

A barricaded gunman or hostage-taking incident represents the kind of high-risk patrol assignment you will not want to face alone. Not ever. In most cases, you will require plenty of help–some of it specialized–to bring the situation safely under control. In the meantime, however, the initial containment and stabilization of the incident will be the responsibility of you and your uniformed peers. What you do in the opening minutes of a barricade or hostage-taking confrontation will have a lot to do with the eventual outcome of the whole event. Think clearly, move cautiously, and act with decisiveness and common sense. By your careful and well-planned actions, you will reduce significantly the dangers of this facet of high-risk patrol.

WHAT IF YOU BECOME A HOSTAGE?

Planning for your survival in the field means at least thinking about the possibility that you could someday become a hostage of an armed offender. It could happen off-duty when you get caught inside a bank while a botched robbery is going down. Or it could take place by your being surprised and overwhelmed on just about any kind of police call.

It shouldn't happen, and hopefully it never will, but what can you do to survive should you find yourself the hostage of an armed offender? Actually, there are a number of things you can do to get out of this sort of crisis alive. They include the following:

1. Remember, as unlikely as it may seem when you are on the hot seat, time really is on your side. Allow it to work for you and against your assailant. Give your fellow officers time to organize and pull off a rescue should one prove necessary.

2. Don't pose an obvious threat to your antagonist–it may provoke him into trying to take you out. Let him think that you–kept alive–may be his way out.

3. Keep a good mental attitude throughout your ordeal. It'll help see you through to an eventual victory. *Believe* that you will get out of it alright.

4. If you have any choice at all about your location as a hostage, stay away from doors and windows. A police sniper may be lining up your captor for a head shot. Try and stay near potential cover, such as heavy furniture. And stay as far away from the hostage-taker as you can get away with.

5. Cooperate with your captor in every way you can without weakening your own position. You don't want to provoke him into violence. Don't bait or argue with him–ever. Avoid abrupt movements or any other actions he might interpret as threats.

6. Remain ever alert, particularly for escape opportunities. But only go for it if you are sure you can escape. If you fail to get away, the retaliation directed against you likely will be highly unpleasant and perhaps fatal.

7. While you are a captive, do your best to be an excellent observer and witness. What you remember may help your comrades later in the operation or serve to convict your tormentor in court.

8. Don't try to be a hero. Attack only if you can be reasonably certain you can win. You probably won't get another chance. Hold nothing back. Attack all–out and fight to win no matter what you have to do. There are no rules here. Accept that the armed criminal's death may be the result.

9. If a rescue force assaults your location, get on the floor and remain motionless. Don't try to help. You could get shot accidentally if you are too "active" during the incredibly tense and sometimes confused moments of a rescue operation.

There is a lot you can do to ensure the safe and successful resolution of a barricade or hostage-taking crisis, whether that crisis is solved before or after tactical specialists arrive. Operating under the guidelines of *time, talk,* and *tactics,* you must call necessary assistance, isolate the offender's location, and commence gathering data on who and what is involved.

You must evacuate or protect in place innocent persons in the area and conduct a continuing assessment of what you are facing and how best to respond to it. You should establish a command post and try to open a conversation with the offender. Your goal is to negotiate his immediate surrender and then plan for its safe implementation. If you are unable to end the crisis yourself, you must arrange for a smooth transition to a tactical unit or SWAT team. Then, when it's all over, talk with your peers about what worked and what didn't. Kick some ideas around. Learn from the experience and get better for the next time.

There is much you can do to win a barricade or hostage encounter. But it is also important to remember that factors totally beyond your control may cause the confrontation to end in violence. If the offender has decided in advance that the incident will end in his death, you may be unable to avoid that result. That's his choice, not yours. Realize ahead of time that a tragic outcome remains a real possibility.

All you can do is the best job you can. By utilizing your good officer safety know-how, your basic common sense, and your excellent decision-making abilities, you can greatly improve the survival odds for yourself, your peers and innocent others.

A RISK REDUCTION CHECKLIST FOR
BARRICADES AND HOSTAGE-TAKERS

1. Before you act, learn as much as you can about the incident, the location, and the people involved.

2. In resolving a standoff safely, follow the experience-proven formula of *time, talk,* and *tactics.*
3. Evacuate or protect in-place uninvolved parties.
4. Set up inner and outer containment perimeters.
5. Obtain needed assistance, including specialized units and equipment.
6. Make contact with the offender and open negotiations, if possible.
7. Enter and search the offender's area of control only as a last resort and even then only with extreme caution.
8. Be sure all your people know the plan.
9. Keep your movements quick and low. Use good cover. One officer moves while the other covers. Remember wraparound door entries.
10. Take the time for a thorough, building-clearing search. Don't relax until everyone and everything is accounted for.

A 35-year-old sergeant with 15 years on the job was killed at about 4:30 p.m. at the scene of a disturbance at a residence. A mentally disturbed man was barricaded inside and had been firing at neighbors and bystanders. After tear gas was fired into the house, the victim and two other SWAT team members, all wearing protective vests and gas masks, entered through a rear door and were immediately fired upon. The sergeant died when struck in the right eye by a round from a .38-caliber handgun. His assailant was arrested.

* * * * *

Upon responding to shots fired at a residence, a 33-year-old sheriff's deputy with 7 years of service was killed at about 2:10 p.m. After attempting to shoot his wife and children, a 57-year-old male barricaded himself in a home and began shooting at passing traffic. The victim officer and several peers approached the house from the rear using trees and outbuildings for cover. The subject exited and fired three times at one officer. The victim deputy then attempted to use a bullhorn to talk the man, whom he knew from previous contacts, into surrendering. Instead, the subject shot the deputy once in the head with a rifle. The offender was wounded and arrested by other officers.

Chapter 10

"MAN WITH A GUN" CALLS

Guns in the hands of criminals, crazies, drunks, and other "misguided" individuals are quite obviously the greatest single threat you face as a peace officer. You already know, or should know, that virtually any contact with the public, any call for assistance, or any apparently peaceful encounter can turn into a life-or-death confrontation involving firearms.

The passed-out drunk at the lunch counter may come out of it with a pistol from a coat pocket, the juvenile hitchhiker may produce a gun from a backpack, or the prostitute you stopped handcuffing the tenth time you arrested her without incident this time can show you a .22-caliber surprise from the purse you didn't bother to search. The guns are out there. So are those who are quite willing to turn them on you.

But as dangerous as all the previously noted confrontations are, they pale in their ability to get your adrenaline flowing when placed alongside the known "man with a gun" assignment. Now you know from the outset that you may be in for one of law enforcement's greatest challenges. What can you do to meet the challenge while minimizing the danger to yourself, your peers, and the public you serve? Fortunately, there are many things that you can (and must) do to overcome the threat.

GETTING THE PICTURE

To start with, the survival-smart police officer anticipates the worst possible outcome of every call or contact he makes. That means that you must recognize the very real possibility that guns and gunplay may turn up unexpectedly at any time. A reported drunk with a bulge in his pocket may turn out to be a robbery in progress by the time you arrive on-scene. A complaint of firecrackers in a residential neighborhood may morph into a sniper firing shots when you get there. By using your imagination along with your good

129

common sense, you can be better prepared for whatever you find.

You also can reduce your risks on the street by playing out the "man with a gun" scenario in all its various possibilities in your head before you face it for real. Mental preparation for facing danger is vital. So is planning what you will do when confronted by that danger. You can run the never-ending variety of "man with a gun" threats through your mind while you are not otherwise occupied on patrol. How would you handle a reported gunman in a supermarket? How about the kid with a gun in his pocket in the packed classroom? Or the person with a gun on the teeming subway train? Meanwhile, you can come up with some proposed solutions, too. When you finally face the "man with a gun" call in reality, it won't be for the first time.

Information gathering is also vital to your welfare as you face the "man with a gun" assignment. You pump your dispatcher for every possible scrap of information. You ask more questions when you arrive on scene. Witnesses, victims, friends and relatives of the armed subject, fellow officers, and even your agency's records can provide answers to such important questions as:

- Who is the armed subject?
- Who else is involved? Are there hostages? Innocent bystanders in the way?
- What is the cause of the confrontation? An interrupted crime? Domestic battle? Pending suicide? Mental subject with a weapon? Or what?
- Is the situation really what it appears to be? In other words, might you in reality be dealing with a toy gun or an off-duty law enforcement officer who doesn't realize his weapon has been seen?

Laying your plans for handling the crisis will be your next on-scene priority. By applying your training and experience to the information you have been able to gather, you must plan your solution to the armed problem at hand. Now, you must answer several more key questions in order to safeguard your own person:

1. How will I approach the armed subject's location, assuming I choose to approach at all?
2. What kind of weapons can I safely deploy?
3. How much assistance will I need from other officers and/or agencies?
4. What special problems (traffic, hostages, lack of cover, etc.) does this situation present?

PLANNING FOR SUCCESS

The planning you commence here will continue until the armed subject call is resolved. Your approach and your options may change as more facts are learned, the armed individual responds, and the overall situation changes. Planning, not unlike information gathering, is a never-ending process.

The planning you undertake must include a continuing assessment process that you will conduct, perhaps with the help of your peers and a supervisor. How great is the danger now? It may change radically as the armed subject himself changes. He may get mad or calm down, become tired or get agitated, and decide to consider surrender instead of fighting to the death. Things also will change (as will your response) if the subject begins firing a gun, harms people or throws out a weapon. (Remember: He may have more.) New information can change the situation and your response to it, too. The sudden availability of the subject's identity can, via a "Wants and Record" check, turn a barricaded drunk with a gun into a wanted murderer. You must be able to alter your plans and your response with equal speed.

With appropriate information (you'll never have ALL you want) and a plan of action (it'll never be letter-perfect) in hand, getting all the help you need to solve the problem without taking unnecessary chances is a must. Safely handling a "man with a gun" confrontation calls for careful teamwork, not *macho* heroics that are likely to get you killed. Once your assistance is on hand, it is vital that everyone knows the plan of attack and his place in it.

Achieving the element of surprise in approaching and confronting your armed adversary is your next objective. You want to locate and target your subject before he does the same to you. That means you turn off your lights and siren far away when you're responding to the scene. You also slow down to eliminate the noise of a racing engine or squealing tires. Once you arrive, you park your police vehicle well away from the scene, out of the offender's line of sight (and fire). You move in quietly on foot.

If you must eventually enter a building to get at your armed subject, consider creating a diversion (breaking glass, a slam against a door, etc.) while you go in somewhere else. To the extent possible, the ground on which you end up facing the armed offender should be your choice, not his.

With a protective perimeter of police personnel in place and uninvolved people kept safely out of harm's way, your confrontation with the armed subject can proceed with greater safety. You and your assisting officer or officers on the arrest team must be clear on exactly what each individual is to do in the operation. You must be clear on both the statutes and department policies regarding use of deadly force. Each team member must also have as complete an answer as possible to each of several vital questions:

- How is the subject dressed? (There's no room for mistaken identities here.)
- What crime has been committed so far?
- Does the offender have accomplices?
- Where is he now?
- What weapons does he possess, if known?
- Does he know that the police are on scene?
- What else do we know about the situation?

Once you are within earshot of the armed subject, it is time to begin taking control of the situation with a verbal challenge. In an armed confrontation, it is oftentimes the one who gives the first order who controls the outcome of the incident. Your challenge must be uttered in a loud and clear voice. And it must be voiced only when you are behind cover with your weapon aimed at center mass on your armed opponent. The challenge itself can be a simple one:

"Police! Don't move!"

Only one officer speaks. If the subject does not respond immediately, the challenge can be repeated, still from behind good cover and with weapon at the ready. Don't make the mistake of leaving cover to approach an adversary who is still armed and not yet under control.

When you do gain compliance or it is at least evident that your initial command has been heard, you can proceed to give further verbal orders, still from behind cover and at gunpoint:

"Turn your back to the sound of my voice. Place your hands on top of your head. Turn all the way around. Slowly. Keep facing away from us."

If no weapon is seen in the subject's hands, he may then be ordered to back up to your position and be taken into custody by an assisting officer. All of this is done with the subject and the general area still covered at gunpoint by yourself and your backup(s).

If a weapon is spotted in the subject's hand, the directions are altered accordingly:

"Facing away from us, bend over and lay the weapon on the ground, now! Do anything else and you will be shot."

Stand by ready to fire until the subject complies. If he does not have a gun in his hand but you spot a firearm in his clothing or on his person, the following verbal instructions may be appropriate:

"We see the gun! Don't touch it or you will be shot!"

The gun is best left where it is until the subject backs up and is taken into physical custody. That's a safer option than telling him to take it out and lay it down–thereby giving him a chance to get the weapon in hand.

The orders are necessarily harsh. No apologies are in order, however. By making it clear to the offender what you are prepared to do, the chances are improved that you won't have to make good on your promise. By gaining control with words, you hope to avoid having to do so with gunfire.

ACHIEVING A SAFE SURRENDER

It is important to keep the subject with his hands on his head, facing away from you until he is totally under control. If more than one armed or believed-armed suspect is involved, they are all kept covered in this position while one at a time is brought backward into your area of control and secured by cuffing and searching. Each subject is secured in a police vehicle under guard before the next one is brought back.

If at any point a clearly armed subject moves to point a firearm at an officer and you have no reason to believe he won't use it, you have no choice but to protect your life and that of your partner by firing at center mass on the offender. To do anything less is to expose yourself and others to violent death at the hands of an armed and menacing offender.

The great danger of a "man with a gun" call is not removed until the suspect is properly handcuffed, thoroughly and repeatedly searched, and lodged in a holding facility. It is worth remembering that even when determined to be clean of firearms, an individual still can remain a serious threat to you via his "personal" weapons: feet, teeth, head, and so on. Be careful. And never be too sure that he really is "clean" of death-dealing weapons and devices. The survival-smart police officer never stops looking for one more weapon, one more nasty surprise.

When it is all over and the adrenaline level has subsided a little, it is time to review in a quieter moment how things went and how your tactics might be improved for the next time. What tactics and techniques worked well? Which were found lacking? Is additional or different equipment or training needed? This self-critique session literally could be a life-saver, so express yourself freely and encourage your peers to do the same. Only an open sharing of information and opinion on the part of everyone involved can help ensure that things will go even better the next time out.

"Man with a gun" calls are among the most hazardous assignments you will receive as a peace officer. You help guarantee your own safety and that of your fellow officers by preparing for them as your top priority. That kind of preparation is ongoing. It requires continuing training, planning, on-scene assessment, and, ultimately, decisive action aimed at controlling an armed and dangerous subject. It is thoughtful, survival-oriented preparation aimed squarely at *reducing the danger to you.*

A RISK REDUCTION CHECKLIST FOR "MAN WITH A GUN" CALLS

1. Start planning your actions before you get there.
2. Approach the problem site quietly and stay out of sight.
3. Obtain as much information as possible before you act.
4. Obtain as much help as you need. Don't shortchange yourself in this vital area.
5. Attempt to isolate the armed subject from bystanders and potential hostages.
6. Continuously update and reassess the situation.
7. Confront and give clear, concise directions from behind good cover.
8. Disarm, secure, and search your opponent carefully.
9. Critique your handling of the incident so you can do an even better job next time.

A one-year patrolman died of a gunshot wound from an 8:40 p.m. tavern incident. The 36-year-old policeman and three other officers responded to a "man with a gun" call at the establishment. As the victim and another officer approached the rear of the building, they were advised via radio that a subject matching the armed man's description had just exited the front of the bar. The two officers entered from the rear and walked through the establishment, passing the actual armed subject, who had apparently never left. The subject fired a .25-caliber handgun at the pair of officers, striking the victim once in the face and the other officer in the chest and groin.

* * * * *

After responding to a "man with a gun" call, a 13-year veteran officer was shot and killed outside a lodge building. The officer had just exited his car when he was struck in the chest with a .30-30-caliber rifle round fired by a 29-year-old male whom the officer was approaching. The subject was arrested by other officers.

Chapter 11

VEHICLE PURSUITS

A number of things can happen as a result of a police vehicle pursuit of an offender of one sort or another:

- The offender pulls over, surrenders, and is taken into custody without damage or injury to anything or anyone.

The rest of the possibilities are not quite as nice:

- The police crash, injuring no one but destroying property.
- The offender crashes, injuring no one but destroying property.
- The police crash. Someone is hurt or killed.
- The offender crashes. Someone is hurt or killed.
- The offender escapes.

It is painfully obvious that a great many police pursuits do not end well for law enforcement. For this reason alone, it is worth a lot of quick but careful thinking on your part before you commit your vehicle, your peers, your department, and possibly your life to a dangerous course of action: the high-speed vehicle pursuit of a fleeing offender.

Basically, a police pursuit occurs whenever an offender elects to flee in a vehicle rather than stop and give up to an approaching police unit. The offender may be a wanted murderer or a scared teen fleeing from a traffic ticket. The danger he creates for you and every other user of the nearby roadways is considerable.

BAD THINGS CAN HAPPEN

Although the statisticians have trouble agreeing on exact figures, it is known that police-involved pursuits injure many hundreds of people annually. Every year, innocent people are killed by pursuing police cars or the vehicles they are chasing. There is no shortage of tragic examples. In one case, a 3-year-old boy was killed in the southwestern United States when the pickup truck in which he was riding pulled in front of a patrol car in pursuit of a fleeing stolen vehicle. The fact that the police vehicle's lights and siren were operating did nothing to bring back the dead youngster.

Police officers can be victims of pursuits, too. Hundreds receive injuries of one degree of severity or another in pursuit-related actions every year. Most years also see one or more officers die because of the felonious actions of fleeing offenders or pursuit-related accidents occurring at high speed. Simply put, *high-speed pursuits are bad news.*

Nonetheless, violators of the law have a legal duty to yield to your properly equipped, properly operated police vehicle. (That means lights *and* siren.) Generally speaking, you have a legal right to apprehend these offenders no matter where within your jurisdiction they are to be found. At the same time, the law has restricted the means you may employ to catch the wrongdoer who runs from you. Your state's motor vehicle codes probably limit your actions to what is "reasonable and prudent." The civil courts of the land and the hordes of attorneys that attend them limit you further.

In addition, any vehicle pursuit you elect to become involved in must fall within the policy and procedure guidelines established by your own agency. There is diminished satisfaction for you in running the crook to ground if in doing so you must face disciplinary action administered by your own department. Worse, you expose yourself to considerable civil liability if something goes bad during the pursuit and it can be proven that you knowingly disregarded or disobeyed your organization's pursuit guidelines.

Very strong emotions are aroused when you are in pursuit of an offender in a vehicle. Adrenaline flows in quantity. Don't fall victim to the pursuit psychology that can result in literally dozens of police cars becoming involved in a dangerous, lengthy, high-speed convoy. If too many police units have become involved in the chase, perhaps by inviting themselves along, it is time for you to do one of two things, assuming you cannot get them to discontinue pursuing. Call off the pursuit if you can. If you cannot, get out of it yourself. Many departments wisely limit by policy the number of police cars that can actively engage in a pursuit to two or three. That's a smart personal pursuit policy for you, too.

If you are not actively involved in a pursuit as either the primary chase car or his backup, you often can be the most help by paralleling (at lawful speeds) the chase route on other streets in case the chase suddenly changes direction or the suspect flees on foot. By heading into the general vicinity where experience and your knowledge of the "lay of the land" have taught you the pursuit may end, you also can be on hand to help set up the perimeter for a ground search for suspects if they eventually take off on foot.

CONTROL YOUR ADRENALINE

Be aware of another danger to you in the high-speed pursuit scenario. It comes in the form of the "cowboy" police officer who deliberately encourages violators to flee because he gets his kicks from the thrill of the vehicle chase. This red lights and siren junkie can get you killed by, among other tricks, turning on his emergency equipment when he is still a couple of blocks behind the car he intends to target. Or he backs off and holds back a little to see if an undecided offender will rabbit for him. This officer is bad news. Stay away from him.

Keep in mind that in an urban area a fleeing traffic law violator is not a very good reason to engage in a high-speed vehicle pursuit in heavy traffic. Granted, he MAY be an escaping murderer, too. But you don't know that, and as an ethical law enforcement officer you can act only on the known facts at hand. Your actions of the moment cannot be justified by what you find out later.

It naturally goes against the grain of any good police officer to "allow" a wrongdoer of any variety to get away, even temporarily. But the truth is that many of these fleeing offenders will be caught later anyway, perhaps when they do not have the assistance of a stable full of horses under the hood. The question you are left to answer for yourself is this one: How much is it really worth to me to catch this jerk right here, right now? Is it worth putting my life on the line and the lives of innocent others at risk? If your honest answer is in the negative, it is time to back off. It's very likely that there WILL be another day of reckoning for this particular offender.

Assume, on the other hand, that you have decided that the pursuit you have just commenced IS worth the risk involved. The offense committed is *that* serious; the offender is believed to be *that* dangerous and he cannot be allowed to remain at large. Assume, too, that you already have decided that your own driving skills and your vehicle's abilities are up to the task. Finally, assume that road (dry), weather (good), and traffic (not too heavy) conditions are such that you can at least begin a pursuit in relative safety. What then?

First of all, recognize that while they certainly can help you, a book or video presentation alone cannot teach you the skills you will need to master for emergency and pursuit driving. These only can be learned under the guidance of an experienced, qualified instructor on a pursuit driving track. Your department owes you the opportunity to take such training. Perhaps more to the point, you owe it to yourself and those you serve.

FOLLOW THE BASICS

Now that you have decided to pursue and have prepared yourself in advance to do so in safety, there are still some principles of high-speed pursuit you must keep in mind. There are a few more preparatory steps you can take, too. First, you should have made a careful, pre-trip inspection of your patrol vehicle before you hit the street. Are all the lights in good working order? How about the tires—do they have good tread and are they properly inflated? Does the steering respond properly? How about the brakes? Your pursuit preparations begin before you ever leave the police station parking lot.

Second, you should have stowed all of your gear so that you don't face any unguided missiles inside the passenger compartment during driving maneuvers. Many good police equipment carriers and holders are on the market and can help you out here.

Third, be sure your lap and shoulder belts are working properly and are in use during normal patrol operations. When the pursuit begins in earnest, it will be too late to hook up. Belts are intended to be used *all* of the time that your vehicle is in motion.

Now that the pursuit has started, here are some more thumbnail sketch reminders to add to your on-the-track training for bringing the chase to a safe and successful conclusion:

- Don't pursue to *catch* the offender and drive up on his trunk lid; drive to *follow* him until he makes a mistake that leads to his capture or until he simply gives up. You do not have to drive faster than he does. You just have to move fast enough to keep him in sight. If you slow up, the violator may follow suit.
- If you are the backup car in a pursuit, handle the radio traffic for the primary car. Keep dispatch and other police units advised of the direction of travel, speed, and new developments, such as the tossing out of evidence or the showing of weapons. If you are the primary car, let your radio partners know the reason for the pursuit, vehicle description and number, and description (if known) of the suspect vehicle's occupants. Also broadcast the speed and direction of travel. When and if you get a backup car behind you in the chase, let him take over the radio duties while you concentrate full time on the pursuit. You'll have

plenty of details to occupy your mind.

- Scan as far down the road ahead of the pursuit path as you possibly can. Don't forget the side roads that intersect with your likely route. Remember that your side vision suffers while you are focusing on the fleeing vehicle dead ahead. Slow up as necessary.

- Try to stay 4–5 seconds behind the vehicle you are chasing. That is, it should take 4–5 seconds for you to reach a point or object on or near the roadway that the suspect has just passed. Allow more time and distance when poor roadway or visibility conditions exist, if you continue the pursuit at all. If you end up crashing into the rear end of his car, your vehicle, with its mechanical vitals up front, is more likely to be disabled than his. By staying back a bit, you are less likely to overshoot and end up in front of the offender if he stops suddenly and decides to flee or take you on. By passing him, you will, of course, be in a bad tactical position if he decides to use firearms against you.

- By the same token, do not pass or draw abreast with a fleeing vehicle. Police officers have been shot to death or died in offender-initiated crashes in just this maneuver. Stay back and wait for *him* to make the mistakes.

- Your normal Code 3 or emergency run procedures are not suspended just because you are in a pursuit. Keep all your visual and audible emergency equipment operating. Pass other vehicles going your way only to the left. Slow greatly or stop at intersections where the traffic signal is against you. Slow up even when you have the "green." Don't worry about the fact that your quarry is busting these intersections wildly and could get away from you. Your obligation to an innocent public is greater than your need to get him.

- Throughout your pursuit, stay in control of yourself and keep resisting the very real temptation to drive just a little faster or push just a little harder.

- Handle your steering wheel firmly but carefully by threading it from one hand to the other rather than by grabbing or jerking at it. This threading technique is best practiced on the pursuit track, of course.

- Do your braking before you enter a curve or turn, not after you are into it. To stay on top of the natural forces that will try and pull your car off the road, don't begin to increase your speed again until you reach the middle or apex of the curve.

- Enter a curve or turn on the outside portion of your traffic lane, make the turn on the innermost portion without leaving your lane, and finish up on the outside portion again. Stay on your own side of the road. Remember: To avoid losing control and spinning out, you want to slow before you go in and apply some power as you come out.

- Always be ready to extract yourself from surprise problems that may befall you. If you find your vehicle fishtailing, for example, ease off the accelerator and steer in the direction of the skid until you regain control.
- Try to pump your brakes as necessary rather than staying on the brake pedal. Jamming them on hard will lock up your ability to steer the car and put you into an uncontrolled skid.
- Make your steering movements smoothly. That will result in improved control over your driving.
- If you slip off the road surface, let off on the accelerator and gradually steer back onto the pavement. Do not jerk the wheel. Abrupt moves of that sort could turn your car over.
- If your vehicle has a blowout, keep a good grip on the steering wheel and ease off on the accelerator. Use the brakes as little as possible as you steer straight ahead and slow to a stop.
- It's not over until it's over. When the suspect's vehicle is disabled or otherwise appears stopped for good, do not allow adrenaline to cause you to run up to the car with the intent of extracting the occupants forcibly. Officers have been killed doing exactly that. Stay behind cover and go into your high-risk vehicle contact procedures. High-speed pursuits have been known to turn into barricaded gunman incidents with the suspect's vehicle serving as the barricade. Pursuit terminations have also resulted in fatal gunfights. Be smart. Issue commands to the offenders from behind cover. Bring them back to you, don't go to them. Stay back, stay covered, and stay alive.

Finally, be aware of the very real tendency to overreact when the pursuit has ended and the adrenaline rush inside you is still powerful. Suspects have been beaten brutally and officers sued successfully and/or charged criminally as a result of such tense moments. Control the suspect(s) with the minimum force required to do the job and back off. Give yourself time to take some deep breaths and walk around a little bit. You may want to ask a less-involved officer to handle and transport the prisoner for you while you cool down. *That's* good officer survival, too.

You'll note that this chapter has not discussed techniques for ramming, cutting off, boxing in, or shooting at fleeing vehicles by the use of police vehicles and weapons. That's because in most cases none of the above represents particularly effective tactics for safely ending a high-speed pursuit. Worse, they are dangerous to you. You are as likely to injure yourself or innocent others as you are to stop the fleeing offender by employing any of these desperate measures. Do not apply such techniques at all unless you have been well trained in their use. Apply them as an absolute last resort and then only as directed and authorized by your agency. But do not overlook the danger to you and others that their use involves.

Pursue as a last resort. Pursue when you must, but pursue in control. High-speed pursuits are very dangerous affairs. You should begin or continue one only as a last resort when you have gathered as much pertinent information as you can, analyzed what's to be gained and what's to be risked by chasing, and made a conscious decision that pursuing is worth it. Once you decide to pursue, remain aware that you retain the right and obligation to call a halt at any point at which you determine that the risks outweigh the potential for a good outcome. Your decision to pursue is not an irrevocable one.

Practice your high-speed driving maneuvers with a competent instructor and follow your jurisdiction's laws, rules, and procedures for pursuit driving. Don't push the envelope when it comes to staying safe. Remain keenly alert throughout a pursuit for potentially disastrous surprises like a tire failure or unexpected side-road traffic or pedestrians. You don't want to get hurt yourself, nor do you want to be responsible for harm coming to innocent others who just happen to be sharing the road.

To better your chances of surviving a high-speed pursuit, avoid multiplying the danger by ramming or pulling in front of a fleeing vehicle. At the conclusion of the chase, remember that the danger is not over until the offender is safely in jail. Don't rush into an ambush by charging a stopped vehicle. Stay in control of yourself and play it safe. Bring the bad guy out to you. Let *him* make the mistakes.

High-speed pursuits are valid law enforcement tactics that must on occasion be used to bring very dangerous offenders to justice. See to it that when you engage in one, you do so with careful decision making. That's what reducing the danger to you is really all about!

A RISK REDUCTION CHECKLIST FOR VEHICLE PURSUITS

1. Be aware of your jurisdiction's laws and your agency's regulations concerning vehicle pursuits.
2. Before continuing a pursuit, ask yourself whether it's worth the risks for what you have to gain. Then, act on your decision.
3. Follow, do not overtake. Pursue in control at all times.
4. Get help and keep everyone advised via radio of the pursuit's progress.
5. Know your limitations as a driver as well as those of your vehicle.
6. Scan well ahead and to the sides. Let the offender make the mistakes.

7. Don't get too close. About 4–5 seconds behind is about right under ideal conditions. In poor driving conditions, open up the distance some more.
8. Be prepared to deal with surprises and driving emergencies.
9. Follow your agency's normal Code 3 or emergency run procedures.
10. Don't rush up to a pursued vehicle when it stops. Follow high-risk vehicle contact procedures.
11. Remember that it is always acceptable to get out of a pursuit that is spinning out of control and escalating in danger to the innocent.

A 22-year-old patrolman with less than a year's police experience was killed trying to apprehend the driver of a stolen vehicle at about 9:50 a.m. The stolen van, pursued by other officers, swerved across four lanes of traffic and hit the victim officer's patrol car head-on. A 19-year-old male was subsequently charged with murder.

* * * * *

A 16-year highway patrol trooper, age 48, was aiding other officers in the pursuit of a stolen car and tried to pull his patrol car in front of the moving vehicle in an effort to make the driver stop. Instead, the fleeing vehicle's driver rammed the trooper's car, causing it to leave the roadway and overturn. The stolen vehicle then landed on top of the patrol car and the officer was killed. A 30-year-old male was charged with capital murder.

* * * * *

A 37-year-old deputy sheriff was fatally shot at about 9:30 p.m. after pursuing a reported drunk driver at high speed. The drunk was reported to have an infant with him in the vehicle. At the end of the pursuit, the suspect fled on foot and was chased by the deputy. Shortly thereafter, the deputy radioed for emergency backup and reported "officer down." Responding units found the lone deputy down with a fatal wound to the chest from a .223-caliber rifle round.

Chapter 12

STICKUP IN PROGRESS

Armed robbery is a big problem—a dangerous problem—in the United States. If stickups are dangerous for citizens, they are no less so for police officers. For that matter, any crime in progress assignment contains built-in hazards for the officer sent to deal with it. The danger is real for a number of reasons, and it begins for the peace officer even before he arrives on-scene.

While the procedural specifics vary from one department to the next, a crime in progress assignment often calls for an emergency response from the officer sent to handle it. That may translate into a Code 3, lights, and siren run over busy streets. Sound emergency driving techniques will make the trip safer for the survival-smart peace officer, but the unpredictable reactions of other drivers sharing the road will not permit the danger to be removed completely. Thus, the need to arrive quickly but safely represents the first safety challenge for the officer answering a stickup (or other major crime) in progress call.

The lack of information often found in critical law enforcement calls presents another threat to the first responder. A lack of data about what is happening can set an officer up for disaster unless he applies everything he knows about defusing the danger of a high-risk assignment. The officer also must confront changes, perhaps drastic ones, that may have occurred on-scene between the time he last received information from his dispatcher and the moment he arrives. Lack of information can kill.

The officer arriving on the scene of a crime in progress may encounter a number of unknowns. How many offenders are there? Where are they? Are they armed? If so, *how* are they armed? Are there additional, undetected offenders, such as lookouts, somewhere nearby? A failure to ferret out *all* of the threats in time could have fatal consequences.

An officer answering a crime in progress call has no way of knowing how an interrupted or a startled offender will react to being challenged by the law.

Will he fight? Start a gunfight? Flee on foot? Will a high-speed pursuit ensue if he is able to reach a vehicle? Will he take an innocent person as a hostage to facilitate his escape? Could a barricade situation result from an interrupted robbery? Escalation of risk is always a possibility when a criminal realizes that his initial plan has gone awry.

Whether you are on or off duty, being present at or near the scene of a stickup in progress can be extremely hazardous to your continued good health. As in the other varieties of high-risk patrol you will encounter, a reliance on good common sense and proven officer survival tactics will considerably reduce the dangers you will face. Proven effective robbery response tactics will be required even before you arrive at the in-progress crime scene. Those effective tactics will require the participation of other police personnel in addition to yourself. Your radio dispatcher, for instance, will be vital to your safe operations.

ASKING THE KEY QUESTIONS

Even as patrol units are being dispatched to a stickup in progress or just-occurred robbery, your communications people should be obtaining and relaying to you and your peers the answers, where available, to such key questions as:

- What is the exact location of the crime?
- What are the descriptions of the robbers?
- Where are they now?
- Were weapons seen? What kind?
- How many offenders have been seen?
- Can you see a lookout?
- How about a getaway vehicle? What does it look like and where is it? Is it occupied?
- Have shots been fired?
- Is anyone known to be injured?
- Direction of travel, if the robbers have left?

Knowing just as much as you possibly can about what is going on at the scene will help you greatly in responding safely to what you find when you get there. Whatever you learn from your dispatcher, it's up to you to move as quickly as you safely can toward the robbery site. Maintaining the element of surprise on your side is vital, so you will want to avoid betraying your presence with a wailing siren or flashing lights near the crime scene.

You must avoid being seen by a lookout as you approach the robbery scene. As a result, you should arrive on a street other than the one the stick-up is occurring on, if at all feasible. You must take care to park out of sight of the immediate scene. But even as you take care to avoid being detected by the armed crooks, you must do everything you can to locate your opponents. What does not look right here? Who or what appears out of place? How about vehicles? Remain alert as you plan your next move. The robbers may no longer be where they were at your dispatcher's last report. You may encounter them many blocks from the crime site. You must be ready to confront armed danger well before you reach the place where you *planned* to encounter danger. Robbers have a nasty tendency to refuse to follow a pre-planned script. That means you've got to remain safely flexible in your own planning and response.

PLANNING FOR SURVIVAL

What else can you do to stay safe while responding to a stickup in progress call? A number of things. First of all, realize that your arrival may be anticipated by your armed adversaries. Many robbers know *their* business, too, and they have learned that many of the targets that are most attractive to them come equipped with silent alarms that will bring the cops on the run, perhaps before they are done with their "business." As a result, they are looking for you and have very likely planned what they're going to do when you show up. They have the advantage of making plans without having to worry about keeping pedestrians and other innocent bystanders safe from any gunfire that may develop.

It's up to you to make plans of your own that provide for your personal safety as you plot the downfall of your criminal opponents. In quiet moments on patrol, play various robbery scenarios through your mind and come up with realistic options for handling the various threats. In other words, "If he does A, I'll do B. If he does C, I'll resort to D." And so on.

Critique your stickup response plans and then plan some more. You are smarter than your enemy. Use that intelligence to defeat him.

No matter how many silent robbery alarms you respond to and no matter how many of them turn out to be false, don't allow yourself to become complacent or *assume* that an alarm is going to be bogus. Making dangerous assumptions like that can make you careless. And being careless can get you killed.

As you make your personal preparations for an armed robbery response, remember that your potential opponents are coming to their work better equipped all the time. They are oftentimes showing up today with larger caliber weapons as opposed to Saturday night specials. Sometimes they are carrying shotguns and even machine guns. Occasionally they are found wearing body armor of their own.

You cannot afford to come to your work any less prepared. Your sidearm must be well maintained, and you must be proficient in its use. If your department permits it (and it certainly should), carry a police shotgun or patrol rifle in a locked rack in your patrol vehicle. If you are truly competent with that weapon, you should be more than a match for the average crook, even if he is armed with an automatic weapon. Wear your body armor, too. There is no acceptable excuse for not wearing it.

If you get into a gun battle with a robber who fails to go down in spite of obvious hits to the torso, take it for granted that he's wearing body armor and shift your fire above and below his armor level. A head shot is most likely to be immediately fatal, but below the belt, the pelvic girdle area presents a bigger, easier target if you're some distance away. Set your sights on one or the other if you suspect your rounds are impacting on an opponent's armor.

Today's stickups may come equipped with their own cell phones, two-way radios, and/or radio scanners to talk to a lookout and keep on top of what you are doing. There's not much you can do about their possession of these things other than to be aware of the possibility. Do that and utilize even more caution every time you respond to a robbery in progress call.

Continue to plan your stickup response even as you are en route and don't forget to include the other responding police units in your plans. Set up via radio who's going to go where. Ideally, you will want an officer at diagonally opposite corners of the building where the crime is occurring. You also will want a couple of roving units in the neighborhood to look for getaway cars and backup crooks. And you will need to plan who will direct police operations on-scene. (It will most likely be the first car to arrive.)

Your planning also will determine who is to issue orders to the crooks when you confront them. Such advance arrangements should prevent confusion that might otherwise result if too many cops are yelling too many things all at the same time. You cannot formulate final plans for every eventuality you will find on-scene. But by engaging in some flexible, thoughtful planning ahead of time, you can minimize the surprises that might otherwise await you.

Remember: No matter how long it takes you to get there, the possibility always exists that the robbers will still be present when you arrive. A stickup may be over in seconds, or it may last 15 minutes or more as the crooks try to have a safe opened for them or otherwise attempt to fatten their haul. Their greed may force them into a confrontation with you. Expect it, anticipate it, plan for it, and then meet it head-on. But always meet it *smart.*

There is at least one other safe assumption you can and should make about a stickup in progress call, as dangerous as assumptions often can be. ASSUME that there is at least one more robber than you are aware of on-scene or nearby. Never stop looking for one more offender—man, woman, or even a young person—perhaps serving in the capacity of a lookout, driver, or outright assassin, placed there to intercept and murder any intervening police (that means you!). Never stop seeking to detect additional threats to your safety. Your life may depend on your continuing survival consciousness and unending state of readiness.

It is almost (but not quite) too obvious to talk about: As pumped up with adrenaline as you may be, NEVER rush inside the location where a stickup may be going down. That major tactical error still takes place with sad regularity, and officers still die tragically as a result. Instead, deploy outside and behind good cover with your assist units and wait for the robber(s) to come out to you. If you have arrived quietly and deployed carefully, the bad guys may not be aware of your presence, and you probably will not have long to wait. In contrast, if you are too noisy, too visible, or otherwise too obvious in your approach and deployment, you may succeed only in bringing about a barricaded gunman situation that is complicated by robbery victims who have just become hostages. A bad situation has now gotten worse.

Even if it looks like the robbers have gone (or were never there), don't go in. Use your voice or your car's PA or the telephone (your best option) to call an employee out of the business and into your area of control. This procedure can be made easier if you have done some advance work with the business owners on your beat and told them what to expect from the police ("We're not coming in; you come out") on a stickup in progress call. You and your agency may decide to work out some verbal codes to be used when calling a locale from which a robbery alarm has been received ("This is the telephone company. Is there trouble there?"). The possibilities are virtually without limit.

Remember: You don't go *in.* They, robbers or victims, come *out.* And never leave cover until you are convinced that the person and situation you are facing outside are safe for you. *Know* that you're talking to the store manager and not the robber and that things really *are* under control before you leave cover. Again, if you've done your homework ahead of time, you already may know what the manager looks like. If you are going to make a mistake, you want to err on the side of too much caution, not too little.

OFF-DUTY DANGERS

Here's something else for you to think about when planning for armed robbery encounters. As one bloody case history after another has demonstrated, it is very dangerous duty indeed for a police officer to work off duty and alone as a uniformed security guard at a financial institution. If a potential robber is worth his salt at all, he already knows that you're present, exactly where you are positioned, and how you are armed. He may have one or more assistants. (You probably don't.) He may have radio or cell phone communications. (You very well may not.) He most likely has no concern at all for what his gunfire may do to innocent bystanders. (You are not so callous.) He, in a very few words, has a lot of advantages on his side.

What the establishment is probably hiring is your uniform in the hope it will deter would-be robbers. It probably *will* scare off some potential stickups, but the ones it doesn't chase off are probably the most dangerous of all. They *know* you're there, and they are coming anyway. They are not at all put off by the possibility that they may have to kill a cop.

If you *must* work as a bank security officer, know in advance what your employer expects and permits you to do. Know, too, what your police agency requires and allows while you are working in an extra-duty capacity. See to it that you have the capability of quick and reliable communication to your department, even if that communication amounts to no more than a prearrangement with specific bank employees to telephone for police help when you signal them to do so. Try and have access to your own two-way radio or cell phone tying you to police aid.

If you elect to accept such employment, know that you are guarding a financial institution (or any other establishment) as a full-time, high-risk assignment that demands your complete attention. It's not a job where you can sit at a desk, put your feet up, and study for that upcoming exam or read up on the latest fishing news. Otherwise, you could find yourself knowing an awful lot about a coming exam or fishing–just before you get yourself killed. You cannot afford to maintain a lower level of officer survival awareness on an off-duty job than you have when you're working the street, particularly when that extra job carries with it the good possibility of a confrontation with an armed robber.

In conclusion: Working off duty as a security officer to deter armed robbers is not the safest of jobs for a police officer to have. If you must do it, take advantage of every possible officer safety precaution that you can. Take no extra chances. Call for backup when it even *begins* to look like you might need some. Plan and plan some more about how you will respond if a stickup goes down. Work to minimize your risks and maximize your use of good cover and other sound tactics. Be supremely cautious.

Whether you are on or off duty, it remains true that you are much better off outside than inside a place where a stickup is going down. It's safer for you and it's safer for the innocents present, who might otherwise blunder into the middle of a firefight. But even with you and your backups properly deployed under cover *outside* a robbery target, you will need to pay careful attention to potential crossfires endangering officers or civilians if a gun battle develops. Be aware of what's around you before you start blasting away. Stay behind cover and do not fire unless you can do so without endangering uninvolved others. There *will* very likely be another opportunity to capture an escaped stickup if you must hold your fire and it comes to that. There *won't* be an opportunity for you to bring back to life an innocent person cut down by misdirected police gunfire.

THE FINAL CONFRONTATION

Obviously, the dangers of an armed robbery confrontation are not over for you just because you have at last confronted the target of your attentions. Until he and his cohorts are safely and securely cuffed, searched, and lodged, your safety remains in at least some jeopardy. As a result, you must utilize everything you have learned about cover, handcuffing, and searching techniques to bring a cornered robber safely into custody. You work closely with a backup. Only one of you leaves cover to secure a proned out or kneeling suspect. That officer makes his approach only when the surrounding area is carefully watched for other offenders and secured. If a robber won't obey your commands to exit and surrender, it may be time to declare a barricaded gunman situation that requires a SWAT unit response. But while SWAT mobilizes, it will be up to you and the other officers already on-scene to secure a perimeter and start clearing endangered citizens from harm's way.

But assuming you don't need SWAT and you *are* able to get your armed robber to come out to you, your job is still not finished. The area still has to be searched and cleared of any other stickups or lookouts. The interior of the robbery target has to be checked out–carefully–for additional suspects who still may be hiding inside. You will need help to carry out these area–securing tasks safely. You will need to take all the time required to do the job right, too. You cannot afford to be in a hurry where officer safety is at stake. There is all the time in the world to do it right *the first time*. If you're very careless, you may not get another opportunity.

None of this changes the fact that answering a stickup in progress call is potentially hazardous business for you. That's a given. What you *can* do, however, is substantially reduce the danger to which you expose yourself. You do that by applying all you have learned about officer safety thinking and officer safety tactics. That thinking and those tactics require that you plan and coordinate your stickup response. They require that you deploy carefully and approach cautiously using cover effectively. They require that you remain as patient as you are alert. And they require that when you decide to act, you do so from a position of tactical strength. That's what reducing the danger to YOU in the stickup in progress challenge is all about.

A RISK REDUCTION CHECKLIST FOR STICKUP IN PROGRESS

1. Understand the risks and dangers and start planning your response long before a stickup confronts you.
2. Plan your approach and arrival to keep your presence and deployment a secret from the robber(s).
3. Communicate and coordinate with your assisting police units.
4. Watch out for lookouts, criminal backups, and escape vehicles as you approach the area of the reported robbery.
5. Don't go in after a robber; let him come out to you.
6. Anticipate the presence and participation of more robbers than you are aware of.
7. Utilize sound building and area search tactics to locate and apprehend concealed or fleeing robbers.
8. Secure and search all captured stickups with extreme caution and thoroughness. They are still dangerous to you.

At approximately 11 a.m., an off-duty sheriff's deputy was working in a bank as a security officer when two male robbers entered. Both robbers wore ski masks; one displayed a .25-caliber handgun, and the other showed a .45-caliber weapon. They demanded the officer's weapon, and both shot him before he could respond. The 53-year-old deputy, who had nearly five years of law enforcement service, died of wounds to the chest and shoulder. Both robbers, who were later captured, were on parole and believed involved in other bank robberies.

* * * * *

A 46-year-old sergeant with 14 years on the job was killed by a robbery suspect at approximately 10:20 a.m. After being stopped by the victim of the robbery, the sergeant gave pursuit of several suspects in a car. The sergeant was shot through his patrol car's door when he pulled his unmarked car parallel with the suspects' vehicle. Four subjects were later arrested and a fifth committed suicide before capture.

Chapter 13

AMBUSH ATTACKS

Ambush. Depending on who you're talking to, an ambush may be referred to as "a trap," "a lying in wait for the purpose of attacking," "a sneak attack," or half a dozen other definitions.

An ambush is all of that and more. When a police officer is the target of an ambush attack, the assailant is expressing to everyone his utter disregard for what the nation's system of laws is all about. By demonstrating his ultimate and possibly deadly contempt for the agents of that system of justice–the police–the ambusher is screaming his total rejection of the principles that most Americans hold dear. He has confirmed beyond doubt his status as an absolute outlaw in society.

But to the police officer on the receiving end of an ambush attack, something a lot more personal than principle is at stake here. It is his life that the sniper, bomber, or other variety of attacker has targeted.

THE CONCEPT OF AMBUSH

For the average police officer, the whole concept of the ambush attack–that a person he may never have met might want to destroy him–is sometimes a bit difficult to grasp. He can understand, at least, the sudden violence aimed at him that might erupt from a police-interrupted armed robbery or domestic assault. It's harder for him to accept that another human being who wouldn't give him another look in the supermarket checkout line now wants to destroy him because of the uniform he wears.

Ambush attacks or even the threat of them can be particularly destructive to police morale. The obvious hatred required on the part of the attacker, along with the unpredictability of the assault, can prove psychologically damaging to the law enforcement personnel placed at risk. As fear and stress mount in individual police officers, relations with the public in general turn sour as everyone not in a police uniform begins to look like a potential ambusher. A vicious cycle begins that can aggravate the situation that may have led to an ambush incident in the first place.

But there is more to know about an ambush than its working definition. Hard experience has taught, for instance, that the average ambush attack, if there is such a thing, is over in well under a minute. While some ambushes are the result of long-term, deliberate planning, most are spur-of-the-moment attacks brought on by some real or imagined grievance the attacker or someone close to him has suffered at the hands of the police, such as a traffic citation encounter. Ambushes can occur in rural areas or built-up urban jungles. They can occur on any day of the week and at any hour of daylight or darkness, although many take place during the dark hours. Not surprisingly, uniformed officers in marked patrol cars are the most frequent law enforcement targets.

The types of ambushes menacing police officers today are limited only by the evil ingenuity of the attackers, but they generally fall into categories of (1) sniping by gunfire, perhaps from a considerable distance, (2) bomb or projectile throwing, and (3) direct assault at close range by a surprise attacker armed with something like a sharp instrument or handgun. On rare occasions, attacks may be complicated and made considerably more dangerous by multiple ambushers working in some sort of prearranged and coordinated plan of attack. In all instances and with all types of ambush assaults, however, the attacker's most effective weapon and possible "edge" remains the *element of surprise.*

It will be up to you as the potential recipient of an ambush attack to defeat your attacker's plans by denying him the advantage of total surprise and then responding with some effective countermeasures of your own. For example, you may be able to detect an ambush in the planning stages by paying attention to what you have been hearing or seeing on your beat. Is resentment growing in some element of the community about a perceived use of excessive force or some other alleged miscarriage of justice perpetrated by law enforcement? Have verbal threats been heard? Is threatening graffiti present? In other words, what is the word on the street?

By tapping into regular sources of intelligence information, you may be able to prevent an attack by spreading accurate information, warning off a potential ambusher by direct or indirect contact, or, as a last resort, intercepting and defeating an attempted ambush. Naturally, you share any ambush-related data you obtain with the other members of your agency. You in turn expect the same of them.

MENTAL AND PHYSICAL PREPARATIONS

You can steel yourself to handle an ambush attack that you hope will never come by preparing yourself mentally and physically to resist and overcome any surprise assault. Your preparations begin with your personal program of physical conditioning to build strength and endurance. They continue when you equip yourself with body armor and the best weapons you can carry. They go further still when you routinely play out in your mind's eye the varying ambush scenarios you might be exposed to and how you would respond effectively to each. And, of course, you further prepare yourself by learning all you can about ambush situations by reading and studying what is available on the subject as well as by picking the brains of those who have faced deadly ambushes and come through alive. There is a lot of officer survival expertise out there if you will just tap into it.

On the street, it is better (and safer) for you to defuse an ambush attempt and prevent it from occurring than defeat the assault once it is underway. You accomplish this by unending information gathering, coupled with constant alertness and a refusal to let down your officer safety shield for even a moment. Once again you are looking for situations and people not behaving as they normally would be expected to do. A street normally bustling with people that is strangely deserted. A false call, perhaps for the second or third time today, to an abandoned building or isolated area. Street lights or other illumination damaged or out in an area where they were working a short while before. All of the situations may be indicators to the wary officer that something is amiss and an ambush may be in the works.

An ambusher may not wait for you to come to him. He may come to where he knows you will be: the station house, the police parking lot, a cop-favored restaurant or bar, a spot where patrol supervisors routinely check reports on the street, and so on.

All of this means that you cannot relax your vigilance for a moment, not even on your agency's home turf. Officers have been assaulted and murdered inside of and all around police facilities and jails. (One mentally deranged woman attacked officers twice within the same month at the same police station.) There is no reason to believe that these places will cease to be magnets for cop-haters in the future. And that means that you must look, listen, and keep your field survival wits about you even when you are not technically in the field. As a result, you keep looking for cars and people that don't belong. You watch out for purposeless loiterers in the public lobby or parking areas. You scan rooftops and secluded places for potential snipers as you enter and leave the police facility. And you always stay ready to respond instantly, on or off duty, to an attack on you from *any* source.

As often as unpredictability presents a threat to you in your dealings with others as a law enforcement officer, unpredictability can be a strong ally in preventing a successful ambush attack against you. You build unpredictability to work for you and make a prospective ambusher's work much harder by declining as much as possible to follow a regular routine in your movements and actions. (This, not surprisingly, generally makes for more effective patrol operations, too!) You avoid a regular, predictable routine by not always going to the same spots for coffee, meal, or bathroom breaks at the same times. You also avoid, to the extent possible, following the same patrol routes or approaching the same individual buildings for a security check each night from exactly the same direction. By avoiding the use of the same spot each shift to write reports or watch for traffic violators, you also help keep a watching, would-be ambusher off balance.

Be wary of the traffic violator who appears deliberately to violate the law in front of you. Consider following him at a distance until you can get back-up assistance with you. Then, consider the advisability of a high-risk vehicle stop as opposed to an unknown risk pullover.

On dispatched calls, keep your feelers out for anything at all that seems out of the ordinary. Is the caller's address obviously a fake? Are there no lights showing at the supposed site of the domestic dispute? (Most people don't fight in total darkness.) Is an unknown "person with information" wanting to meet you at a remote location? Look out!

If you smell a rat, don't go without plenty of assistance. Even then, do not approach along a logical, expected route. Consider just sitting back some distance, behind cover, and watching for developments. Plan some surprises of your own, too, such as aerial surveillance (if your agency has that ability) or several patrol cars approaching with sirens from opposite directions while remaining outside of the actual danger zone. *Now* what is starting to happen?

Look for any indication of a trap. If you really know your area, you will already have a feel for what's normal and what is not. Be suspicious. Be cynical. And be gone if you don't like the looks of what your senses tell you. It's far better to be wrong about pending danger and be mildly embarrassed than to plunge carelessly ahead and be unembarrassed but dead.

Remaining alert to the possibility of an ambush requires that you attempt to see past that which appears to be the obvious. An abandoned, stolen car found in a remote area may be just that and nothing more. A smashed store window that activated a burglar alarm may be just what it looks like. But do not become so focused on the obvious that you fail to look around you and consider other possibilities. There *may* be a sniper in the brush beyond that stolen car. There *may* be an ambusher with a gun hidden just across the street from that smashed store window. Check around you thoroughly before you allow your attention to become fixated on any one task at hand. Even then, remain alert for sudden and perhaps barely perceptible changes around you. Somebody just might be trying to paint a target on your back.

IMPLEMENTING A RESPONSE

If you do come under ambush attack, your response options are relatively limited. You can run or drive out of the zone of attack as fast as you can move. (That's probably the best of all options. You can return later with enough help to solve the problem.) You can take cover and call for help. (Not quite as good–you still may be somewhat vulnerable.) Or you can attack immediately and forcefully with everything you have available. (A reasonable alternative only if your ambusher is quickly and directly within your reach, such as standing in the open within pistol range.)

You are showing good street survival sense if you opt to retreat in the face of an unknown but clearly dangerous threat. By withdrawing from the immediate area of attack, you give yourself time to gather reinforcements, seal off the area against the ambusher's escape, and plan an effective counterattack. It makes no sense to spend any extra time in the danger zone, especially when you are not absolutely certain where the threat is coming from, what it is (rifle fire? pistol fire? firecrackers?), and how many attackers are delivering it.

Get out, if you can, and survive to fight back later with a much-improved chance of winning. Make good use of cover in effecting your retreat. Slump very low in the seat if you are driving a squad car out of the area. Move quickly and stick to good, solid cover if you are moving out on foot. Don't expose any part of yourself unnecessarily.

What if a barricaded street, overwhelming gunfire, or other adverse conditions make it impossible for you to escape right away? In this case, you must protect yourself in place even as you radio for reinforcements and plan a successful response. Keep using cover. If you are still with your car, put the vehicle's engine compartment between you and the source of incoming rounds if you can determine their origin.

If you cannot figure out where the attack is coming from or your position at your vehicle becomes too hot, you may opt for other cover, assuming it is both solid and very close by. Fire hydrants, big trees, concrete barriers, and the corners of brick buildings all can furnish good cover. Once you get there by moving quick and low, keep any body parts you want to retain behind cover. Take a peek for the location of your opponent if you think he is moving or about to overrun your position, but make it a quick one. Don't look twice from exactly the same spot. Call for help, if you have not done so already, and keep looking for the next cover possibility in case you have to move because your location is being approached. Move only if you must, however.

Remember: Your option of attacking and turning the tables on your ambusher should be attempted only if you can see your target clearly and he is physically reachable and relatively close at hand. If your tormentor is on the street or otherwise at your level and within reach and you are still behind the wheel of your car, you might try driving right over his position. This tactic assumes, of course, that your armed attacker can be reached quickly and is not behind substantial cover that a vehicle would be unable to take out.

Follow up your vehicular attack by preparing to assault your adversary with gunfire if he is still able to hurt you. Don't forget that he may have helpers in the area. And don't stand around admiring your handiwork. Get behind cover until help is on-scene and you are really sure the area is secure. After all, there's very little satisfaction in taking out one bad guy if his partner still manages to do you in. Keep repeating to yourself the same old field survival advice you have heard many times before: never stop looking for one more offender. If you succeed in spotting him, start looking for the next one.

If you are away from your vehicle when you come under attack, react promptly and return fire if you can see and identify a target. In other words, don't fire blindly or shoot at shadows. You help no one, including yourself, by blasting innocent civilians. But if you safely can retaliate against your attacker, do so with the intent of stopping his assault once and for all.

If your attacker is far enough away or so well concealed that you cannot reach him with effective return fire, stay behind cover and try to remain as calm as you can. Panic can get you killed. You may get the chance to turn the tables if he is stupid enough to show himself. If he doesn't, stay put and wait for the help you have summoned to arrive.

And on the subject of rescues: Whether you are the one needing saved or part of the relief force responding Code 3 to the rescue, you have certain obligations to your fellow officers. If you are the one trapped in an ambush, you have more than your own life to worry about, as big a concern as that must be. You also may hold in your hands the key to the safety of those who come to help you. As a consequence, it is up to you to use whatever communication you have at hand (hopefully including a working portable radio) to tell your rescuers what's happening on-scene before they get there and get ambushed themselves. They will need to know, for instance, your exact location, your attacker's locale as best you can ascertain it, the number of attackers you believe to be involved, the kind of weapons being used in the attack, the safest approach routes to the scene for the rescuers, and anything else that may reduce the danger for these officers.

You also owe it to your rescuers not to make the situation worse than it already is. That means you don't take foolish chances and get yourself shot, thereby complicating the incident by forcing a downed officer rescue effort. Instead, stay behind cover, provide your help with the best, most current information you can, and stay alert for changes in the ambush picture. You are not out of the woods yet, and it would be particularly distasteful to get yourself murdered with help close at hand!

If you are part of the rescue force, you must be no less cautious than if you were the "main attraction" at the ambush attack. No "cowboy" heroics are needed here. Whatever you decide to do, you must do it in coordination with the other members of the relief force. This is not the time for solo tactics.

If you are dealing with a hidden sniper still firing after your arrival, your primary goal is to get your colleague out of danger without placing yourself at grave risk. That may mean keeping a sniper's head down with suppressing fire if you can spot his exact location while other officers drag a wounded comrade to safety. Then it will be time to cease fire, seal off the area with a tight perimeter, and evacuate uninvolved persons while you wait for adequately equipped and specially trained SWAT personnel. Once your colleague has been rescued, the ambush may turn into a barricaded gunman incident requiring the special tactics associated with a barricade situation. Now, time is your ally. There is no need to rush the outcome of the incident.

If an ambushed officer is found to have been wounded, his apparent condition may influence your tactics on scene. Influence, yes. Dictate, no. You only complicate matters if you get yourself shot while trying to save a downed officer. A number of factors can influence your response to the aid of a wounded officer: his location, the apparent severity of his injuries, his vulnerability for getting hit again, the location and weaponry of the ambusher, and so on.

If an officer is down and clearly not moving (actually or by design), he may be unlikely to be shot at again, particularly if the shooter is quite some distance away and has other targets to worry about. It may thus be unwise for you and other officers to draw fire on yourselves in a hurried rescue effort. At the same time, be prepared to direct suppressing fire on the ambusher's position if he resumes his attack on a downed officer. Then a "quick and low" rescue while your peers put up covering fire may be the only reasonable course of action.

SPECIAL AMBUSH THREATS

There is another, somewhat unique ambush threat to your welfare that you should be aware of. Granted, bullets can do you in. But so can dropped or thrown objects. Objects like scrap metal or garbage cans tossed off tenement roofs. Objects like rocks dropped off roadway overpasses. Objects like bolts and ball bearings propelled from a slingshot. Objects like gasoline bombs and Molotov cocktails tossed by your friendly neighborhood ambusher.

Many of the aforementioned threats can be avoided if you remain constantly alert to your surroundings, particularly the people who are around you. You would not, for example, want to spend a lot of extra time in a narrow alleyway in a hostile neighborhood without a pretty good idea of who might be on the roof or behind a dumpster. You also would not want to cruise mindlessly beneath a freeway overpass without at least glancing at who is up there doing what. Application of some good old common sense should keep you out of a lot of hazardous circumstances that might otherwise be brought on by things that go "whoosh" in the night.

Incendiary devices pose a somewhat different problem. They are relatively easy to both make and use. And their use is regularly demonstrated on the evening's television news as everybody watches the cops in Pakistan, South Korea, or some other hot spot of the moment dance to get out of the way of the flaming devices.

The ingredients for the poor man's incendiary device—oil, gasoline, bottle, rags, and a match—are quite easy to come by. There are various refinements to the construction of the thrown incendiary device, but the basics remain about the same. Technically, there is a difference between the gasoline bomb and the Molotov. The former is fueled entirely by gasoline, whereas the latter includes a dose of motor oil to add to the heat and intensity of the burn.

Some fire-bombers may add bits of Styrofoam or rubber to the mixture they put in their bottles to cause the flaming substance to stick to the surface it comes in contact with. Other ambushers have added sugar, potassium chlorate, and sulfurous acid in various containers and combinations to fuel their incendiary devices. Whatever the exact composition of these infernal concoctions, they pose a threat to you. How you meet that threat will help determine your safety on streets that may bring you face to face with a fire-bomb ambusher at any time.

First of all, it is worth noting that firebombs of all sorts may produce dramatic effects that look worse than they actually are. A lot of flames and smoke can scare people nearly to death. Hopefully, you will not be among them because there is absolutely no reason for you to be. If you are outside, you obviously want to get away from an incoming incendiary device. (It's burning wick probably will be fairly easy to spot.) Move quickly but don't panic and cause yourself greater injury in trying to get away than the firebomb likely would inflict on you.

If someone (like a fellow officer) gets the flaming contents of a gasoline bomb or Molotov cocktail on his clothing or person, what you do for him could well mean the difference between negligible injuries and serious injury or death. Because a person with flames on him tends to panic and run while flailing at the fire, your first task may be to tackle him low and bring him to the ground. There you can wrap him in a coat or blanket if one is readily at hand or just roll him against the ground if no other smothering cover is available. Try to protect the victim's face from the flames and watch out for your own hands. Do not leave them in extended contact with burning or smoldering garments. If you can, rip off any of the victim's clothing that is still on fire.

Call medical help for the burned victim of a fire bomb ambush. Don't forget to obtain medical attention for yourself if you have been burned during the flaming attack or your rescue efforts.

If you do get flaming liquid on you or if your clothing catches fire during a blazing ambush, drop to the ground and roll to smother the flames. Whatever else you do, avoid running and beating at the fire with your hands. You will only fan oxygen to the flames and burn your hands and arms by doing so. You also could get shot at or bombed again while you are running about.

Once you have extinguished the flames and gained cover, come up with your sidearm ready to repulse further attack or start one of your own. Call for help and scan the area carefully for your attacker. Use caution. A fire-bomb may be followed up by another device or by gunfire. Move out of the immediate area if it looks like you can safely do so. Stay alert. It is entirely possible that the attack is not yet at an end.

Police vehicles, occupied and otherwise, tend to draw a lot of attention from firebomb throwers. If you are in your patrol car when it is hit by a Molotov or gasoline bomb, stay inside and drive out of the vicinity of the attack. Assuming you have been patrolling with your windows rolled up, the flames should stay outside the passenger compartment and will go out fairly quickly. Things probably look a lot worse from inside than they actually are. Victims of firebomb attacks on vehicles have been known to leave the relative safety of the car's interior and run right into the path of gunfire or more bombs.

If you are unable to drive out of the area because your vehicle is disabled or the path is hopelessly blocked, wait for the flames to die down some and then roll low out of the car door that is nearest to decent cover. Stay close to the ground in moving quickly to cover. Be ready to return fire from there. By all means, let your dispatcher know what has happened and get some help on the way.

Whether the weapon of your attacker is a handgun, a high-powered rifle, a machine gun, an incendiary device, or something else, ambushes can be defended against and defeated. They can be as terrifying as they are sudden, but they also can be overcome by survival-trained police officers determined to win and stay alive.

Surviving an ambush on the street will require all the sound experience and common sense you can muster to your aid. It will demand restraint on your part at the same time it calls for personal courage. By being prepared to meet the ambush threat, you effectively reduce the danger of yet one more variety of high-risk patrol. In reducing that danger, you increase considerably the likelihood of reaching a happy retirement with all of your physical and mental faculties intact.

A RISK REDUCTION CHECKLIST FOR AMBUSH ATTACKS

1. Remember that an ambush attack can occur virtually anywhere at any time and can be carried out by just about any sort of individual. Stay constructively suspicious.
2. By taking away an ambusher's element of surprise, you help defeat him. Look for the out of the ordinary to tip you off that there's trouble brewing.
3. Avoid establishing a predictable pattern or routine in your activities to the extent possible.
4. Retreat may be your best option in an ambush attack. By staying alive now, you can win later.
5. If you elect to fight, fight to win with everything at your disposal. Use good cover and overwhelming gunfire to neutralize an ambusher who is trying to kill you.
6. Don't get tunnel vision. Never stop looking for additional threats and more attackers.

A 33-year-old deputy was killed at approximately 8 p.m. after responding to a call of a disturbance at a residence. Getting no response at the door, the 2-year deputy and another officer were returning to their vehicles when the victim officer was shot in the head with a .22-caliber rifle fired from a window of the house. The adult male assailant was later killed when he pointed a rifle at SWAT officers entering the house.

* * * * *

At approximately 8 p.m., a 28-year-old patrolwoman with over six years police experience was shot to death while she sat in her patrol car writing a report on a residential street. A single shot from a .30-30-caliber

rifle struck the officer in the head. A 43-year-old male was arrested for the officer's murder and later committed suicide.

* * * * *

Around 10:20 p.m., a police sergeant was killed in an unprovoked attack. According to witnesses, the sergeant was sitting in his patrol car when a man ran up and fired five rounds from a revolver. The officer was hit in the arms, hands, and head. The killer fled in a vehicle but was arrested several days later. He was found to be a drug dealer with prior convictions.

Chapter 14

EMOTIONALLY DISTURBED AND MENTALLY ILL PERSONS

There is no such thing as a guaranteed harmless nut. That simple statement could serve as the tragic yet accurate epitaph for some American police officers. Every jurisdiction in the country has its share of local characters, oddballs, and not-quite-right citizens. Most of these people will go through life being not much more than a minor irritant to the average police officer. A few, however, will one day kill themselves, the neighbors, a stranger, or a peace officer. The great problem for you is identifying the dangerous ones before they pose a serious threat to you or those you are sworn to protect.

The bearded, wild-eyed man marching nude down Main Street reading poetry aloud is an obvious crazy who *may* prove dangerous to you. Less obvious in her danger is the severely depressed housewife with a pistol in a pocket of her bathrobe. Ditto for the 16-year-old you stop for a red light violation while he's on his way—armed—to a suicide appointment in the park.

Some radio calls for police service will come to you plainly labeled for what they are: mental subject at the bus station, suicide attempt on the tracks, jumper on the roof. But mentally ill people representing a big threat to you also can be a part of ambulance runs, domestic disturbances, bar altercations, assault calls, traffic accidents, and code enforcement or noise violations.

There are some obvious and not so obvious things you can look for to help you spot the mentally disturbed individual on a call, in the street, amid the crowd. Is he abnormally excited or agitated for the circumstances? Are his facial expressions normal or is he scowling, clenching his teeth, or showing a pronounced nervous twitch? Is what he is saying nonsensical, obscene, or outrageous? Maybe he's just drunk, stoned, or angry. Or maybe he is mentally deranged.

WHAT TO LOOK FOR

Some more symptoms to look for in the mentally disturbed man or woman:

1. Disorientation—a break with reality that cannot be explained or attributed to drugs or alcohol.
2. Delusions—having beliefs contrary to obvious reality.
3. Hallucinations—seeing or hearing persons, objects, or events that do not exist.
4. Acting out—bizarre behavior that may include conversation with persons not present, taking off clothing for no apparent reason, spinning or rocking, or agitated swaying of the limbs, again for no apparent reason.

It is important to remain mindful that perhaps 3 percent of the American population is in some way or degree mentally or emotionally troubled. Most of these people do not pose a threat to police officers or the public. But a very few of these individuals *are* dangerous to you and others. Recognizing them solves a part of the problem you now face as a police professional. The remaining difficulty is found in dealing with them safely for all involved, particularly if you must take the mentally disturbed individual into protective custody for transport to a medical or mental health facility.

One of the cardinal rules that you must keep in mind when handling an intoxicated individual will serve you equally well in dealing with the mentally ill subject. The mental subject, in this aspect like the drunk, is UNPREDICTABLE above all else. The little old man who is smiling and babbling one moment may attack you without a word the next. The surly but submissive disturbed juvenile may turn suddenly violent and go for your sidearm for no readily apparent reason. Be kind, be sympathetic, but *be careful.* You cannot afford to relax your vigilance for even a moment while in the presence of an individual you suspect of being mentally disturbed.

Most of the same techniques that will serve you well in working with any potentially dangerous person should work just as well when you must investigate and handle the emotionally disturbed subject. First, you need to gather as much information as possible on the situation and subject involved before you directly confront the problem person. Who is he or she? What is his prior record or history with law enforcement or mental health officials? What is his current demeanor? If he is upset or agitated, is it possible to learn exactly what the source of the real or perceived aggravation is? Is the subject known to be armed or does he have immediate access to weapons?

You should have adequate help on hand before you approach a subject who has been identified as a possible mental subject. When you do approach, keep outside the 10-foot danger radius surrounding the subject within which he can get to you very quickly. Keep your handgun side turned away from the subject and stay alert.

Address the troubled individual in a voice that is calm yet authoritative. Screaming threats along with your directions will only confuse and, possibly, further agitate the subject. Instead, tell him clearly what you want him to do in direct, simple terms: "Police! Put your hands on your head. Interlace your fingers! Turn your back to me! Move!" Or whatever oral instructions appear appropriate to what is happening or has already happened.

You easily can worsen the situation by inappropriate handling of the apparent mental subject. Talking "down" to the person as if he were a young child could set him off. So could saying anything that might be seen as ridicule or insult by someone who may already be expecting a put down from a "hostile" world.

Take your time and avoid invading the suspected mental subject's "personal space" unless you are ready to take him into custody with the help of a cover officer or two. If forced custody appears to be the only reasonable option in dealing with the mentally troubled individual, be sure you have adequate reinforcements on hand before you begin the custody process. There are numerous, well-documented cases of mentally deranged people exhibiting superhuman strength, so be careful and work together.

You must be patient, kind, and empathetic in dealing with mentally or emotionally disturbed persons. Speak in a normal tone of voice. Listen attentively to what he has to say. Do not lie. Don't reinforce his delusions by agreeing with him when he is perceiving things that simply are not existent. Be supportive and nonthreatening but also mean what you say. You can be empathetic and firm at the same time. Remember that you may have to work with this individual again. He very well may remember how he was treated and respond accordingly next time.

Stay patient with the individual who may be verbally abusing you. Repeat your questions and directions, if necessary, without losing your temper. It simply may take your subject's troubled mind longer than normal to process and act on your instructions. Meanwhile, stay on your guard in case it is the subject who gets impatient or angry and attacks you. If you are menaced, utilize the minimum amount of force you can to overcome resistance and protect the both of you. Follow contact and cover tactics with your backup. Remain in control of your own emotions as you act to effectively control the severely mentally or emotionally disturbed person.

Be sure your weapon is snapped in tight and kept well covered during a close quarters confrontation with a potentially violent mental subject. Do not, however, intentionally disarm yourself by locking your sidearm in your car trunk or leaving it elsewhere during an on-the-street crisis with a mental party. And don't hand it to a bystander to hang onto while you fight with a violent subject. (This has really happened!) Thus disarmed, you could find the last few seconds of your life most troubling if your adversary suddenly produces or gains access to a deadly weapon of his own. Practice top-notch firearm-retention skills.

Remember that deranged individuals can and do confront police officers in the guise of "normal" crooks, too. Mentally deranged people have shot up shopping centers, robbed banks, taken hostages, and ambushed police officers. These are dangerous people. You must assume that what would be a "normal" response from a "normal" criminal may not hold true for a severely disturbed person on a violent crime rampage. He may laugh at your drawn gun and keep advancing on you. He may attack in the face of obviously superior numbers and weapons. He may press on even though critically wounded and refuse to give up even when confronted with near-certain death. You cannot, then, expect him to respond logically to what you say or do. He remains UNPREDICTABLE above all else.

SUICIDES ARE DANGEROUS

A particularly dangerous mental subject deserves your special attention—and extra special caution. The *suicidal* individual poses a danger to you because he may not care one bit who he takes with him in his act of self-destruction. Worse, lacking the final courage to take his own life, he may try to force the police to kill him by menacing or perhaps murdering an officer. This big danger to you is sometimes referred to as "suicide by cop."

More women than men attempt suicide, but more men actually succeed in killing themselves. Women are more likely to overdose on drugs, while men tend to rely on more violent means such as firearms. The elderly account for a great many suicides, but Native Americans, business and professional people (including police officers), young adults, and even youngsters contribute to the total, also.

Although suicides in this country may number 25,000 a year, recognizing the potential suicide is not always an easy task even for the mental health professional. Probably 80 percent of these eventual suicides give some sort of a cry for help via statements, actions, or actual suicide attempts prior to their final act of desperation. You may be able to pick up on some of these danger clues from friends, relatives, or coworkers of the suicidal person or get them from the subject himself. Thus forewarned, you can better defend yourself while helping the self-destructive human being. Some possible indicators of a pending, self-inflicted death include the following:

- The depressed person blames himself, realistically or not, for all of his own or his family's troubles.
- The individual makes statements about the uselessness of life and his belief that he would be better off dead. The talk may include comments about methods of self-destruction.
- Heavy drinking binges may accompany the plunge toward suicide. Drugs may be taken along with booze as the person's desire to live diminishes further.
- The potential suicide may neglect the basics of personal grooming, lose weight through refusing to eat, and display extreme fatigue brought on by the inability to sleep.
- The self-destructive individual may show a lack of interest in anything, including work, family, or recreation. An interest in living may be replaced by a black depression that includes a feeling of complete hopelessness.
- The potential suicide may have experienced a recent crisis or crises that he has felt unable to cope with, including the death of a loved one, loss of a job, drastically declining health, or breakup of a marriage or relationship.
- The subject has carried out actual preparations for suicide, such as buying a gun, stockpiling pills, or even "testing" his wrists or throat with shallow, hesitation cuts.

The standard legal criterion for taking any mentally disturbed person into protective custody against his will generally requires that he is clearly an imminent danger to himself or others. The would-be suicide falls well within this requirement, but getting him into custody safely requires some careful handling on your part. You will, among other officer safety concerns, want to consider the following suicide intervention techniques that can be applied to the apprehension of any potentially dangerous mental subject:

1. Watch out for weapons in the hands of the subject or in his vicinity.
2. Don't put yourself between a potential suicide and an obvious "target" for him, such as a roof edge or bridge railing. Otherwise he may take you with him if he is determined to destroy himself.
3. Don't yell, bluff, bluster, or threaten. Do speak with a firm, authoritative voice and mean what you say.
4. Don't make promises that you know cannot be honored. (Example: "Come with me and you won't be handcuffed." You may have to deal with this individual again, and he may decide to get even next time for

your past deception.

5. Persons taken into custody as dangerously mentally ill, including potential suicides, should be handcuffed behind their backs during transport for their welfare and yours.

6. Suicidal or otherwise mentally disturbed detainees must be searched just as carefully as criminal suspects. Before they are placed in a secure facility, a thorough search that includes clothing and underwear must be completed. Persons seriously contemplating self-destruction have been known to hide blades and other tools of death in some pretty imaginative places.

Suicidal or homicidal, the mentally ill individual presents a very real threat to you as an easily recognized symbol of authority. The caution, alertness, and good common sense with which you respond to that threat will determine the degree of personal safety with which you handle the emotionally disturbed subject.

SOME SUICIDE WARNING SIGNS

1. Threats of Suicide. Take them seriously. They may be a last warning before the act is attempted.

2. Extreme Depression. The presuicide individual shows little or no interest in doing much of anything or seeing anyone.

3. Sudden and Dramatic Attitude Improvement. A sudden and pronounced lift in spirits may mean the depressed individual is relieved at having reached a decision on a "solution" to end all of his problems: suicide.

4. Preparations. Giving away personal, prized possessions or putting affairs in order, such as writing a will, *may* indicate that the individual is seriously contemplating suicide.

5. Prior Attempts at Suicide. Any suicidal acts in the individual's past may indicate that he or she is at high risk to try again.

6. Radical Behavior Changes. Big changes in appetite or body weight, sleeplessness, disappearing sex drive, and withdrawal from contacts with other people *may* all point to a severely disturbed and possibly suicidal person.

SOME DO'S AND DON'T'S OF SUICIDE INTERVENTION

DO take your time with the suicidal individual.
DO really listen to what he has to say.

DO show through your words and actions that you want to help.
DO try a new approach if the first fails.
DO keep the potential suicide talking.
DO keep your own safety foremost in dealing with the suicidal person.
DON'T try to shock or challenge the threatened suicide. ("Go ahead—you don't have the guts to do it!")
DON'T argue with the troubled individual.
DON'T play psychiatrist or try to analyze the endangered person.
DON'T blame yourself if the subject carries out his act of self-destruction, now or later. It is not your fault. He made his own decision and acted on it.

Mentally ill and emotionally disturbed people need your help. They need your understanding. But they do not require that you sacrifice your own safety in order to help them. Always look to your own survival as you seek to help these troubled human beings.

A RISK REDUCTION CHECKLIST FOR EMOTIONALLY DISTURBED AND MENTALLY ILL PERSONS

1. Gather as much information as possible before you decide on a course of action.
2. Be as truthful, objective, and nonthreatening as you can in dealing with a mentally disturbed individual.
3. Be conscious of your weapon at all times—your potential opponent probably is.
4. Remain aware that the suicidal individual may attempt to use you as the instrument of his death in a "suicide by cop" scenario.
5. Leave yourself an escape route in case things go sour in your contact with an emotionally disturbed individual.
6. Have adequate help on hand before attempting to take a mentally disturbed person into protective custody.
7. Use careful handcuffing and searching techniques on the mental subject taken into custody. He or she presents as great a potential danger to you as the criminal offender.

Shortly after midnight, a 26-year-old officer with four years of police experience was slain by a male adult with a history of mental problems. The officer and a backup had gone to a report of a possible shooting at a residence and on arrival found a wounded woman in a vehicle. The second of two shots fired from the house as the officers were assist-

ing the dying woman struck the victim officer in the chest. A .30-06-caliber rifle was the death weapon. A barricade standoff ensued. Hours later, the 39-year-old subject ran from the house firing at officers and was fatally wounded.

* * * * *

At about 12:30 a.m., a 53-year-old sergeant was shot and killed at a disturbance call. Upon arrival, the officer confronted a nude male armed with a broken bottle and a board. In a struggle, the sergeant lost his sidearm to the subject. The officer ran to a nearby store to call for assistance, but his assailant followed and fired four rounds through the closed glass door. Three rounds fatally wounded the sergeant in the back.

* * * * *

A 44-year-old woman who was later determined to be a drug user with mental disorders was involved in a disturbance on a city bus. The driver flagged down a 60-year-old police officer who then attempted to take the woman into custody by himself. The two struggled and fell to the ground. The woman seized the officer's sidearm and shot him fatally in the front of the head. She then used the weapon to fire at other officers before being wounded and taken into custody.

Chapter 15

SPECIAL DANGERS, SPECIAL RESPONSES

You already know that the world you work in can turn suddenly, violently dangerous. There are people out there who are only too willing to hurt you. You are well aware by now that there are dangers inherent in responding to stickups in progress, domestic disturbances, man with a gun calls, and a dozen other varieties of high-risk patrol. But there are other dangers lurking out there. *Special* dangers that will require *special* responses and solutions from you.

The special hazards you may confront as a police officer can range from human to inanimate in character. They can come from animals or viruses as easily as from knives and bullets. They can even spring from accidents and carelessness on your part. Taking a look at some of these special dangers and how you can shield yourself from them is definitely worth your time.

TRAFFIC ACCIDENTS

Statistically, at least, you are in more danger from traffic mishaps occurring during routine driving than from high-speed pursuits. During the sample year of 2008, 68 American police officers were accidentally killed in the line of duty. Of this total, 39 officers died in automobile accidents, 13 were struck by vehicles, and six were killed in motorcycle accidents. The figures were provided by the FBI's Uniform Crime reports. Clearly, vehicular traffic poses a significant threat to your safety. Obviously, that risk is multiplied if you are assigned to uniformed patrol duties as opposed to support functions in a law enforcement agency.

Your driving duties are made somewhat more hazardous than those faced by the civilian motorist by a number of factors. You are, for example, doing other things at the same time you are driving in many instances. You're working the radio or emergency equipment, writing down information, scouting the vicinity visually for violators, or experiencing other situations requiring your intervention. In other words, your attention is divided. If you're not extra careful, you can eliminate yourself from competition for the safe driver award!

Your driving is also made a bit more hazardous by the fact that you are often on the road during the most difficult and extreme conditions: during traffic rush hours, in extremely bad weather, during disaster situations, and throughout the hours when the most drunken drivers are on the streets. You may face more driving hazards during your shift than the average motorist encounters in a month of puttering about town.

Additionally, you may be more at risk for a vehicular encounter of the nastiest kind by the situations and positions into which you must put your police vehicle (and sometimes yourself). When you park your vehicle on the roadway to protect an accident scene or a violator's car, you run the risk of having an intoxicated or head-buried motorist climb up your trunk. When you step out onto the pavement to direct traffic, you invite these same people to leave tire tracks on your nice, clean uniform.

Despite the traffic dangers built into your job, you *can* make it a lot safer. You *can* reduce your risk-taking. You can, for instance:

- Be sure your patrol vehicle does not add to your risks. Check it thoroughly before you take it out at the start of your shift. Examine the tires for excessive wear and proper inflation. Check the brakes for the proper amount of "pedal." Be sure the lights, horn, and wipers work. Check the emergency lights and siren. See if the steering responds properly. Ascertain that the windows and mirrors are clean.
- Always wear a properly functioning lap and shoulder belt. Not only will your belts significantly reduce your chances of being seriously hurt in a collision, they'll also help you control the vehicle during extreme driving maneuvers by keeping you in place behind the wheel.
- Wear your body armor. It can protect your torso in a car crash just like it can save you from an assailant's bullets.
- Don't drive if you are sick and taking medication that can make you drowsy. Get enough rest before you go on duty. A fatigued or sleepy driver is an accident-prone one.
- If you work with a car partner, get into the habit of talking to him without gesturing or looking in his direction when you are driving. Keep your eyes on the road and your hands on the wheel.
- Reduce your speed accordingly for adverse weather, road, or traffic conditions. Realize that increased speed means a considerably increased distance required to react to danger and stop safely. At night, do not overdrive your headlights. In other words, don't drive so fast

that you no longer have time to stop before reaching something your lights reveal in your path.

- Allow your eyes to precede you well down the road. Don't just look for potential threats a car length or two ahead; scout for hazards a block or more down the street. Those distant hazards can include pedestrians, cars just starting up, blocked traffic lanes, and oddly behaving vehicles. Keep looking ahead. Slow down and start planning your avoidance strategy when you spot potential trouble.

- Get out of the car. Get some fresh air and exercise your muscles a little by walking a bit *before* you start feeling really drowsy behind the wheel. It's good accident prevention. These mini-breaks—perhaps three or four of them per hour—are especially important if you are working a very quiet tour. Exiting that metal and plastic cocoon from time to time will improve your observation skills and police work, too.

- Don't stare at a perceived police problem or other "situation of interest" while your car continues in motion. Bring your vehicle to a safe stop, *then* examine the situation to your heart's content.

- Know your own driving limitations as well as those of your vehicle. It's a fact of life that you generally do not respond as quickly to road dangers as you get older. Adjust your driving speed accordingly. And remember that your four-door family car with red lights and a special paint job is not a high-performance sports car. Don't expect it to handle or respond like one.

- Try to stay out of another driver's blind spots. A good rule of thumb: If you cannot see his face, either directly or via his mirrors, he probably cannot see you, either.

- Don't follow another emergency vehicle "running hot" closely through an intersection. Most motorists will still be watching the lead vehicle and may move right into your path without ever seeing you.

- If a crash is imminent and unavoidable, try to maneuver to avoid a head-on collision or one that involves your being hit in the driver's door. Toward the rear of your car's right side is the "best" place to be hit; toward the rear of the left side is probably the next "best."

- Remember that the majority of police vehicle accidents occur at very low speeds (under 5 mph) and while the car is backing. As a result, be extra alert when traversing crowded parking lots and consider *backing* into a parking space. That way you can drive out forward when you leave, a real benefit if you are in a big hurry.

Don't forget that you can be hurt or killed as a pedestrian just as you can come to grief when you are behind the wheel. Stay alert to the moving traffic around you when you are out of the car and on or near the roadway.

Don't stand between two vehicles–ever. It's a good way to get your legs crushed. If you are directing traffic, wear a high-visibility reflective vest. Try not to turn your back on moving vehicles for more than a couple of seconds at a time. Leave yourself an escape route to the sidelines, so to speak. Some dangers are best handled by getting out of their way, and quickly.

By just applying some commonsense precautions to your operation of a police vehicle, you can reduce your traffic risks greatly. Stay alert for danger before it collides with you.

EXOTIC WEAPONS

You can be hurt or even killed by things that would at first glance appear harmless enough. The hard-core criminals and ultra-disturbed members of society have gotten pretty good at disguising and adapting their deadly toys. Only by being extra attentive to what you see and handle can you avoid their potentially fatal traps and infernal devices.

Belt-buckle derringer pistols, for instance, are available on the weapons market. Often firing a single round, they may give the appearance of harmless buckle ornaments. Handle carefully any such items you encounter on your prisoners or potential arrestees. Naturally, you always will remove all belts from prisoners you plan to book or lodge anyway.

Check the undersides of prisoners' belts for knives or blades that fit into the buckle area, too. Some really ugly "survival" blades are sold to be fitted into belts and buckles. Handle with care.

As you no doubt are aware, virtually any kind of normally harmless object can be fashioned into a weapon of sorts by one so inclined. Tire gauges and ball point pens have been altered to fire a small-caliber bullet. Walking canes can become sword canes. Rings can be designed with ragged edges and points to tear flesh. Belts can be constructed from motorcycle chains. Everything from a wallet to a car door can be rigged to conceal a firearm. So can a small, personal communication device or a briefcase. Keep your eyes open and use your imagination.

Even harmless looking balls of tinfoil have proven injurious to officers searching the haunts of dope dealers and extremist groups. These booby-trap weapons are created by mixing certain chemicals together and then sealing them off from the air by wadding up the foil tightly. When an unsuspecting officer unwraps the foil in his search for drugs, the contents can ignite explosively upon being exposed to oxygen.

The message for you in all of this is as simple as it is direct. If you do not know for sure what it is, leave it alone. Get expert advice before proceeding further. Depending on what you think you are dealing with, expert advice could mean a drug lab or firearms specialist or even a bomb squad technician. Take your time and take no chances. The extra minutes and effort will be worth it in lives saved and injuries prevented.

Don't overlook the potential threat posed by a portable, hand-held device designed to deliver a powerful electric shock to whomever is touched by its probes. Intended as a self-defense weapon for police as well as law-abiding citizens, these tools have turned up on occasion in the hands of violent criminals. The devices, when used properly and held against a subject's body, can disable him temporarily. If you are menaced by one of these or a similar device in the hands of a crook threatening to use it, you may be forced to view the situation as a potentially life-threatening one and respond with appropriate force to stop the threatening action. After all, if you are knocked down or out, even temporarily, your sidearm is up for grabs, and that in itself constitutes a threat to your life.

If you elect to use deadly force against an offender who has threatened you with an apparently functional electric shocker, you can count on being asked afterward if there was anything else you could have done to thwart the attack without resorting to fatal (or potentially fatal) force. Could you, for example, have retreated beyond your attacker's physical reach? If you could have and didn't, why didn't you? Or so the questioning may go. Be thoughtful in your response.

There is another key point for you to take in here: Always try to leave yourself a route to retreat if it becomes necessary. It's not cowardice, it's just good common sense. It takes into account the truth that killing or being killed should not be the only choice left open to you when you can avoid it. A tactical withdrawal can be a perfectly acceptable option until you can rearrange the odds in your favor. After all, the law does not say you *must* use deadly force in a given set of circumstances. It says you *may*. Don't overlook the difference.

There are, of course, other things out there that can pose a real threat to your continued good health. Primitive blow guns and their metal-tipped darts are popular in some locales among juveniles and even survivalist types. These projectiles can cause serious injury if they strike a vulnerable spot, such as the face.

Nunchakus or nun-chuks are still around, particularly among the Bruce Lee imitators of the land. This potentially dangerous striking instrument consists of two lengths of wood or metal connected by a short piece of cord or chain. In the hands of someone who knows how to use them, nunchakus can cause injuries by means of squeezing, crushing, jabbing, or striking blows.

The throwing star, or shuriken, is also popular with juveniles and the martial arts set. Throwing knives might be lumped in with these flying weapons, too. Once again, any of these devices can prove quite nasty in the hands of a skilled user. Some can be hurled with considerable accuracy for 30 feet or more.

SHARP AND POINTED WEAPONS

A crusty old cop who had spent nearly thirty years in law enforcement had been both cut and shot in his time on the job. He had no problem deciding which he preferred: "I'll take a bullet anytime. Knives are *nasty*."

The veteran's opinion of sharp blades and similar weapons appears to be shared by a great many peace officers. There is just something about a sharp or pointed weapon that can produce a deep, jagged, gaping wound that sends chills down the spine of the bravest street cop. Although he knows intellectually that a speeding bullet can make him just as dead, there is still something particularly frightening to him about the cold steel. It is a fear that is well placed.

Sharp or edged instruments do kill police officers virtually every year in this country, the land of cheap and readily available firearms. Perhaps it's because they are quickly at hand and easily concealed. Perhaps it's because they are largely unregulated. Whatever the case, knives and similar instruments remain the weapons of choice in many assaults on police officers. With that grisly fact in mind, it becomes worth your while to know more about countering these deadly weapons.

Awareness of your surroundings is probably your first line of defense against an attack by a sharp instrument. Keep looking around you when you are on the job. Watch the hands of likely assailants. Don't forget that the most dangerous blade is the one you don't see, so don't allow your senses to relax for a moment.

Keep your distance as much as the situation allows from those you suspect may attack you. You'll want to maintain at least a five- to six-foot separation between yourself and a party you are contacting initially. That's assuming he does not appear about to produce a sharp or pointed instrument for use against you. If you believe from his words or actions that he's about to pull a weapon of *any* sort, back off and seek good cover. Draw your own weapon and be ready to use it to protect your life.

In actual, hands-on tests, officers have discovered that you will need *at least* 21 feet between you and a man with a knife to escape getting stabbed or cut if he has his weapon out and you don't when the attack begins. (This point has been made graphically clear in some of the excellent officer survival seminars put on by Calibre Press, Inc.) If the blade wielder is in full possession of his motor skills and physical agility, he will be able to cover almost all of that distance before you can draw your sidearm and get on target with shots to center mass.

Try to leave yourself at least 25 feet as a buffer between you and a blade-armed subject. Also try to preserve an escape route behind you if you know you are likely to face an offender with a sharp or pointed weapon. Draw your sidearm and bring it onto your target. Try to disarm and dissuade him verbally: "Police! Drop the knife! Drop it now or you will be shot!" Keep him covered as you await compliance and remain aware of your route of retreat. Just remember that it's difficult to talk and shoot accurately at the same time. You may have to abandon the talk option in a hurry, so be ready. Keep the distance between you if he tries to move forward, assuming you have room. But do any retreating slowly and deliberately. This is no time to fall down. If he charges you with a blade and you have no other out, *shoot to stop his threatening actions.*

In the old days, self-defense instructors taught moves and tactics intended to stop a close-quarters knife attack with a police baton or even your bare hands. Some still do. The fact is that for most officers these tactics aimed at disarming a knife-wielding attacker work far better in the classroom where the "bad guy" is relatively cooperative than they do in the real world of the streets.

There are indeed some police officers who are quite capable of neutralizing the average knife attacker with hands or baton. These physical tactics experts are relatively few in number, however. Most police officers simply do not use or practice unarmed defense against sharp or pointed weapons often enough to be proficient at it. Chances are you may be one of those officers. And the fact remains that unless you are *extremely* proficient in these baton or bare-handed disarming tactics, there is a very good chance you are going to get cut or stabbed if you decide to tackle a knife wielder on his own terms.

Your safest and most reliable option when faced with an edged, sharpened, or pointed weapon is to keep your distance—preferably 25 feet or more—from it. Rely on cover or other physical obstructions to prevent your being charged successfully. Try your verbal skills at convincing your opponent to drop it. Maintain a route of retreat. Finally, if you are attacked without any other safe means of escaping the assault, shoot to protect your life or the life of a third party. When you do shoot, you shoot for center mass to stop the life-threatening action of the offender.

OFFICER DOWN RESPONSES

There is probably no more chilling a radio call than that of "officer down, shots fired." At such a moment, the most well-trained and disciplined agency or officer can start to come apart in the urgent emotions of the moment—the desire to do *something* to rescue the downed colleague and respond to his assailant.

It is at just such a moment that yet more police officers can be wounded or killed in ill-conceived rescue attempts. It has happened before. You have a duty to yourself and your wounded and unwounded colleagues to see to it that your response to the officer down challenge is a measured and careful one destined to end successfully.

Your first obligation to all of your peers is to see to it that you don't do anything without some sort of plan, however basic, in mind. It does not have to be anything fancy. In fact, the simpler it is, the better chance for succeeding it probably will have. Whatever you do, you will almost certainly need help—possibly quite a bit of it. Each person will need to know the plan and his part in it before the rescue effort commences. And all of this will have to be done quickly if a downed officer is to be saved from serious consequences.

If a wounded officer is unable to move himself to cover and yet is close enough to it to be dragged there by peers who do not have to extensively show themselves, the rescue may be a relatively easy one. But oftentimes it's not that easy. If your wounded colleague is down in an open area, such as a street, parking lot, or yard, within the field of fire of an assailant, your task will be complicated. As a result, don't start anything until you have sufficient police manpower on hand to get the job done right. Additional casualties will not help the situation.

You will need to create a diversion to distract your armed and possibly firing opponent just as the downed officer pickup begins. Use your imagination in providing an appropriate diversion. It may be a siren suddenly activated on the other side of your adversary from where the rescue will take place. It could be a rock through his window on that same side. Or it might be one of your peers on a P.A. system ordering him to surrender, again from a direction well away from your actual rescue operation. Whatever you choose for a diversion, it must be timed carefully to commence only seconds ahead of the beginning of your officer pickup moves. It must not endanger the police personnel carrying it out from behind cover.

Your obvious goal should be to get your wounded colleague quickly behind cover and to medical care while minimizing the risk to his rescuers. You can accomplish both by placing some sort of portable cover between you and hostile gunfire as the rescue is carried out. An armored car or—even better—a tank should work very nicely. Unfortunately, it is unlikely that either will be available in time to affect the outcome of a real-life rescue effort. (One department did successfully utilize a large dump truck, however.) As a result, you likely will have to settle for a patrol car, complete with its assets and limitations. Its assets include the fact that you are familiar with the vehicle and have it instantly available. On the downside, it is far from bulletproof.

In order to use a patrol car for an officer down pickup, you'll probably want to jerk out the back seat, if possible, to give you more room. You'll want a car without a cage, if one is available, for the same reason. If you can get some body armor from officers who are uninvolved in the operation, hang those vests over the side windows on the side of the car that you will be presenting to the shooter during your rescue attempt.

You'll need three volunteers for the rescue operation. One will drive the patrol car while slumped as low as possible behind the steering wheel. The two pickup officers position themselves on the back floorboards, crouched low. They, like the driver, wear body armor. The car is piloted quickly to a point where its side is to the offender and the downed officer is within 4 to 5 feet of the rear door with the car between him and possible gunfire. The pickup officers exit low out a rear door, scoop up the wounded cop, slide him in quickly, and pile in with him. The driver then moves quickly out of the danger area and turns the downed officer over to medical professionals.

It may be advisable to have covering officers not involved in the pickup provide suppressing gunfire if your rescue party is fired on while in the open. Such suppressing fire only should be permitted if the officers firing have a clearly identifiable and presently threatening target to shoot at *and* their fire will not endanger innocent others in the area or the rescuers themselves. Once the rescued officer and his rescuers are safely out of harm's way, the covering gunfire should cease.

The officer down pickup is dangerous. It involves some risk-taking for the rescuers as well as the rescue subject. It should not be attempted if the officer is obviously dead or if there is any other realistic means of saving the downed policeman.

Obviously the vehicle pickup cannot be used in areas where a car cannot gain access. In such instances, including those inside structures, such as apartment or tenement hallways, the rescue team will have to utilize whatever cover is available in making its move. If you can get SWAT-type portable shields quickly to the scene, by all means use them. It is conceivable that a rescue cannot be attempted at all without sacrificing additional personnel. That, too, is part of the decision-making process that goes with reducing the danger of high-risk patrol. The decision not to send rescuers in under existing conditions will be an excruciatingly painful one, but it is one that may have to be made. It, too, is a part of officer survival.

Meanwhile, if *you* become a downed officer, try to keep in mind that even if you are in the open, there is a good chance you will not be fired at again if you stay down and remain motionless. Particularly if there are other officers present for him to worry about, your assailant may not be all that interested in you anymore. If good cover is very close, it may be worth your while to roll quickly to it. Otherwise, stay put unless you are clearly in the open and drawing fire. Don't spur your peers into a dangerous rescue attempt unless you really need immediate help.

VICIOUS ANIMALS

Can an animal pose a danger to you? You bet. Unless you do your policing in one of the exotic lands where the bad guys are said occasionally to rely on roosters, pigs, or jungle cats for guard duties, the animal you are most likely to encounter on unfriendly terms is man's best friend.

Although battle-trained pit bulls have gotten all the media attention as the bad guys of the canine world, Dobermans, German Shepherds, and multibreed mixes can hurt you just as badly if given the opportunity. The key for you is not to give these four-legged bullets a chance to sink teeth into any part of your anatomy.

You may encounter a hostile canine when you go to arrest a wanted party, begin wrestling with a domestic assault offender, or participate in a drug raid against a target guarded by canine sentries. Or you may be met by protective, flashing teeth when you seek to help a downed elderly person in a residence or on the street. The question you face now is how to overcome this additional danger and still carry out the duties that brought you to the scene in the first place.

If you have any advance warning at all that you are about to come under canine attack, you may be able to confuse or distract the animal long enough to get your job done and stay out of his reach. You can, for instance, chase away some hostile dogs by hosing them down with a fire extinguisher or waving a burning road flare in their direction. A screaming siren in very close proximity will scare away some troublesome mutts if the noise doesn't upset your mission plans. A blanket flailed at them will put to flight some of the more timid guard dogs. Some of the newer aerosol irritants containing oleoresin capsicum are very effective against dogs that tear gas has traditionally had little or no effect on. A conducted energy device may work well, too. Of course, if you have the luxury of time on your side, your best bet may be to call in an animal control officer with a capture pole and other specialized equipment.

Listen to the tales related by officers from around the country and you'll hear accounts of attacking dogs that took any amount of physical abuse—including numerous bullets—and yet persisted in their assaults. One pit bull took three .38-caliber rounds to the chest without serious effect. Another was hit with pistol rounds and run over by a car yet carried on his attack. In one incident in Colorado, a pit bull exited a vehicle while an officer was attempting to arrest the car's driver on felony charges and bit the policeman 11 times. The animal reportedly clung to the officer's arm even after he shot the dog to death. The message for you here is not to underestimate the staying power of a canine opponent.

If other measures fail or are impractical and you are facing an attack-trained or just plain vicious dog, your only chance to save yourself from serious injury may be your sidearm. Dogs—especially the really muscular ones like pit bulls—often will not go down easily, even with multiple pistol hits to the body. Your best chance probably will be a shot to the head of your attacker. If your position in relation to the animal allows it, your best shot may be through the eye or open mouth and back into the brain. You may need to fire more than a single round to stop the attack.

If a big dog has already sunk teeth into you and you're not in a position to shoot, police canine trainers advise that your best bet may be to grab the beast hard by the coat and skin and lift him off the ground. Some canines lose their concentration and their nerve when they lose traction from being hoisted completely off the surface. If you can get him up off the ground, try to direct a powerful kick to his largely unprotected underside. The belly or gonads are good targets. Keep striking until you hurt him enough to make him release his grip and retreat. You're going to be hurt, but you are not going to die. Shield your own vitals—your groin, face, and throat—from a possible counterattack. Get out of his reach as quickly as you can. Just because he has released you doesn't mean he won't attack again.

INFECTIOUS DISEASES

Not everything that can bite you, so to speak, has four legs. Or two. By the nature of your job, you are at least somewhat at risk from a whole collection of diseases carried by the less than pristine "clients" you must deal with. Hepatitis is one malady sometimes encountered in the drug-dependent people you arrest and handle. Acquired Immune Deficiency Syndrome (AIDS) is another, although it is not seen as often nor is it as easy to contract as hepatitis. Tuberculosis (TB) is also showing up in the United States with increasing frequency. When you add to the list the various colds, flus, infections, skin diseases, and other health problems frequently harbored by this rather unwholesome group, you have a pretty sickly scene indeed.

You must protect yourself against coming down with the same diseases and conditions suffered by these unfortunates. Not surprisingly, prevention is by far the best solution. You can go about preventing disease and protecting Number One in a number of ways.

One way you can stave off illness is by living healthy yourself. That means eating enough of the right kinds of foods, exercising sensibly, watching your weight, and avoiding smoking. (You already knew that!)

Avail yourself of protective vaccines that are available from modern medicine. Get a tetanus booster shot if it hass been many years since you had one. There is also a series of shots you can take to immunize yourself from hepatitis B, an extremely unpleasant disease that eventually can do you in.

Equally important to the prevention of infectious diseases are good personal hygiene habits. That means keeping your fingers away from your eyes and mouth (and out of your nose!) while you are working. In addition to the people you've touched, the steering wheel of the police car probably has been handled by a great many others who have left their own germs to pass along to you. Watch where you put those dirty hands!

You also can protect yourself from your "clients" with a practice that doctors and nurses use in their own germ-laden environments: wash your hands a lot. Whenever possible, wash your paws with soap and water when you have finished searching, fingerprinting, or otherwise handling a prisoner, his clothing, or his personal effects. If you have to handle him again, wash up again afterward. It's just good common sense and self-preservation. When you're in the field, consider carrying some of those foil-packaged, premoistened cleanup towlettes in your briefcase or uniform pocket. You also can carry (and use often) a small, plastic bottle of alcohol-based hand disinfectant. All of these can help with the cleanup duties until you have a chance to wash properly. They are also handy when you've gotten dirt, fingerprint powder, or blood on yourself.

A good pair of disposable, latex gloves should be included in the equipment you carry with you. If your department won't furnish them, you can buy a box yourself fairly cheaply at a drug store. Carry them on your person on duty and put them on before you deal with an individual you can see has blood or other bodily fluids on him. You also may want to put them on before dealing with a really foul, down-and-out drunk or transient. The latex will give you a decent degree of protection against disease organisms that would otherwise end up on your skin. But don't continue to carry dirty, used gloves with you. Discard them for a fresh pair.

You also can protect yourself against AIDS and other maladies by avoiding the needles that drug users frequently have on them. Squeeze clothing softly from the outside as opposed to jamming your hands into pockets until you are sure there are no needles there to hurt you. Have *him* empty his pockets for inventory once you are convinced there are no weapons present.

Before you start your detailed search process, use a simple technique that many veteran street cops have found to work well: ASK him what he has on him before you search. Ask him specifically if he has needles or syringes in his clothing. You can work out your own speech, but one experienced patrolman uses the following pre-search address and claims it has never failed to unmask any hidden dangers: "I need to know right now if there's a needle or anything that could hurt me in your clothes. Tell me now because if I get hurt on something you told me wasn't there, we're both going to be sorry." The key is in his "sincere" delivery, it would appear.

If you do get cut or stuck with a needle or other object, unless the wound is gushing, permit it to bleed and wash it thoroughly. Fill out the necessary injury report for the record and see a physician right away. He may be able to prevent problems by cleaning the wound properly and administering a shot of tetanus antitoxin. But whatever else you do, do *not* ignore such an injury that breaks the skin. A minor wound that seems inconsequential now could cause complications later. Don't take any chances. It doesn't require a brave person to ignore a dangerous injury. It simply requires a real fool.

WOUNDS AND INJURIES

First aid has been referred to as the immediate and potentially lifesaving care given to a person who has been injured or taken ill. It includes self-help and care that you provide for yourself until professional medical care is present. Competent self-help can sometimes mean the difference between living and dying when you have been seriously wounded or otherwise hurt. It can mean the difference between temporary and permanent disability for you. And it can spell the difference between a quick, uneventful recovery and a lengthy stay in the hospital.

Your minor bumps, bruises, cuts, scrapes, and breaks, uncomfortable as they may be, generally can wait until you have a chance to be treated by the medical professionals. It's the really critical stuff–maintaining a heartbeat, blood supply, and breathing–that you have to worry about immediately. Generally speaking, the heartbeat will take care of itself if you worry about the other two. You do that by maintaining an open airway and stopping to the extent possible any external, serious bleeding.

Ahead of any other self-aid steps you may take, you multiply your chances for survival by staying as calm as you possibly can under the circumstances. Try to follow this line of reasoning because it's true: *If I am conscious and alert enough to know I am hurt, I am going to make it.* If you are still with the program to that extent, you are obviously not shot through the brain or heart. *You should be alright.* Don't quit now.

Your mental attitude may very well make a big difference in your survival chances. You doubtlessly have heard of officers who received relatively minor, survivable wounds and yet went into shock, gave up, and died. You also have heard of cops who received massive injuries and who by all rights *should* have died but refused to do so. Decide in advance that you belong to the latter category of officers. Don't give up. Know that you are going to survive. And *know* what to do to ensure your recovery.

Circulation (Controlling Blood Loss)

Your circulation obviously cannot continue if there is no blood left to circulate. Your task, then, is to control blood loss if you are wounded or injured. You accomplish this in several ways.

Minor bleeding from a laceration or other injury won't kill you. It may even help cleanse the wound. Severe bleeding, however, can result in shock, loss of consciousness, and eventual death. Your first method for limiting serious bleeding is to apply pressure directly over the wound. Use a bandage compress, wadded up towel, folded handkerchief, or even the palm of your hand to apply the pressure. If professional medical care will be delayed, you can hold a pressure dressing in place by means of bandaging. But do get to medical care as quickly as possible. You will need treatment against infection as well as to prevent resumed bleeding and possible shock.

If direct pressure over the wound does not stop the blood loss, you should elevate the injured part, as well. Raise the injured hand, arm, leg, or foot above the level of your heart. An exception to the elevation rule may occur if you suspect a fracture to that area.

If serious bleeding continues in spite of your first two efforts, the use of a pressure point may be required to pinch off a supplying artery for a short time. Use the pressure point technique in addition to, not instead of, the other measures. Don't use the method any longer than absolutely necessary. That generally will mean that you have turned yourself over to medical professionals for emergency care before you cease your efforts.

If a hand or arm is involved, you can apply pressure to the brachial artery by pressing it against the arm bone on the inside surface of your arm roughly midway between the elbow and the armpit. With the flat surfaces of your fingers, press inward toward your thumb, which remains on the outside surface of the injured arm. Your grip should compress the artery against the bone and slow or stop the blood loss. If you are physically unable to do this yourself, you may be able to instruct a helper to do it for you.

If a foot or leg is gushing blood, the pressure point you'll want is the femoral artery pressed against the pelvic bone. To make it work best, you'll need to lie on your back with the heel of your hand (or your helper's hand) pressed against the front crease of the affected leg where it joins your groin area. A second hand may need to be pressed down immediately atop the first to increase the pressure and close off the artery. Again, this blood-stopping action is itself potentially hazardous and should only be carried out until professional medical aid takes over.

Breathing

It is true enough that you cannot give yourself mouth to mouth, but you at least can do some things to be sure your breathing continues on its own. If you are lying down, for example, consider lying on your side if wounds don't preclude this position. That way fluids can drain from the side of your mouth, if necessary, without collecting in your throat and blocking your airway. If you wear dentures, remove them so as to help preserve an open airway if you go unconscious. If possible, have someone stay with you until medical help arrives. That way you have somebody there to maintain your airway or start resuscitation efforts if you pass out and it becomes necessary. Loosen any constricting garments or leather gear or have someone do it for you. Try to stay calm and concentrate on breathing at a normal rate. You are going to be alright, so take it easy.

Traumatic shock, a potentially dangerous condition resulting from depressed function of a number of vital organs, can accompany any serious wound or other injury. Shock may be indicated by general weakness, pale, cold, clammy skin, a rapid but weak pulse, irregular breathing, and nausea. You can act to minimize its harmful effects through some additional self-help, prevention, and treatment measures.

If your injury permits, remain lying down. Cover yourself enough to prevent the loss of body heat, but do not become overheated. You need insulation between your body and the ground, too, so make sure your cover extends there. If you do not have a head injury, raising your feet a little higher than the rest of your body also can help prevent shock.

You combat shock by treating whatever other condition—such as continuing loss of blood—may have caused it in the first place. Medical care by professionals will, of course, need to follow your self-care efforts to address shock.

By relying on your own, good common sense, bolstered by some of the special responses described here, you can control and overcome these and other special dangers of your special work. It is, after all, *your* job and *your* life. What you do to make the former safer and the latter longer is up to you.

A RISK REDUCTION CHECKLIST FOR SPECIAL DANGERS, SPECIAL RESPONSES

1. Always follow good defensive driving practices.
2. Use your lap and shoulder belts when you are on vehicular patrol.
3. Remain alert to all traffic possibilities when you are standing or walking on or near the roadway.

4. Be alert for weapons that don't *look* like weapons. Be suspicious of unidentified items or objects on or around a subject you are dealing with.

5. Don't try to disarm a subject armed with a sharp-edged weapon by using your hands alone.

6. Have a definite plan before you rush in to rescue a downed officer under fire. Remember the value of body armor, cover, and diversions.

7. Anticipate and plan for the presence of vicious dogs on raids, arrests, and other operations.

8. Rely on good hygiene habits and carry disposable rubber gloves and cleanup materials as personal protection against infectious diseases. Guard against needle injuries by using caution in where and how you use your hands for searching.

9. If you are wounded or seriously injured, your main tasks will be controlling blood loss, maintaining an open airway, and preventing shock. Stay current on your first aid skills and know how to handle a self-aid situation.

At approximately 2:45 p.m., an urban patrolman was slain after responding to a disturbance involving a man with a gun. Reportedly, a dispute between two male adults resulted in the call for police. A gun battle ensued upon the officer's arrival. The 22-year-old officer was reloading his weapon when his assailant walked up and shot him in the head with a 9-mm semiautomatic handgun. The dead officer had two years of police service.

* * * * *

A male subject, age 51, was reported armed and pouring gasoline at various points in an apartment complex. The man barricaded himself in his apartment before police arrived at the 9:30 a.m. incident. Responding officers forced entry, and a 41-year-old police lieutenant was killed with a rifle round to the front torso. After negotiations failed to produce the subject's surrender, at about 2:00 p.m., a tactical unit forced entry, and a 39-year-old officer was shot fatally with the same rifle. The officer was hit in the rear upper torso in an area unprotected by his body armor. The offender was killed during an exchange of gunfire. He reportedly had a history of mental problems.

Chapter 16

OFF-DUTY CONFRONTATIONS

Consider this scenario: You are minding your own business, off duty with your family, enjoying a meal in a crowded, local pizza restaurant. Without warning, two armed robbers burst in with sawed-offs and announce a holdup. You're armed. What do you do?

If you're smart, you do *nothing* beyond being the best witness you can be. Doing anything else is simply too risky for you as well as all the other innocent people present.

Now, change the scene just a little. Same restaurant, same off-duty you and your loved ones, same innocent crowd, same armed-to-the-teeth robbers. But something is different. This time the creeps murder the manageress right in front of your eyes. They promise to do some more shooting unless everyone present gets on the floor and offers up their valuables. Do you respond any differently this time?

A homicide has just occurred in your presence. You are a police officer charged with enforcing the law. You are armed. But you are also very alone except for the liability of a crowd that is already terrified. Your screaming family is at your elbow. You would be justified if you did nothing besides being a good witness and preparing to respond in case the robbers attacked others. Other officers would argue, however, that you would be negligent if you did not respond with gunfire of your own as soon as the restaurant employee was shot. These same officers, however, may be overlooking the additional dangers to others imposed by letting still more lead fly in a gunfight inside a crowded establishment.

A final version of this hypothetical but all-too-possible picture: same setting, same armed robbers, same you and your family and crowd, same murder of a restaurant employee. But now the killers begin searching each of the terrified and proned out customers. They are going to find your weapon. They are going to find your police credentials. They have already killed once. *Now,* what are you going to do?

187

In this scenario, most officers agree that they would have to act and risk the application of deadly force against the criminals, even though serious drawbacks (in the forms of innocent bystanders, their own loved ones, and being outnumbered and outgunned) still exist. They would elect to take their destiny in their own hands rather than risk execution at the hands of their adversaries. Still, not all of their peers agree. Some would still not act, perhaps placing their fate in the hands of Lady Luck—or Divine Intervention. They point out that there is no guarantee of success against heavy odds if they choose to take the murderers on. Obviously, there is not a single, correct answer to the preceding, tough scenarios.

AN EVER-PRESENT DANGER

Off-duty confrontations are an ever-present possibility in the life of a law enforcement officer. They can occur when and where they are least expected: at home, in the middle of the night, at high noon, in the corner barber shop, while you are picking up the kids from school.

Most off-duty confrontations do not result in life or death matchups. Many involve no more than obnoxious drunks, panhandlers, and juvenile vandals. But others do present the specter of armed attack against the intervening officer. Some are *extremely* dangerous—dangerous for you.

When all kinds of off-duty enforcement encounters are taken into account, peace officers win far more than they lose. Crimes are prevented or solved and good busts are made on a regular basis by off-the-job cops.

But the potential risks are considerable. Every year in this country, officers are seriously injured as a direct result of off-duty enforcement activities. Most years officers die in some of these extra-duty encounters. The risk to you is great. But there are things—effective things—you can do to reduce your personal risks and dangers as you honor your oath to serve and protect, off duty and on. Thinking about these things now, in advance of confronting them on the street, is the smart thing to do.

The reality of the matter is that you face added dangers from more than one direction when you elect to take police action when you are off duty and away from the human and logistical backups you count on to help you do a difficult job in relative safety. Not only do you face your adversary or adversaries alone, you also run the risk of being confronted by police or citizens who mistake you for a "hostile" because of your actions or displayed weapon. It is no secret that police officers have been shot to death by peers who mistook them for armed opponents. The tragic result of a mistaken identity likely will occur again.

Your dangers, then, originate from at least two sources when you decide to wade into trouble when you are in an off-duty capacity. You face increased danger from the criminals you confront, and you risk mistaken identification by police officers and others who subsequently may threaten you. Both represent significant hazards requiring specific countermeasures to reduce or remove them. Of the two, the danger from the criminal offender is probably the greatest threat.

CRIMINAL CONFRONTATIONS

It is not negative thinking to assess realistically the added risks you face if you elect to take off-duty enforcement action against armed opponents. First of all, you are most likely acting alone and without the big advantages provided by human backups and radio communication. If you are like many officers, you may be carrying a less capable weapon, such as a small-caliber semiautomatic, instead of your service weapon. You may have a limited supply of ammo with you as well. Off-duty you will almost never have quick access to a heavy-duty backup weapon, such as a police shotgun. And, if you are like many of your off-duty peers, you will not have quick access to other vital tools of your trade, such as handcuffs.

Another significant shortcoming you will face in an off-duty encounter is a lack of body armor to protect your torso. This is a serious deficiency that could make all the difference in the world if a gunfight erupts. Think about that in your planning *before* you identify yourself as an officer and swing into action.

There are somewhat less tangible disadvantages you must overcome if you choose to confront danger when you are off-duty and out of uniform. For example, every kind of thug from a disorderly drunk to an armed felon may be less likely to obey your commands when the symbol of your official authority—your police uniform—is missing. Displaying your badge and credentials is certainly better than nothing, but it will be unlikely to have the same impact.

You also may be on slightly shaky ground if you decide to take enforcement action when you are out of your own "comfortable" jurisdiction. You may be less familiar with your surroundings and potential threats. Just as bad, the citizens and police of that jurisdiction are probably unfamiliar with *you* and may mistake you for a bad guy if you whip out a weapon or begin grappling with someone. Bullets mistakenly fired by a "vigilante" citizen or an over-eager officer will kill you just as dead as those fired by a criminal.

Fortunately, there are some basic steps you can take to better your chances of coming out of an off-duty encounter in good shape. Your first priority here is to decide early on whether the situation really merits your forceful and immediate intervention or merely a telephone call to the on-duty peace-keepers. Law enforcement lore is full of tales of officers who got themselves into big trouble by intervening in situations that would have been better left alone or at least handled another way. One off-duty officer lost his job after he fired shots at a reckless driver. Another off-the-job copper intervened in a petty shoplifting caper being carried out by three burly juveniles–and got himself pounded to a pudding for his efforts. Yet another policeman intervened off duty in a boyfriend-girlfriend argument inside a bar while he was somewhat under the influence himself. Before the ensuing brawl and its fall-out had settled, he found himself brought up on criminal as well as departmental charges for his well-intentioned but overzealous efforts. And none of the incidents mentioned here ended the way too many do: with the critical injury or death of the off-duty officer.

The message to you in all of this should be a clear one: You should be very selective in the enforcement duties you involve yourself in when you are off the job. Most crimes you observe in progress should merit a fast phone call to the police of the appropriate jurisdiction, your best work as a professional observer and witness–and nothing more. You should not strive to be your neighborhood's policeman for every tiny infraction of the law on an around-the-clock basis. That sort of approach to your profession is not healthy for you, emotionally or physically. You need some time off from the work and worry of your job just like everyone else.

Property crimes such as theft and vandalism generally can be referred to your on-duty colleagues for appropriate handling. It is in the area of crimes against persons–as found in the scenarios that opened this chapter–that the necessity for taking some kind of direct action arises, even if you are off duty and less than ideally equipped and backed for a potentially dangerous confrontation. Don't forget, however, that you help no one and actually make the task harder for your fellow officers if you act rashly and become part of the problem, perhaps by becoming a hostage or a wounded victim.

You avoid acting ill-advisedly by planning before you act, even if that planning is forced by events to be only a few seconds time in duration. In that time, you'll want to size up the opposition and your chances. Look carefully around you. How many offenders, possible lookouts and backups included, are you apparently confronting? How are they armed? How are you armed? Where is the pending confrontation going to take place? A crowded store? A busy parking lot? Can you afford to wait until a more opportune time and location to force a showdown? Perhaps most important of all, ask yourself: What are my chances of winning and coming out of this confrontation unscathed if I force the issue?

Try to call for help *before* you commit yourself to off-duty action. If you cannot use the telephone yourself, ask two or three different people, if possible, to call the police for you. That way you hopefully can guarantee that the message will get through. Specify that an off-duty police officer is committed and needs help. Describe yourself and your clothing, if you have time and end up making the call yourself. Specify what type of help you need. If you already have your offender in custody or the situation is not critical, you don't need emergency assistance. Say so. You don't want one of your fellow officers to get hurt or killed rushing to your aid when speedy help is not vital. If you *do* need emergency help, say that, too. If your opponents are armed and dangerous, alert your help to that fact. Provide as much information as the developing situation permits.

Keep assessing the situation even as you get involved. Watch out for unexpected criminal backups and accomplices to appear. Look to your own needs for good cover. Be alert to the actions of any victims you are intent on rescuing. They may react unpredictably, particularly if your identity as a peace officer is not readily apparent.

If you are unarmed, do not try to intervene in an in-progress crime that requires an armed response, such as a stickup or assault with a weapon. Don't try to run a bluff. It may get called with unfortunate results for you. Carry an off-duty weapon that is adequate to any realistic challenge you are likely to face. (A small-caliber Saturday night special is *not* what you need.) You have an immediate advantage if you carry the same weapon you rely on when you are working, particularly if you utilize a semiautomatic on the job. Carry an extra magazine or speedloader of ammunition. Have your handcuffs close by, if at all reasonable. And never go out without your police credentials if there is even a remote chance you may become involved in an armed, off-duty confrontation. It's survival smart.

Rely on your good judgment and common sense to keep you out of off-duty trouble. Before you commit yourself to a full-fledged assault on the bad guys, be certain that they really *are* bad guys. One off-duty deputy sheriff called for help and prepared to intervene in an apparent kidnapping in progress at a fast-food restaurant. He learned just in time that the local high school's drama class was filming a mock crime scene.

Common sense also says you should not make a practice of hanging out where you are likely to run into troublemakers you have met on the job or find new ones. After hours clubs and other drinking "joints" with bad reputations are examples of spots you shouldn't be caught dead in, so to speak. Don't invite trouble and you are much less likely to find it, particularly when you are less well equipped to handle it than you would be on duty. That, too, calls for a liberal application of good common sense.

If, while off duty, you come across an officer you feel may need some help, be careful in how you approach to offer it. He is not ungrateful, but if he is smart he will be cautious in accepting you until he's sure you are on his side. (You, hopefully, would do the same.)

If you are in your personal vehicle at the time and your on-duty peer is conducting his business on or near a roadway, be sure you park off the road so that your vehicle does not block his vehicle's emergency lights or otherwise create a traffic hazard. Approach slowly with both of your hands in open view. When you are within earshot, identify yourself as a peace officer and ask if you can help. If he replies in the negative, feel free to be on your way. If he says yes but doesn't immediately give instructions, ask what you can do and then follow his directions.

Do not do anything at any time that distracts the officer from watching the situation he is involved with. Once more, you do not want to create a problem greater than the one you were trying to help solve.

Off-duty or extra-duty jobs pose special risks for the law enforcement officer. You can avoid those risks by declining to work in a potentially hazardous location without backup(s) present to assist you. Rough bars provide a good example of places you should not be working in by yourself, if at all. Banks and other financial institutions are also potentially dangerous locations for the off-duty officer working security. If you must work one of these jobs, be sure you have a plan worked out in advance with the civilian employees so they know how to react and what to do if a stickup goes down. That plan should include detailing who will telephone for help, activate an alarm, and so on. They also should know better than to give you up if you are working in plain clothes. They should be familiar with the institution's policy on responding to cash demands and bomb threats, as should you. Some rehearsals involving all of the civilian employees are a good idea, too, if these people are to be expected to respond sensibly in a crisis.

Whatever else you decide to do about an off-duty, criminal confrontation, remember this: Assess your chances for intervening *successfully* before you give away your identity and commit yourself to action. Once you've done that, it's too late to go back to being the proverbial innocent bystander. Realize that at times the only reasonable action you can take is to be an excellent observer witness and nothing more.

If you do decide to take enforcement action, call for help first if at all possible. Identify yourself as a police officer. Then, act decisively utilizing the principles of good cover and personal positioning. Keep your eyes open and the rest of your senses alert for unexpected dangers, such as hidden weapons. Don't let down your guard for as long as a potential threat exists.

MISTAKEN IDENTITY DANGERS

If there's anything more "irritating" than being menaced (or worse) by the bad guys, it's being threatened (or worse) by the guys in White Hats. Again, however, there are some commonsense steps you can take to significantly reduce the danger to you. As noted already, if you anticipate taking police action off duty and you are not in uniform, try to telephone the police of that jurisdiction (or have someone do it for you) *before* you act. Let them know that a plainclothes officer will be on-scene and, if time permits, give them a description of yourself and your clothing. This is no time for a case of mistaken identity.

In another off-duty scenario, you may find yourself pulled over by an officer of your own or some other jurisdiction. If you are armed, visibly or otherwise, you want your on-duty compatriot to know it immediately so that he realizes he does not have to treat you as a dangerous threat. That way you hopefully can forestall a nasty turn of events that results when he sees your weapon and reacts to it. The key is that he realizes that the armed person (you!) is also a peace officer.

Once you have brought your vehicle to a stop, leave your hands in view atop the steering wheel. If you happen to be a passenger, place your hands on the dash or on top of the seat in front of you. As soon as your fellow officer is within hearing distance, tell him who you are and which agency you are with. Do not reach for identification unless and until he tells you to go ahead. Otherwise your movements may be interpreted as threatening. Tell him if you are armed and let him know where the weapon is located. If you are given the go-ahead to get your credentials, tell him where your hands will be going and move slowly as you retrieve the documents. (Remember: Do not carry an off-duty weapon at all unless you also carry proof that you are a legitimate law enforcement officer.)

Consider adopting hand signals or verbal code words to be used by all members of your department or agency for establishing their identity to fellow officers when off duty or in plainclothes. This sort of arrangement is particularly necessary for large agencies in which employees do not know by sight all of their peers. Keep in mind, however, that smart crooks may eventually pick up on the code and use it against you. To maintain security, codes and signals should be changed from time to time.

But what if you are challenged by an on-duty officer while you are engaged in off-duty enforcement or plainclothes work? The important thing here is to do whatever you are told in a slow, deliberate manner. Do not do or say anything that could be construed by the officer as threatening to him or her. Do everything you are told, even if it means allowing a suspect you have just collared to get away. Holding onto your catch is not worth dying for. You can hash it all out with your challenger later. Right now do as you are told.

Freeze in whatever position the challenging officer tells you to assume. At the same time, shout out that you are a police officer and state the agency that you are with. Don't reach for your credentials until told to do so. Otherwise this sudden move could get you shot.

If you happen to have your weapon out and trained on your subject when you are challenged, freeze in that posture. *Do not turn toward the challenging officer. Do not move the weapon.* Shout your identity and wait for further instructions, all the while watching your subject to prevent a sudden assault or grab for your gun. An obviously explosive situation has just developed. Don't do anything to set it off.

If possible, you should have your police credentials out and in hand before you attempt off-duty or plainclothes enforcement action. Not only does your subject and any innocent others in the vicinity have a chance to see them, they'll also already be out and in evidence if you are confronted by another peace officer. Some plainclothes officers wear their badges on their belt or clothing near their weapons for that reason. If the holstered weapon is seen accidentally while they are not in uniform, hopefully the badge will be seen, too, and a quick call for the police short-stopped in that fashion.

If *you* are the officer called on to challenge what *may* be a plainclothes or off-duty cop, you have your own safety to worry about. If you see a firearm in the hands or on the person of a "possible" police officer, operate just as you would when facing any other "unknown situation, weapons involved" call or contact. In other words: draw your weapon, get behind good cover, and then verbally challenge your possible adversary: "Police! Don't move! Stay in that position!"

When and where possible, approach your "unidentified" subject from behind and out of sight. Evaluate carefully what you see and hear going on. Look for weapons, handcuffs, and identification. Note who else is present and what they appear to be doing. Does it look and sound like a legitimate police action? Don't jump to conclusions, however. Things are not always as they appear. Robbers sometimes use handcuffs. And drug dealer rip-offs sometimes include offenders claiming to be narcotics plainclothesmen.

Once you are in position and have made your identification announcement and commands, EXPECT sudden, panic reactions to your intervention, even from a police officer. Do not be too quick to open fire, particularly if you have the advantage of good cover. Try to allow things to sort themselves out and become clearer. Meanwhile, keep watching everyone present very closely.

Consider ordering the "officer" you have challenged to slowly holster any in-hand weapon, raise his gun hand over his head, and slowly bring out his credentials with his other hand. (Remember: fake police credentials are not all that hard to obtain.) Stay suspicious and alert. If you are in doubt, cuff and disarm everyone involved once adequate backup is on-scene. He can explain his case in far greater safety for everyone that way. If you feel you need to make an apology, you can do that a little later. But do not lose sight of the fact that it was *his* actions that brought about the risky confrontation in the first place.

Make no mistake. Off-duty confrontations are dangerous for you. They are much more so if you enter into them without advance planning and due caution. Fortunately, the commonsense precautions you take can lessen the risks you experience. By planning your moves, summoning help when needed, and making it crystal clear who you are and what you are doing, you can remove a majority of the danger. It is surely worth the doing for the life it can save: *yours.*

A RISK REDUCTION CHECKLIST FOR OFF-DUTY CONFRONTATIONS

1. Be highly selective in the enforcement activities you decide to get involved in off duty. Don't try to be the neighborhood policeman 24 hours a day.
2. Before you get involved in enforcement action off duty, call the local police agency for help or have someone make the call for you.
3. If you are challenged by an on-duty officer while attempting to take enforcement action off duty, don't move and do everything you are told. Do nothing that could be perceived by the officer as a threat to his safety.
4. Assess your chances of winning an off-duty encounter with one or more offenders. If you can't win, don't initiate police action.
5. Be very selective in where you choose to work at an off-duty enforcement job. When you do accept a position, make some emergency plans with your coworkers there.
6. Realize that sometimes the only responsible course of action available to an off-duty officer is to be an excellent witness and nothing more.

An off-duty probationary police officer, age 27, was slain at approximately 2 a.m. when he apparently tried to thwart a stickup. Confronted by two males, the officer was beaten and his service weapon was taken. Clinging to the hood of the subjects' vehicle as they escaped, the officer was shot three times in the neck with a handgun.

* * * * *

An off-duty officer, age 25, was working security at a lounge and assisted another officer in arresting a subject creating a disturbance. Upon release later, the subject returned to the lounge with three male companions, evidently looking for the officer. Upon locating him, they opened fire. The victim, with nearly two years of law enforcement experience, was struck fatally in the head with the blast from a 20-gauge shotgun. Four males were subsequently arrested.

Chapter 17

PRISONER CONTROL AND TRANSPORT

News item: "Three men pulled razor blades and an ice pick from their clothes moments after being convicted of murder in a New York courtroom. Eleven court officers were injured in a melee that lasted several minutes. The men, who had been in jail during the trial, had been patted down before being brought into the courtroom."

Also, consider this report from the FBI's yearly summary detailing incidents of law enforcement officers murdered or assaulted:

Two sheriff's deputies arrested a 26-year-old male for drunk driving. He was patted down, handcuffed, and driven to the county jail for a breath test. The deputies secured their weapons, took him to the testing room, and removed his restraints. During the testing process, the subject removed a .32-caliber handgun from his clothing and killed both officers with shots to the head. He then escaped in a patrol vehicle.

Or consider another case from the FBI report:

Two deputies were walking three prisoners back to jail following a court appearance. The prisoners, handcuffed to one another, were walking between the deputies with a deputy walking at the front of the group. A prisoner suddenly began to struggle with that officer, used his one free hand to get the deputy's sidearm, and shot him three times. He then shot the other deputy once in the chest. The first deputy survived his wounds. The second did not.

More than 30 years ago, pioneer officer survival expert Pierce R. Brooks, a veteran LAPD police investigator tired of investigating the killings of his peers, pointed up poor (or no) handcuffing, poor (or no) searching, and plain officer apathy as frequent contributors to police deaths. Those same factors continue to kill and maim police officers today, as plainly indicated in the three recent incidents detailed here.

Approaching, controlling, and transporting an individual you are taking into lawful custody remain among the riskiest actions you undertake as a police officer. In addition to the known-dangerous persons you encounter, you also may be confronted by a surprise at the point of arrest. The individual you are attempting to seize is, unknown to you, wanted by another jurisdiction, perhaps under another identity. The game is up for him as soon as he is brought in and booked on your matter. He may feel he has to attack you in order to preserve his freedom.

Or a prominent citizen or "family man" caught in a compromising situation may panic at the thought of the public exposure that will result if you arrest him. Particularly if he is under the influence of alcohol or other drugs, he may assault you in a last-ditch attempt at saving his reputation.

Or an individual may be so frightened at the prospect of being jailed or otherwise introduced into the criminal justice system that he or she will lash out at you in a desperate try at avoiding a fate he or she sees as absolutely unacceptable. Some juvenile offenders could fall into this category of resister. A fellow peace officer involved in a personal crisis might be included here, too, and feasibly could react in a similarly violent and unpredictable manner.

You are endangered by your own complacency when you assume that just because a given individual caused no problems and offered no resistance the last time he was arrested he won't this time either. People differ from day to day, hour to hour, minute to minute, and situation to situation. For that matter, you will not react to an offender in *exactly* the same way you did the last time the two of you met. For you to expect him to be predictably the same is dangerously unrealistic. It is just plain dangerous as well. Never assume anything about your "regular customers" other than the fact that they are potentially dangerous to you *every* time you meet them. Proceed accordingly.

Remember, too, that hazards may lurk in the witnesses, bystanders, and friends of your arrestee who may be nearby. Do not attempt to take your party into physical custody while others are within grabbing distance. Try and move your subject out of a crowd before you finalize the physical custody process.

Once a subject is in custody, forbid his physical contact with others. The chance for the furtive transfer of weapons or contraband is simply too great. These associated people should be kept out of the patrol vehicle. The car should have all of its doors locked. And you should drive away from the arrest site as expeditiously as possible. "Out of sight, out of mind" seems to be at work here, and by removing your prisoner, you may prevent a violent rescue or an escape attempt. Ask your questions and do your paperwork elsewhere, preferably in the secure confines of the receiving facility.

The process of controlling and transporting your prisoner can be divided into several essential stages. They include approach and positioning, handcuffing and searching, and transport. For convenience's sake, they are examined separately here.

APPROACH AND POSITIONING

When you approach the subject you intend to take into custody, you present him with perhaps his best opportunity to attack and overcome you. The closer you bring yourself and your weapons to him, the more you improve his chances of escaping by assaulting you. As a result, everything you do during the approach and arrest process must be aimed at guarding your own well-being even as you effectively control your prisoner.

The entire arrest operation begins with a safe and successful approach. This book has already covered the vital aspects of proper use of cover and backup assistance. These necessary tactics and techniques merit a re-reading now. In addition, it is important that you remember that every situation and every individual you encounter will vary from every other, to one degree or another. What was good cover and tactics in one situation may not be equally good in another. At any rate, always remain mindful of where your closest good cover is every time you go into a possible arrest encounter. You may need to seek it out quickly, even on the most routine of arrests for the most petty offense you can imagine.

Meanwhile, when you are going into a *known* high-risk arrest situation, get behind cover without fail before you verbally challenge your arrest target. Have your firearm out and at the ready, leveled center-mass on your opponent, where the situation warrants. *Then* you can shout your identifying challenge: "Police! Don't move! Put your hands on your head!" Or whatever words the circumstances dictate.

In the best of all possible worlds, you should never attempt any full-custody arrest without a covering officer present. That requirement should be mandatory for felony or other known, high-risk arrest situations. In reality, however, many "lesser" confrontations will dictate that you take a nonresisting (as yet!) minor offender into physical custody without the help of a back-up officer.

Whether you are working with or without a cover officer, approach your misdemeanor or unknown-risk subject from his rear whenever possible. If he's facing you, order him to turn away from you as you identify yourself as a police officer. Advise him not to move unless instructed to do so. Tell him to spread his legs wide apart and clasp his hands together, fingers interlaced, atop his head. Repeat your directions if need be and wait for him to comply. Stay out of his arms' reach until you are convinced that all is well for the moment. Do a careful visual inspection for weapons to the extent that you

can. If you see any move quickly to the cover you had scoped out in
advance, draw and point your firearm and proceed from there as for a
known felony or high-risk confrontation.

If no complications are noted immediately, scan the area for any companions of the arrestee who may be nearby. Then you can move in, keeping
your holstered weapon turned away from your misdemeanor or unknown-
risk subject. Still moving from behind, grab onto his interlaced fingers with
one hand and squeeze them as a control hold. Bring his arms behind him,
one at a time, for cuffing. (More about handcuffing later.) If at any point he
begins to struggle, you can always pull him down to the ground, step back,
and draw your baton if you are unable to immediately overcome his resistance to handcuffing. Be ready to defend yourself.

If you are fortunate enough to have a cover officer with you during this
contact, make sure that you stay out of his line of sight and fire throughout
the approach and actual seizure of the arrestee. Immediately tell your partner if you see a weapon. His degree of readiness to apply appropriate force,
if necessary, should rise when he receives this information.

If you are the cover officer in this situation, stay to the rear of the subject
and spread out at least a couple of arms' lengths from the primary control
officer. Stay alert and be ready to intervene with whatever degree of force is
necessary to overcome surprise resistance to arrest. Meanwhile, keep an eye
on the general vicinity for possible interference.

A *known* felony or high-risk arrest offers you at least a couple of choices
for the positioning of your arrestee. Again, you approach carefully from the
rear whenever possible. But this time you stay behind cover with your
weapon pointed at the subject throughout your oral instructions and his compliance. Do nothing more until a backup is in position nearby. It will then be
up to one of you (as the initial contact officer, you decide who) to approach
and handcuff the subject. This is done while the other officer covers at gunpoint, still from behind good cover.

Before anyone approaches, order your subject to clasp his hands together,
fingers interlaced, atop his head. When he complies, order him to turn
around slowly 360 degrees so you can look for obvious weapons in his possession. Let your partner (and the subject) know orally if you spot any, but
leave them in place for now. Have the subject face away from you again. You
now have at least a couple more choices of positioning before you or your
backup approach and handcuff. One choice has him drop to his knees, cross
his ankles, and remain still with his hands on his head. The other has him
drop to his knees, then fall forward flat on his stomach, head on the ground,
hands atop his head, legs spread wide apart. Both positions work. The "down
on your knees" positioning may be more likely to gain suspect compliance
depending on the existing weather and ground conditions as well as the

degree of cooperation you are getting from your subject.

If you are the officer detailed to secure the known high-risk offender, stay out of your covering partner's line of sight and line of fire as you approach. Holster your own weapon before you get within arms' reach of your suspect. Then, cuff as before moving as quickly as possible while keeping the subject off balance. If you are using the subject kneeling position here, place one of your feet on his crossed ankles. Go easy on the pressure here. You are not trying to break bones, just keep him under control. If the offender makes a grab for your weapon or otherwise resists violently, shove him forward with one hand and draw your firearm as you back out of his reach. Be ready to react further if he pulls a weapon or tries to get yours.

If you elect to prone out your high-risk suspect, get him cuffed and off the ground as soon as you have checked him for weapons. Do not apply continuous pressure on the back of a prone individual. You may hamper his breathing and eventually cause him to suffocate. If a proned-out prisoner does begin to experience difficulty in breathing, get him into a sitting or standing position, still handcuffed, call for medical assistance, and monitor him carefully in case rescue breathing becomes necessary.

Once your party has been handcuffed, whatever his arrest positioning, remove any visible weapons and conduct a thorough search for hidden others. (More about that shortly.) Continue to maintain a lookout for more offenders or hostile bystanders. Get yourself and your prisoner out of the area as soon as possible if you have any doubts about your continued safety there.

Occasionally you may encounter a party who is so "out of it," in one way or another, that he cannot understand your verbal orders about the positions you want him to take and what you want him to do next. He may put his hands behind his back for you, for instance, but be unable or unwilling to put them on top of his head. Use your own best judgment in handling such glitches. He may honestly not understand for any number of reasons what it is you want him to do. Or he may be trying to sucker you into attack range. Wait for a backup before you get in close. If very unusual circumstances dictate that you must go it alone, do so with the utmost caution and be prepared to disengage, back away, and respond with necessary force instantly if indicated.

HANDCUFFING AND SEARCHING

Your handcuffs are among the most important pieces of police equipment you carry. But they have limitations. They are, at best, temporary restraining devices. They do not fully immobilize a prisoner, even when properly applied. They can be slipped out of and even broken open. Remember that when you use them. Use them on all full-custody arrests, not just the known-risky ones. It's hard to be wrong for handcuffing a lawfully arrested subject. It's easy to be wrong (and perhaps hurt or killed) for *not* handcuffing that same individual.

Still, never forget that even excellent quality handcuffs (and that's the only kind you should carry) can be defeated. If they are not double-locked, they can be shimmed and opened with a thin metal strip inserted into their ratchet mechanism. They can be opened by sticking a modified ball point pen filler into the keyhole to work like a handcuff key. Some crooks have even succeeded in breaking their cuffs apart by pinning the cuffs' chain swivel into a slot on their seat belt buckle and applying pressure and leverage. (This should not happen if the cuffs are properly behind, not in front of, the prisoner.) They even can be opened by a real handcuff key the criminal has hidden under his belt or elsewhere on his person or clothing. None of this is mentioned here to cause you to lose faith in the handcuffs you are carrying. It is intended to make you think again about your personal safety and not rely TOO much on the protective value of restraint equipment of any kind.

Following proper handcuffing techniques reduces your chances of being injured during this potentially hazardous phase of prisoner handling. Always approach and cuff from the prisoner's rear. Retain a firm grip on the cuffs throughout—a loose cuff is a vicious weapon when attached to a wrist and swung with force. Do not handcuff a subject with his hands in front of him. He can still use both of his hands and the cuffs as dangerous weapons. He can seize your own sidearm and kill you with it. *Handcuff prisoners with hands behind the back, palms facing out.*

In handcuffing, you start with the subject's hands atop his head. Control his first hand by bringing it down off of his head in a wristlock and to a lower back position. Follow your physical tactics instructor's exact teachings on this. With that hand in control, use your own free hand to press the closed arm of your cuffs firmly against the wrist of the hand he still has on top of his head. (Don't perform a TV cop's slap of the cuffs against the wrist. Just press firmly.) The free arm of the handcuff should swing around the wrist and catch on the teeth on the other side, assuming there are no obstructions such as clothing in the way.

Tighten the cuff down enough that your subject cannot withdraw his hand through it. Do not tighten it so much that blood circulation is cut off to the hand, however.

Once you have brought the cuffed hand off of his head and down to lower back level, secure the hand that you have been gripping down there into the cuffs. Before you do so, however, pass the cuffs behind the subject's belt if it is possible to do so. Check the just-applied cuff for snugness. Remember: It will be harder for your prisoner to tamper with the handcuffs and easier for you to work with them if you face his palms outward and the cuffs' keyholes up or toward you.

Double-lock the handcuffs at this point by following your particular brand's instructions for doing so. This prevents them from tightening up from your prisoner's movements and injuring him. It also prevents him from claiming that they have tightened up so he can get you in close to attack you when you attempt to relieve his "discomfort." Double-locking also makes it a bit harder (although not impossible) to defeat the locking mechanism. After you have double-locked the handcuffs, you can use a finger to press down on each cuff arm to make sure they are double-locked. If they tighten up, they are NOT double-locked.

A couple of pieces of precautionary advice concerning the use of handcuffs are in order here. Do not handcuff yourself to a prisoner and do not handcuff a prisoner to any part of the interior or exterior of a police vehicle. The former tactic could get you assaulted or disarmed, and the latter could get you sued successfully if the vehicle is involved in a fire/accident or the prisoner is injured in some other way.

While there would rarely be justification for handcuffing a prisoner with hands in front of his body, an injury keeping you from bringing his arms behind him may present an unusual exception to the rule. If you MUST cuff in front, slip the handcuffs under his belt after moving the belt buckle around behind him. Failing in this, use a cord or a plastic, flexible tie to secure the cuffs at waist level in his front. The main point here is that the front-cuffed subject must not be able to raise his hands or maneuver them freely for an attack or escape attempt.

You always should carry two pairs of handcuffs with you when you are working patrol duty. If you must restrain two prisoners with one pair of handcuffs, however, consider handcuffing the right wrist of one subject to the right wrist of the other. By facing palms outward and passing the cuffs under the belt behind one of the subjects you limit the actions of both to some degree. It will be harder that way for them to coordinate their moves to attack you or escape. Don't forget, however, that it is far better to handcuff each prisoner separately, hands behind backs.

In addition to two pairs of handcuffs, you should carry as a part of your personal equipment a short length of nylon rope with a loop at one end and a gate-latch-type catch at the other as a quick restraint device or hobble for flailing, kicking feet that might otherwise damage your vehicle's windows or interior equipment–or your body. Some officers carry several of the commercially available plastic band ties for the same purpose. Monitor your prisoner and the restraints closely. They can injure him if he continues to resist violently. An officer needs to remain with the restrained subject in order to monitor as well as control him. Do not haul a violent arrestee all by yourself.

To be effective, your handcuffing techniques need to be practiced regularly under the supervision of a skilled physical tactics instructor. Your approach, positioning, control, and handcuffing techniques should mesh smoothly to ensure maximum safety for you. That's something you cannot perfect by reading a book or watching a video. Don't fail to get the hands-on experience and training you need.

A final word on handcuffing: Carry at least one spare handcuff key concealed on your person. It will be more than a little embarrassing if you lose your first key and cannot remove the bracelets you snapped on. Much worse, if you end up handcuffed yourself without an extra key, you could be in the deep stuff rather quickly. By hiding a key—under the rear of your belt, in your shirt pocket, sewn into your vest carrier, or wherever—you will leave yourself a fighting chance to escape.

Every person you take into physical custody should be searched at least three times: the first time as soon as he or she is handcuffed, a second time before being put into a vehicle for transport, and a third time when he or she reaches the booking facility. Each succeeding search should be increasingly detailed and thorough as the surroundings under which it is conducted become more and more secure—the street, at the car, or in the stationhouse or jail. If a prisoner is to be transported from one facility to another, such as from a hospital to the police station or the station to the county jail, he must be searched at the start and conclusion of the transport. In this way, weapons, homemade or otherwise, can be picked up before they are turned against law enforcement personnel.

Always follow the time-proven rule of HANDCUFF FIRST, SEARCH SECOND. He can still hurt you even though he's cuffed, but his best weapons to do it with have just been immobilized behind his back. In the field, having him in the kneeling or proned-out position is the safest route for you when you are dealing with the search of a high-risk offender. Otherwise, search him from behind while he is standing, off-balance, cuffed with his legs spread apart. Do not attempt to search several subjects by yourself no matter how well-cuffed they are. For multiple prisoners (and multiple searches), you need at least one cover officer to ensure your safety.

Every prisoner search you do should be conducted in an orderly, systematic manner. In general, your thorough search should begin at the top of his head and extend down to his footwear. You are looking for anything he could use to hurt you or anyone else with. Any contraband or other evidence you recover in this officer safety search generally will be considered admissible in court against him. Your first search, conducted as soon as you get your subject cuffed and under some degree of control, should consist of a pat down and squeezing of the arrestee's clothing to seek out any weapons with which he could injure you. Check visually as you pat and squeeze his clothing—under arms, along his chest and back, around his waist, and inside as well as outside of his pants legs. Check shoes and boots for concealed weapons. Don't omit an exploration of all pockets to be found on any of his garments.

One note here: Before you begin any search of a detained subject, ASK him if he has any weapons, including pocketknives, on him. Many offenders will tell you right then and there if they are packing a weapon. Naturally, if he tells you he's clean, you still do not take his word at face value. You search anyway. It's the only survival-smart way to operate. Also remember to ask him if he has any needles or other sharp items on him that might hurt you. Make it clear to him that you both will regret it if you are injured by something you blunder onto during a personal search.

Your second search, carried out just before you transport your prisoner, is done in more detail yet, top to bottom. Keeping him off balance, legs spread wide apart, remove and check any headgear for weapons or contraband. If he (or she) has long hair, run your fingers through it carefully in a check for weapons such as razorblades or pins. (You will want to be wearing your leather or latex gloves for all of these street searching operations.) Check under shirt and coat collars. Check for a chain or cord around his neck. It just might have a weapon tied at the other end. It also could be used later in an attempt to strangle someone—someone like you. Pat, squeeze, and probe clothing once again as you work down first one side of the body and then the other. Remember to do your searching *only* with your subject under close control and faced away from you. Check his belt for concealed weapons, a handcuff key, or a metal strip that might be used to shim the cuffs' mechanism. (Later, take the belt for safekeeping.) Run your hand around the inside waistband of his pants as you continue your probe for weapons. Check for a string that may dangle a small gun or knife down into the crotch area of his underclothing. He may assume that you won't search him there. Don't omit a pat down of his groin area in spite of his questioning your sexual preference. Obviously, this particular part of the search should be done by an officer of the same sex as the arrestee.

Check the small of your prisoner's back for concealed weapons, too. After all, the TV cops and robbers like to stick their guns back there, so the crooks do, too. Again, run the backside of your hand along all sides of his legs in a weapons check. Don't forget to pull up his pants legs to expose weapons strapped to a leg or an ankle or protruding from socks, shoes, or boots.

As noted, yet another search should be conducted when you reach your destination for booking or jailing your subject. Repeat what you did previously, but this time remove any of the prisoner's property that may still be on him and pose a threat of harm to anyone, including himself. In addition to his belt, his shoes, boots, chains, necklaces, matches, lighters, ballpoint pens, and like items must be removed and inventoried for return when he is released. Sharp-edged jewelry such as rings must be seized, too. All of this property should be promptly packaged and put out of the subject's reach.

An additional piece of advice about your search efforts: Don't stretch or reach too far and lose your balance and control while you are reaching around your party from behind to search his frontal area. Consider searching to his front centerline from one side of his rear and then move around to the other side to search the rest. The key here is not to make yourself vulnerable by stretching too far. If at any point the subject, still cuffed, begins resisting, push him forward and away from you and step back. Be prepared to respond if he tries to attack with feet, head, or other personal weapons.

As noted previously, searching a prisoner of the opposite sex can present extra problems for you. The problems extend beyond searching a purse or handbag, of course. Male and female officers should do thorough, careful weapons searches of prisoners of the opposite sex. But searching the groin area of any arrestee or the breast region of a female arrestee by an officer of the opposite sex should only be done when there is clear and convincing evidence that a weapon has been secreted there (ex: a clear bulge in the clothing or a part of a weapon showing). If it's a weapon you suspect, go get it without delay regardless of your arrestee's protestations and promises of lawsuits. Your safety requires such action. Otherwise, if no weapon is indicated, wait for an officer of the same sex as the arrestee to complete the "personal" search of the still-handcuffed and carefully monitored prisoner. Meanwhile, maintain close observation of your prisoner.

Never stop searching for one more weapon no matter how many have been discovered already. There are more than a few crooks out there who put just as much value in backup weapons as you do. And there seems to be something about a true knife nut that requires him to have not one but numerous blades on or about his person. Never quit looking, searching, probing. Your life could depend on your persistence.

TRANSPORT

Moving your prisoner from one place to another is still a very dangerous time for you. Virtually every year, peers of yours are injured and killed doing just that. Often the indirect cause of their personal tragedy is that old, familiar bugaboo: *complacency.* It appears that there are at least two ways in which complacency hurts law enforcement officers involved in prisoner handling duties. In one scenario, officers get into trouble because they handle dangerous arrestees (or any arrestee at all for that matter) so infrequently that they don't know how to do it right and as a result get careless. For want of a better description, they face obvious danger so seldom that they may simply forget how to be cautious.

On the other hand, other officers are seriously endangered because they handle so many potentially vicious arrestees in their battle zone environment that the whole picture becomes routine. Routine, as you well know, *can* breed carelessness, apathy, and danger. You already know what can happen next.

From the moment you first take custody of a prisoner, stay alert to your personal safety responsibilities. When you accept him (or her) you likewise accept accountability for your own safety, the safety of those around you, and the safety of the prisoner himself. That regard for safety means, for one thing, that you must always remain conscious of the location of your sidearm in relation to the arrestee. You must keep your weapon snugly snapped into its holster and the holster on your side turned away from the arrestee, including during the time you are walking him to and from a vehicle. Once you reach the jail or booking facility, your weapon is locked away so that neither your prisoner nor anyone else can get at it.

Never walk between two prisoners and never, as noted previously, handcuff yourself to a prisoner. You want your arrestee's movements limited, not your own. Keep a grip on your subject as you walk him to or from a car or anyplace else. That does not mean you try to squeeze the circulation out of his arm with a death grip–that will lead only to resistance and possible excessive force complaints. But do hold onto him. It will help you control the prisoner as well as sense right away if he is tensing up for an assault or escape attempt.

If the subject in your custody is resistive, you may have to walk him while keeping one of his wrists in a compliance hold behind him. By applying a little pressure when he acts up, you may be able to convince him to walk with you, thereby avoiding the Big Scene that results when several officers have to drag him literally kicking and screaming to his destination. Simply tell him how things work at the outset: "Your discomfort will cease when you come with me peacefully. I have no desire to hurt you, and I don't intend for you to hurt me, either."

Be careful what you hang onto while you are walking your prisoner. Handcuffs do not make a good handle for you. They can leave you with a nasty cut and a lot of pain if your subject knows how to manipulate the cuff chain to trap and hurt you (the hinged-style handcuffs are an excellent choice for you here). In the final analysis, firmly hanging onto his arm instead of the cuffs is a better arrangement.

You should have checked your patrol vehicle for "stray" weapons when you went on duty. Now, check on, around, and under the seat again before you put your prisoner inside. Seat belt him in on the right rear seat behind your protective screen or cage. If you have no protective barrier (*not* a good idea), belt him into the right front seat and have a second officer sit immediately behind him. Do not transport a hostile prisoner in the front seat by yourself–ever. It's a great way to earn a set of false teeth.

If your prisoner is violent or promises to become so, hobble his ankles and place him in the backseat with an officer in back to ride with him and provide restraint, if need be. And for your own sake, if he tells you he's going to kick your butt when his restraints are removed, *believe him* and take proper precautions, such as having plenty of backup on hand. Watch him like a hawk the whole time he is in your custody and take no chances.

Regardless of how peace-loving your arrestee appears, search the car again after he is removed from it. He may have abandoned a weapon or other evidence there. Law enforcement lore is full of stories of weapons, likely and unlikely, recovered from backseats. Unfortunately, that does not say much of a positive nature about the quality of searches performed by too many officers.

Your responsibility for your prisoner has not terminated until you have surrendered him to someone else. Monitor him very closely during any booking or questioning procedure. Do not overlook your obligation to search him that third time when you reach your destination. And don't forget to remove from his control anything with which he could hurt anybody, including himself. That always includes shoes, belts, and other potential weapons. If you have a feeling you may have missed something, search again. And yet again, if necessary. Your safety is not something you can afford to get sloppy with.

Strip or skin searches are a topic on which you will have to follow your own agency's procedural rules and policies. Generally speaking, they are conducted only when reasonable grounds exist to believe the individual has secreted a weapon or contraband under all of his garments. They are also frequently done as a regular part of processing a prisoner who is to be lodged in a lockup facility. When done, they must be carried out in privacy with at least two officers of the same sex as the prisoner in attendance. If weapons or other contraband are believed to be concealed *inside* the prisoner's body or some orifice thereof, they must be retrieved only by medical professionals, not by police or corrections officers. That is a facet of *career* survival for you.

If you receive for transport or processing a prisoner who already has been moved or otherwise handled by another officer, remember that you are obligated to search him again to make him "safe" for you. Don't bet your safety on the sufficiency of a search done by someone else. It's just good survival sense, and the original handling officer should know that. By the same logic, do not object when your peer re-searches a prisoner you have handled first. He, too, is demonstrating good survival smarts by doing so.

Safe prisoner handling practices require that you assume nothing other than the presence of potential danger every time you touch an individual who is in police custody. Never stop looking for one more means by which your prisoner could hurt you and/or effect an escape. Never become complacent about the prisoner handling process. Always remain alert to your responsibilities for the well-being of yourself, your peers, innocent others, and your prisoner. It's the only way to remain truly in *personal* control of the prisoner control operation.

A RISK REDUCTION CHECKLIST FOR PRISONER CONTROL AND TRANSPORT

1. Every arrestee should be properly handcuffed for transport with his hands behind his back. But remember that handcuffs are temporary, fallible restraints.
2. Every arrestee should be searched for weapons at least three times: at the point of arrest, before transport, and upon arrival at a destination.
3. Don't accept someone else's word that a prisoner is "clean." Search him again for your own safety.
4. Keep your prisoner off balance and yourself well balanced during a weapons search of his clothing and person. Do not overreach.
5. Remove from your prisoner any item with which he might hurt himself—or you.
6. Do not allow non-law enforcement people to come to close quarters with your prisoner.
7. Practice your handcuffing and searching skills on a regular basis.
8. Never allow yourself to become complacent about the potential dangers of handling and transporting prisoners. *They're real.*

At 6:15 a.m., a deputy sheriff, age 48, was shot to death while transporting a prisoner for arraignment on a murder charge. The unhandcuffed 20-year-old male was riding in the front seat of the patrol unit when he gained control of the deputy's weapon and shot the officer twice in the chest. The victim deputy had 13 years law enforcement experience.

* * * * *

At approximately 5:30 p.m., an 8-year veteran deputy was killed while on solo patrol. The 41-year-old officer located a vehicle known to be stolen and involved in an earlier armed robbery. The deputy was attempting to handcuff a suspect when he was shot three times with a .38-caliber handgun. He died of a head wound.

Chapter 18

TERRORISTIC THREATS

Amer`merican law enforcement's regard of terrorism changed forever after the events of September 11, 2001. Terrorism was not, of course, unknown to American peace officers. Law enforcement had long dealt with the race haters, anti-government zealots, and other violence-prone extremists long before the commandeered airliners crashed. But with the September 11 events came the realization that American law enforcement would now have to deal with carnage on a scale previously experienced only on foreign soil, the 1995 bombing attack in Oklahoma City excepted.

Those events also brought home the realization that law enforcement officers would now have to deal with extremists who were willing to die in order to kill those they regarded as "infidels." As those officers already knew, anyone willing to perish for a perverse cause would be difficult indeed to forestall from carrying out plans for large-scale destruction.

As a consequence, you as a twenty-first century peace officer will need to reevaluate how you look at terrorists and terrorism. You will need to examine your tactics for both terrorism prevention and terrorism response and determine if they are relevant in a changed world. You likewise will have to remain mindful that seldom do future terrorist attacks mimic precisely what has been done before. As law enforcement officers learn from bloody experience, so do the perpetrators of that bloodshed. As terrorism evolves, so must your tactics for countering it.

To the peace officers who must deal with these in-earnest but badly misguided zealots, the political leaning of the violent, terroristic criminal makes little difference. These officers realize that the bombs or bullets of one will kill you just as dead as the instruments of the other. Instead, the survival-smart officer concentrates on implementing anti-terrorist tactics and techniques that will keep him safe no matter what the political agenda of his attacker. That survival-smart officer must be you.

Safety, of course, comes with increased knowledge of the threat faced. That calls for recognition of the enemy.

WHO ARE THEY?

The terrorist of today can be just about anybody with a grievance, cause, or belief so strong that he is willing to kill others, perhaps large numbers of them, to achieve his goal, whatever that goal happens to be. He may be quite willing to perish himself in the attainment of that goal.

The thinking of a terrorist can be particularly hard to understand because he likely does not view the world as you do. He and his kind hope to influence public opinion and government policy by committing acts that are so threatening and terrifying–translate that to mean bloody–that belief in the status quo or normal way of doing business and living life is radically altered. The terrorist is playing to an audience. He seeks to convince that audience that he and his companions are so powerful that government and its agents are helpless and unable to stop them from reaching their objectives.

That helps to explain the terrorist's eagerness to attack law enforcement officers and facilities. The message intended for public consumption is that if government cannot even protect itself from terrorism, how can it protect its citizens? Perhaps it is time to come over to the terrorist's way of thinking for your own good, or so the thought process is supposed to go according to the terrorist's textbook.

Today's terrorists run the length of the political spectrum. They include both domestic and foreign dangers to the safety of the nation's citizens. The agents of terroristic, fanatical fundamentalist groups such as Al-Qaeda represent an especially dangerous threat. Some of these extremists already have demonstrated their willingness to carry out suicide attacks against America, the "Great Satan." Some of these people are lying low but are very much out there today. You must remain conscious of the dangers they present, now and into the foreseeable future.

At the same time, many of today's terroristic threats remain home-grown. Some of their handiwork was seen in the catastrophic bombing attack on Oklahoma City's federal building. But it would be a mistake to view the country's domestic terrorists as somehow united either logistically or in dogma and goals. While some of the extremist groups and individuals share the same party line, there is oftentimes not only disagreement but outright hostility among various factions. Some not only fail to agree on how their desired ends are to be accomplished, they cannot even agree on what the ends *are.*

Some of the disagreements even can be attributed to personal feuds over who is to be in charge of a particular organization or subgroup. It should come as no surprise to you that individuals who cannot get along with the rest of the world oftentimes cannot get along with their fellow extremists either. Nonetheless, the domestic terrorist's internal bickering and antisocial tendencies can make it even harder for law enforcement to track his activities as he periodically abandons one group of zealots to join or form another.

America's domestic terrorists include a few of the old-fashioned race haters who preach racial supremacy and prejudice and direct violence against members of targeted minority or ethnic populations. As distasteful as their rhetoric may be, it is not a crime for these people to advocate the position that one race or group is superior or inferior to another. The racial supremacist—White, Black, or otherwise—only becomes a legitimate problem for law enforcement when he begins to advocate or execute criminal acts against the targets of his hatred.

The government haters also are out there. The extremists among these groups go far beyond grousing about taxes and government giveaway programs. These people go to the point of advocating the overthrow of the government and violent attacks against its agents, including law enforcement officers. The extremist anti-government survivalist types and some of the loosely titled, self-appointed militia movements may represent some of the most heavily armed and potentially dangerous threats to American peace officers today.

Once more, it is not a crime to hate, even if the objects of your venom happen to include the government and its employees, some of whom just happen to be law enforcement officers. But when that hatred includes the intent to launch attacks against government employees and property, protest has crossed the line into criminal conduct.

Some of today's far-right fringe groups make no bones about their willingness to attack those who oppose them, including those they see as the law enforcement agents of ZOG, the illegal, unconstitutional Zionist Occupational Government fictionalized by the extremist right. Statements attributed to the members of some of these groups include specific threats to murder law enforcement officers. With even a handful of these fringe "thinkers" out there espousing such views, only the foolish law enforcement officer would not be interested in remaining alert to the activities of these people.

The lines separating some of the violence-advocating extremist groups are constantly fading and shifting, making it hard to differentiate among them. Some race-haters, for example, also may be members of extremist, fundamentalist religious groups advocating violence against government officials and others, such as homosexuals and those seen as "different." In recent years, a small number of these far-out fundamentalists have posed a danger to law enforcement after attracting cults of followers, some of whom arm themselves heavily and engage in compound living arrangements intended to keep outsiders—particularly agents of the government—at bay.

But not every potential terrorist who represents a threat to law enforcement dons camouflage clothing, wears a gun on his hip, and runs around in the woods spouting anti-government rhetoric. Indeed, some of these people look and sound a lot like you—up to a point. It is when their hot buttons get pushed that they become a potential threat to others. They may be most dangerous to their identified enemies. Many, however, will not hesitate to take you on if they perceive that you are standing in their way.

Included in this latter group of potential threats to you are the eco-terrorists, the animal rights extremists, and the fringe anti-abortion crusaders. There are others, too. Any or all of these people may hold beliefs with which you strongly agree. The difference between you and them is that you as a law-abiding citizen will not engage in illegal and perhaps life-threatening behavior to make a point or further a cause, no matter how well-intentioned the goal. The mainstream members of such groups are almost unanimous in disavowing the crimes engaged in by their far-out supporters. The offenses committed by these extreme believers may include arson, vandalism, intimidation, sabotage, and even murder.

Clearly, the truly fanatical, out-of-touch supporters of causes of one kind or another may be dangerous to the law enforcement officers who encounter them. That holds true even if the officer was not the original target of their depredations. You might, for instance, be placed in danger if you have interrupted what was initially intended as a crime against property. By accidentally encountering an incendiary or explosive device planted by one of these terrorists, you could end up just as totally destroyed as the intended target. You might want to think about that if you discover a suspicious package or device during your investigation of a break-in at an animal experimentation facility or abortion clinic. "Well-intentioned" terrorism can kill or maim you just as surely as the infernal device planted by an anti-American suicide bomber from another country. It amounts to terrorism, all the same.

The face of terrorism does not remain static for long. It is safe to assume that terroristic groups and goals will change as the causes and issues that excite people also change with the times. Some groups will go quiet, shrink, or wither and die as political, economic, and social conditions change. New groups with at least the potential for violence will form, some with the members of older, faded groups on their rosters. It is vital that you, the law enforcement officer who may be called on to deal with their future threats, remain current on who's out there and how they are going about their strange business.

HOW DO THEY OPERATE?

As has always been the case, terrorism requires human participants who can be led to take part in acts of violence against innocent others in order to further some identifiable greater purpose. Terrorism today still requires weapons of destruction, ranging from firearms to mammoth, vehicle-carried explosive devices. Beyond that, however, terrorism has been modernized to take advantage of technology in the Information Age. Technology played a role in the aircraft bombs that split American skies on September 11, 2001.

Terrorism still relies on charismatic speakers and writers who make at least occasional sense and put into words what their audience may already be thinking. In some cases, today's front men (and women) for the extremist and violence-prone groups are better educated and much slicker than their predecessors. It may be, for instance, hard to argue with the speaker's goal of "doing away with welfare." It is only later that the listener discovers that the speaker intends to end welfare by killing off many of its recipients.

It is in the means of communicating its message that terrorism has changed its method of operation today. Some of the more far-out, violence-preaching groups are seeking to ride the cutting edge by utilizing the Internet to spread propaganda, sell their hateful or anti-government materials, seek donations, recruit new members, and communicate with one another. They may refer the curious sympathizer to the electronic addresses of other, like-minded groups and individuals.

In addition, some groups have added professional quality video material such as DVDs to the old standby of printed hate literature to further their race-hating or anti-government agendas. CDs and audiotapes are also available—for a price. Radio broadcasts may carry the violence-inspiring messages of some of these extremist groups.

Some of today's violence-preaching organizations count ex-cops and even current law enforcement officers among their members. They want more. Current officers can furnish information from police databases and other files as well as news of pending law enforcement operations. As a consequence, such peace officer participation, no matter how small or passive, poses a threat to you, the "government agent" and avowed enemy of the more far-out of these extremists. That's bad news.

It may be hard not to sympathize just a little with the well-dressed, well-spoken zealot who looks a lot like you and says he's anti-crime and anti-criminal and wants to dump the whole lot of left-leaning, liberal politicians who seem bent on driving the American working stiff straight to Hell. But you need to listen a little longer to find out exactly *who* the speaker includes among his enemies and just how he plans to deal with them. You might find that you as a government employee appear somewhere on his enemies list if you do not agree with him on every facet of extremist dogma. You might even learn that he plans to whittle down that enemies list with violence when the time comes.

Pay particular attention to the zealot who wants to get really close to you. Your new pal may have ulterior motives. Regard the information you get from him as suspicious even though it may be of interest to law enforcement. It may be part of an organized effort to plant false information. Then remember who and what you are sworn to protect and keep your distance. That, too, is a part of officer survival.

Realize that the terrorists who pose a danger to law enforcement are not necessarily the poison-spewing media stars who bring attention to themselves by spouting their violent rhetoric for media sound bites. These attention-craving performers may not be the people who actually pose a physical threat to you when you cross paths on a traffic stop or check of a rural campsite. Terrorists who are very serious about their plans for destruction are likely to shun publicity, work alone or in small groups, and say nothing when you catch them dirty, perhaps with quantities of weapons or explosives. Do not regard their lack of flash as a trustworthy indicator that they do not pose a risk to you. They do.

DEALING WITH THE THREAT

As an American peace officer, your safety is threatened by terrorists, foreign and domestic. While terrorism should by no means be your *greatest* worry as you go about your peacekeeping tasks, you should nevertheless be aware that the terrorist's threat is real whether you work in the big city, a suburban community, or rural America. But as with every other threat you may encounter on the job, the personal risks can be minimized by your application of a few, sound officer safety and survival practices. Consider the following as a starting point for your terrorist survival regimen.

Know the Opposition

Stay abreast of law enforcement intelligence pertinent to your geographic location concerning which violence-prone extremist groups may be active in your vicinity. Police professional publications often can provide you with background information on the identities and activities of the more well-known groups and causes. Even staying up with the news via television and the Internet can tell you a lot about who is out there and what they are upset about. Do not overlook the intelligence provided in the regular bulletins disseminated by state and federal agencies, such as Homeland Security and the FBI.

In other words, do not neglect your "current events" knowledge. What are the issues of the day and who has said what that sounds potentially threatening? Is the threatening organization well organized or does it consist of one or two loudmouths? (They can be dangerous, too.) Is the group known to be armed and threatening violence against specific targets? Do these individuals or groups reside or have meeting or training facilities in your jurisdiction? Information can mean safety. You cannot have too much of either where potential terrorists are concerned.

Naturally, complaining about the state of the world in general and the government in particular does not constitute a crime. Advocating or carrying out violent acts to "solve" the problem does. Stay current on what's going on and increase your safety margin.

Recognize the Terrorist's Fingerprints on "Routine" Crime Scenes

Terrorists do not restrict their unlawful activities to blowing up things and assassinating their enemies. Terrorists and would-be terrorists sometimes drive drunk, beat their girlfriends, and get into beefs with their neighbors, too. In some cases, they may steal vehicles or commit armed robberies in order to finance their terroristic plans. They also may engage in thefts and burglaries to supply themselves with weapons, ammunition, explosives, communication gear, and other items. Watch for evidence that the person you have just contacted may be more than a "plain vanilla" crook. Keep an eye out for potential giveaways like hate literature, automatic weapons, and oral statements that may tell you that you are dealing with something special (and potentially hazardous). Protect yourself accordingly.

Look for the Warning Signs

In all of your contacts, keep your senses attuned for evidence that you may be involved with one or more members of a terroristic group or perhaps one of their sympathizers. Look for things like:

- Unexplained, unusual, or illegal weapons and ammunition. Unexplained, unusual quantities of ammunition or explosive components also could signal danger. Further inquiry would be advisable.
- Immediate and intense hostility toward you as a "government agent." Lots of people do not particularly love law enforcement officers, but extreme verbal attacks could be warning you of extra trouble ahead. Don't be slow in getting assistance. Then, really *listen* to what is said. He may tell you more than he intends about just why he does not like

you and what he intends to do about it. Don't unnecessarily provoke him. Stay professional and let him talk. You could learn a lot.

• Hate literature or anti-government propaganda, perhaps in a vehicle, business, or home you encounter in your duties. Putting your far-out opinions into mass circulation is not a crime, of course. Advocating violent acts against others may be.

• A "bunker mentality" evident in a subject you have contacted. He does not have to be wearing a helmet and flak jacket, of course. He simply could be mentally unstable. But he might be a member of an extremist group willing to visit violence on its perceived enemies. (He could be both.) Again, listen to what he has to say. Encourage him to talk, but realize that you are unlikely to win a debate with him. Just listen and learn more about what you are facing.

• Refusal to display a license plate or driver's license. Neither makes him a terrorist, but some far-right groups do deny a government's authority to require either of these. Have a backup present when dealing with this individual. In a vehicle stop situation, signs or bumper stickers on the vehicle may give you early warning of the potential problem ahead. Take whatever enforcement action you normally would take, but stay alert for violent surprises, including those involving weapons. Remember: Dissent from politically correct opinions does not make anyone a terrorist. Carrying dissent into criminal acts is a whole different matter.

Expect Unusual Tactics

A dyed-in-the-wool terrorist whom you contact may not respond to you like an ordinary criminal. He may be wearing body armor or even a suicide belt of explosives. He may be very heavily armed. He may be in possession of explosive devices, including military ordinance such as hand grenades. He may demonstrate knowledge of police or military tactics and attempt to apply them in confronting you. He may, in a few words, be especially dangerous to take on alone. Get help on the way fast if you have any inkling that you may be dealing with a member or members of a terrorist organization. Let your responding assistance know what you suspect. Consider a temporary, tactical withdrawal if clearly you are overmatched.

Also know that the devout terrorist may display a very different mindset from the rest of the lawbreakers you encounter. He may have done more than run around in camo gear and practice maneuvers in the forest. He also may have determined that, like you, he is going to win any encounter with an opposing force. He may be absolutely certain that God or Allah is on his side. He may be willing or even eager to die for a cause he believes in. That makes him very dangerous indeed. Do not take chances in responding to the extreme threat he represents.

Practice Good Survival Skills

The same, basic safety practices that serve you well in handling the other threats to your continued well-being will work against the terrorist, too. Watch for the danger signs, make no unsafe assumptions, and obtain necessary assistance. Rely on the sound tactics and techniques you have practiced before as you confront a terroristic threat of any sort. Don't get sloppy or allow bad habits and shortcuts to get you into trouble. Remain observant and expect the unexpected. You just may encounter it. And never forget that you are more than a match for a terrorist of any stripe. Stay confident in your ability to overcome any threat.

Prepare for New Threats

Acts of terrorism do not occur in a vacuum. They are carried out by human beings, alone or in groups, who plan, organize, and then execute their illegal acts. It is up to you as a survival-smart law enforcement officer to know what to watch for as those individuals prepare for a terrorist attack. Here are some of the things you need to be on the lookout for.

Surveillance

Once terrorists have chosen a site for an attack, they generally will visit it more than once in an attempt to gain information and practice their assault. They are looking for strengths and weaknesses of the target, including security arrangements such as law enforcement personnel. They may be seeking the best spot to place an explosive device to attain maximum damage as well as the best routes for approach and escape.

You should be tipped off that hostile surveillance is going on if you note activities like suspicious persons diagramming or photographing the area. Individuals who have blueprints or floor plans of government and other installations also merit your attention. Questions should be asked to determine why they are in possession of such items. There may be absolutely innocent explanations but you won't know unless you dig further.

Solicitation of Information

People asking questions about the functions or layout of likely terrorist targets (power plants, ports, airports, tunnels, reservoirs, water and sewer plants, government buildings, etc.) should earn your attention. Terrorists or their sympathizers may seek information on flight or shipping schedules, personnel, and products found at the target location. Once again, you should ask questions of suspicious persons and document who they are and what they have to say. This kind of information should be passed along to regional fusion centers and anti-terrorist law enforcement units.

Security Tests and Rehearsals

Terrorists intending to attack a specific site oftentimes will conduct a dry run to gauge how difficult it is to gain access. They also may be looking to gauge law enforcement's presence or likely response. They may try to penetrate a secure area and have a plausible excuse ("I was lost") if they are challenged. Be alert to such ruses. Young people or women may be used for this assignment. Terrorists may even seek to gain employment at the future target in order to size up the facility's layout and internal security measures. Be observant, be suspicious, and challenge anything or anyone that does not feel right to you.

Gathering Equipment and Supplies

A stolen car or truck may be loaded with explosives and used as a bomb. Weapons or explosives may be stolen and fashioned into an improvised explosives device. Stolen emergency responder uniforms, vehicles, and radios may be especially prized by those intending terroristic mayhem. Badges and official identification cards also may be purloined to equip terrorists intent on penetrating secure areas.

In today's world, it just makes sense to inquire further when you encounter anyone in possession of items that could be used in a terrorist attack. Stay suspicious and act on your suspicions, but do so with caution. If he suspects that you are onto him, a terrorist is unlikely to have any reservations about murdering a law enforcement officer.

Suspicious Persons

This indicator does not call for racial or ethnic profiling. What it does require you to do is what peace officers do very well: Remain ever on the lookout for the person who just does not fit in the environment. It could be a stowaway on a ship or airplane, a person sneaking across the border illegally, or someone in possession of quantities of weapons, chemicals, or hate literature. Question this individual and report your findings. Pass along what you learn. You always can offer an apology if the individual turns out to be involved in legitimate activities.

Deployment for the Attack

The last and probably the most dangerous (for you) moment leading up to a terrorist attack may come as the terrorists are actually on their way to attack their target. This is likely the last chance for intervention before the attack occurs. This could mean that the terrorists are actually in a vehicle loaded with explosives en route to oblivion.

Whatever the situation you have uncovered, you are obliged to keep your distance out of harm's way until you have adequate law enforcement resources to confront the threat. Act as quickly as possible but realize you help no one by becoming one more victim. Have a plan before you act. Then, take on the threat with plenty of assistance.

BOMBS AND BOOBY TRAPS

Bombs seem to be the favorite weapon of terrorists the world over. America's home-grown and foreign-origin terrorists do not pose an exception to the rule. The key for you is to remain alert to the possibility of a terrorist's explosives attack at any time or place, no matter how unlikely the scenario.

You already know that law enforcement facilities and vehicles make attractive targets for terrorists of all kinds. Realize that individual law enforcement officers can become targets of hate groups, too. In exchange for arresting or even ticketing a fanatic, you could find yourself the recipient of a threatening letter—or a letter bomb. It has happened before.

Bombings attributed to terroristic groups and individuals are clearly on the upswing throughout the world today. There is every indication that the trend will continue into the immediate future. While federal law enforcement officers and facilities have caught the brunt of the terrorist's hatred of late, state and local officers can take little comfort from that fact. The average terrorist's mind would appear to discriminate very little among the authority figures he faces. It is no secret that some of the more extreme voices of domestic terrorism have called for neutralizing all agents of law enforcement. The minions of violent Mexican drug gangs can be included in this group of dangerous people.

Terrorists and their criminal kin like booby traps, too. One California police department recently found itself besieged by gang members who attempted to injure or kill police officers and destroy law enforcement facilities and vehicles. One officer narrowly missed being hit by a round fired from a firearm placed as a booby trap.

Drug traffickers are known to place booby traps for law enforcement at their grow and drug manufacturing sites. There is nothing to say foreign- or domestic-trained terrorists will not do something similar. They already have the will and the technical skills to do so.

The familiar, ordnance expert's advice should serve you well here: If you don't know for certain what it is, leave it alone. Do not touch or handle it. Get away and call in the experts. You just might save your hand or your life by doing that.

If you are a law enforcement officer serving anywhere in the United States today, you are at risk, however small that risk may be, from terrorists and terrorism. These criminals, foreign or domestic, remain relatively few in number, as do the extremist organizations that attract them. On average, you certainly have a much greater chance of being harmed by a "plain vanilla" robber or burglar than a race-hater or anti-American fanatic. But the threat exists. The danger is real.

You limit the dangers of terrorism by practicing virtually the same officer safety tactics and techniques you rely on to shield you from the other hazards of your potentially hazardous profession. Practice them regularly. If your antagonist turns out to be nothing worse than a loud-mouthed extremist, you have lost nothing from your application of extra caution. If he (or she) is actually something a lot more dangerous, you may well have saved your own life.

A RISK REDUCTION CHECKLIST FOR TERRORISTIC THREATS

1. Know if any terroristic groups or their sympathizers have a presence in your area.
2. Realize that you may encounter a heavily armed member of a terroristic group involved in a "regular" crime, such as a traffic offense, shoplifting, or robbery.
3. Stay current on the tactics and operations of known terrorist groups, such as entrapment bombings, sniper attacks, or ambushes.
4. Watch for the warning signs that you may be dealing with a terrorist organization or individual: bulk quantities of violence-advocating hate literature, unexplained and unusual amounts of heavy weapons or ammunition, or a "bunker mentality" accompanied by verbal threats.
5. Expect the possibility of unusual tactics from a terroristic individual or group, such as the wearing of body armor or the possession of military ordinance.
6. Recognize that an extremist may attempt to curry favor with you or even seek to get you to join his organization.

7. Realize that a dedicated terrorist may be willing or even anxious to die to accomplish his goals, which may include killing you.
8. When dealing with potential terrorism, always keep looking for the next threat.

In the Midwest, a highway patrolman was shot to death after making a traffic stop. Unknown to the officer, who was Black, the vehicle contained a wanted, far-right-wing fugitive with avowed racist beliefs. The killer's van was found to contain weapons, a large supply of ammunition, and explosives. The officer's killer was captured, convicted, and eventually executed for the murder.

* * * * *

Two officers were killed by a bomb blast that accompanied an attempted bank extortion. A hoax device was found earlier in the day at another bank in the same community. A suspicious metal box was then discovered outside a bank. Bomb technicians and other officers responded. The box was x-rayed and was believed to be another hoax device. Due to heavy rain, the box was taken inside the bank for further examination. When a bomb technician attempted to open the box, it exploded, killing him and another officer. A third officer received life-threatening injuries but survived. Two men were later arrested in the case.

Chapter 19

REDUCING YOUR EMOTIONAL RISKS

It is impossible to talk about your emotional risks without talking about stress. What, exactly, *is* stress? Stress, for the police officer, is facing a 300-pound bully who has a pool cue in his mitt. It's driving 95 mph in a hot pursuit after an armed robber. It's exchanging shots with a would-be cop killer–and winning. It's facing the internal maneuverings and power struggles within your own organization. Indeed, stress comes from a lot of different directions for today's peace officer. For you.

The psychologists define stress a bit differently. But when you cut through all of the psychobabble, it comes down to something like this: *stress amounts to normal bodily reactions to abnormal situations*. It is from stress that many of your emotional risks are fashioned. Reducing those risks to an acceptable level is what this chapter is all about. But before you can manage your emotional risks, you will need to know a little more about their root cause: job stress.

THE STATS ARE NOT GOOD

Statistically, police officers do not fare too well when it comes to surviving the emotional risks of life. Suicide rates for peace officers are two to five times higher–depending on whose figures you want to believe–than for the general population of the United States. Divorce rates for police officers are high. Alcoholism and drug abuse problems among police people are higher than for the general populace, too. Average life spans for officers have been said to be shorter than for the general public as well.

What are the stress factors that influence the emotional risks borne by police officers? There are both external and internal stressors impacting you and your colleagues. On the outside, stress factors intruding on the officer's peace of mind include negative public attitudes, in some cases, toward police, unfair news media treatment, frustration with the miscarriages of justice built into the criminal justice system, and unreasonable demands from the public.

Frequent internal stressors include inadequate support from the police brass, extensive and time-consuming paperwork, sometimes-poor training, low pay, poor equipment, and the harsh demands of shift work. At some well-run agencies, the stressors are much reduced. At others, they are worse. Taken together with the external stress factors, these mental as well as physical aggravations can lead to frustration, anger, fear, a feeling of helplessness, boredom, and eventual job burnout. And all of that can put you at extreme emotional risk.

THE SYMPTOMS OF STRESS

Your emotional health can be endangered by a slow, cumulative buildup of stress as easily as it can be by a sudden, traumatic experience such as a fatal shootout with a suspect or the violent death of a fellow officer. The symptoms of a stressed-out cop can vary widely. They can, however, include the following physical, emotional, and behavioral indicators:

1. Constant fatigue
2. Abuse of sick leave
3. Abuse of alcohol or other drugs
4. Tendency to be accident prone
5. Sleeping on the job; sleep disturbances off the job
6. Increased number of citizen complaints of misconduct
7. Deep depression
8. Extreme defensiveness, sensitivity, or outright hostility
9. Abrupt mood swings
10. Steady deterioration in work habits
11. Sexual promiscuity or impotence
12. Persistent nausea or digestive problems
13. Severe headaches
14. Difficulty in concentrating or solving problems
15. Nightmares
16. Startle reactions
17. Flashbacks
18. Amnesia about a critical incident
19. Refusal to attach importance to anything but the incident

Obviously, every one of these symptoms is not going to show up in every individual whose emotional condition is edging into the red. Some may approach their detonation point more quietly. But inside, the damaging effects of emotional stress are taking their toll.

There are other by-products of the severe emotional shock wrought on the police person, too. Following a single, high-stress incident or from the cumulative effects of a series of high-stress situations, an officer may repress his emotions in an attempt to deny that what happened really *did* happen. This denial may be accompanied by an orgy of second-guessing. Was there something else he could have done to avoid having to use deadly force? Did he really have to shoot? Did he have to make the arrest at all? What if he had stayed home from work? And so on.

The stressed-out officer may show signs of anger displacement over having been put into an emotionally supercharged atmosphere in the first place. He may unleash his misplaced anger on family members or coworkers. Or he may direct it against the people he deals with on the street. Citizen complaints of discourtesy or excessive force may go up sharply.

The troubled officer may be feeling the effects of unspoken but very keenly felt dreads. Will he have to face a similar threat again? What will he tell the family of the man he shot to death? He may feel an overwhelming sense of guilt at his actions even though he knows that he acted properly and lawfully. He may experience continuing nightmares about the incident(s) and have difficulty sleeping. In his deepening depression, he may intentionally isolate himself from those most able to support him: his friends, fellow officers, and close family members.

If you are involved in a critical incident—a situation that includes the death or serious injury of a suspect, victim, or peer—you may find yourself experiencing immediate as well as delayed or indirect consequences of the happening. It is important that you be aware of them and give them some thought now so that they do not surprise and overwhelm you should you encounter them following a real-life incident. For instance, many officers report that time greatly slows down during a critical incident, such as a shootout with an offender. Later, they may say that an event that actually took five seconds to unfold was played out over a period of several minutes. Other sensory distortions can occur, too. Officers have reported that they actually saw bullets leaving the barrel of a suspect's gun or their own weapon. Others have said that the offender's weapon itself appeared several times larger than they knew it to be.

Yet other officers report feeling numb or dazed as a critical incident played out with them in the middle of it. They recall a powerful sense of absolute disbelief, a feeling that "this can't possibly be happening to me." Some also claim no recall of certain events or sensations that were a big part of the incident. They may, for example, state that they never heard a shot even though several were fired. They may have no recollection whatever of how they got from Point A to Point B, and they may insist they were never at a spot the physical evidence shows that they were.

Officers involved in traumatic incidents may experience an immediate feeling of nausea. They may vomit. They may feel an overpowering need to urinate or defecate. They may sweat profusely. These are *normal* reactions for many people to a very *abnormal* situation. Later, the same officers may experience digestive or bowel problems, headaches, appetite changes, unusual nervousness, or changes in their sex drive. Although some of these conditions may require relief through medical or psychological assistance, there is no reason to believe that any are permanent or long-lasting in duration. They *do* pass. Things *do* get better. How soon depends on a great many variables, not the least important of which is the individual's prior mental conditioning for dealing with this sort of emotional trauma. (And that's something you can start working on right now.)

In the aftermath of a shooting or other highly stressful incident, you also may experience less-immediate consequences or effects. Other officers have before. You may, for instance, find that you are now less aggressive in your contacts on the street. There may be less desire to get into a situation that could result in a confrontation similar to the stress-causing one that occurred before. You may become more introspective about your role as a law enforcement officer. You may find yourself pondering a lot more about job-related things that you used to do more or less without thinking.

Following your involvement in a critical incident, you may find that other officers seem to treat you differently, perhaps with something resembling fascination, particularly if you used deadly force against someone. At the same time, you may sense that the department's brass hats are keeping their distance from you, at least until it is crystal clear that your actions, whatever they were, met all the ethical, legal, and procedural qualifications for propriety. That, too, is a fact of life in many police organizations, and it is one you must be aware of if you are to avoid adding to your personal stress load.

Tragically, the figures show that some police officers involved in very critical incident scenarios—particularly those involving the killing of a suspect by police—leave law enforcement soon thereafter. Worn out by the stress of repeatedly rehashing the critical encounter in their minds while enduring the emotional fallout of the event and its aftermath, they seek escape in other work with a less sacrifice-demanding lifestyle.

WHAT CAN YOU DO ABOUT IT?

There is no need for you to cheat the law enforcement profession of a highly valuable human asset by pulling yourself out of police work in the wake of a traumatic occurrence. Likewise, there is no mandate for you to cheat *yourself* of a career that has been (and can continue to be) emotionally and otherwise rewarding to you. You *can* overcome and get through the emotional risks that sometimes accompany a critical incident.

This critical incident "first aid" requires you to do some commonsense things to overcome or mitigate the negatives that *may* come your way following a situation (or a whole series of them) that was emotionally stressful for you. These self-help suggestions, collected from the experiences of officers who have survived their own bouts with high stress and its results, are not intended to replace professional counseling or medical help that may be indicated following a stress-charged event. But they have helped your peers or prior occasions. Chances are they can help you, too. Your emotional risk reduction following a critical incident or other stressful situation can begin with some of the following steps and suggestions.

Exercise. Particularly during the first couple of days immediately following the traumatic event, get lots of aerobic exercise by jogging, walking, swimming, biking, or whatever else appeals to you. When alternated with periods of relaxation, exercise can help lessen some of the physical reactions you might otherwise experience as a result of stress.

Stay Busy. Don't vegetate. Structure your time but stay involved with whatever is happening on or off the job. A sense of *normalcy* is important to you right now, so keep yourself occupied both mentally and physically.

Don't Self-Destruct. That means laying off the alcohol or other drugs, prescription or otherwise. Alcohol won't make you forget, but it *will* deepen the blue funk that you already may be in. Other self-destructive behavior is taboo, also, such as displaying an unwanted and unnecessary supply of "cowboy courage." Don't do it.

Talk to Others. Specifically, seek out other officers who have been through what you are now experiencing. You will no doubt find some sympathetic ears as well as a good source of sound advice and consolation.

If your department is a very small one, you may have to go to another agency to find these folks. But it is definitely worth your while to seek them out for the help and understanding they can offer. There are even formal and informal groups or associations of officers who have weathered critical incidents in several parts of the country. It may be worth your while to find one on the Internet.

Don't overlook the importance of talking freely with others who may have gone through the traumatic incident with you. They can help you at the same time you benefit them in a free exchange of thoughts and feelings.

Keep Talking. Talk about what you just went through with those who mean the very most to you, too. That includes, where possible, your spouse or "significant other." They should be supportive of what you have to say. Reach out to these people for understanding and backing. They *do* care about you.

Realize That You're Normal. Remember: You are going through normal human reactions as a result of having experienced a very abnormal situation. You are not going crazy or anything even close to it. Don't label yourself as somehow abnormal. Nothing could be *more* normal than what you are going through as a consequence of great emotional trauma. *You will be alright.*

Be Patient. What you are experiencing will go away, but it probably won't go away overnight. Don't disappoint yourself by expecting it to. Emotional healing takes time, just as it takes awhile to mend a broken bone. Don't rush yourself. It'll come.

Accept It. It is mentally healthy for you to accept what happened and resolve to go on. It is far too late to change the outcome of events. Replaying the scenario over and over in your mind will sap your emotional energy. Accepting reality for what it is leads to emotional healing, too. Life must go on.

Don't Go It Alone. Spend a lot of time with supportive others. You can assist your co-workers who may have been involved in the same gut-wrenching incident by sharing your own feelings and providing an attentive ear for theirs. This is generally not a good time for you to go off and be by yourself. You need people and activities to occupy your thoughts.

Practice Your Ignoring Skills. You may have to ignore well-meant but ill-advised comments from your friends and coworkers who are trying to cheer you up or get your mind off the incident. "Nice shooting, Deadeye!" is not what most officers who have been involved in a fatal shooting want to hear. Just remember that the speaker most likely meant to help, so ignore the content of what he had to say.

Ignore the News Media. If the incident you were involved in stirred up considerable news media interest, you may be approached with requests for interviews. To keep from getting yourself worked up over improper or misleading questions and their resulting, inaccurate stories, it is probably best that you ignore the press altogether. Don't read about the incident or watch it on the television news just now. You can always check out what the media had to say when you are feeling back to normal.

Try Self-Calming. Implement self-calming techniques when you feel your stress level (and your blood pressure) rising. Try breathing slowly and deeply. Close your eyes while seated comfortably and imagine yourself in a favorite, peaceful spot or activity. Consciously think about relaxing your body's muscles, one by one. Refuse to allow disquieting thoughts to enter your mind at all.

Don't Hide Your Feelings. Give yourself permission to feel temporarily rotten and let go of all that practiced self-control for a little while. Big boys (and girls) really *do* cry on occasion. It's absolutely alright to do so when you feel that the situation warrants.

Make Decisions. Keep your mind busy. Exercise your decision-making skills. It will give you a sense of increased control over your life, something you may need more of at this point. The decisions don't have to be major ones. Just be sure you make some yourself. If, for instance, someone asks you what you want for supper, answer them specifically: a Triple Slime Dog with double onions and garlic, or whatever. (Now you'll have a new set of problems to worry about!)

Do What Feels Good. It sounds like simple advice, and it really is. You need to keep yourself pleasantly preoccupied just now. If you like to go fishing or skiing, then do it. Ditto for taking a hike or going on a short trip. If you feel that working your regular duty shift would feel good to you, then do that. The key here is to feel good about yourself and what you are doing.

No Big Changes. This is not the time to make any big changes in your life, like getting a divorce or changing jobs. Wait until things have settled down a bit before you implement any major alterations in the way you live. You may feel differently about a number of things soon.

Remember: You're Normal. It's worth saying one more time. You are experiencing normal human reactions to an abnormal situation or event in your life. Others have felt much as you do now. Others have gotten past it. So will you. You are NOT unusual.

It is especially vital that you also realize that none of the symptoms and feelings described here may apply to you. THAT IS NORMAL ALSO. A good many officers who are exposed to a critical incident–including one with fatal consequences–do not go through any of these personal passages. If you are one of these officers, there is nothing wrong with you, either. It simply may mean that you are more comfortable with your job and the tragic consequences it can sometimes make you witness than another officer may be. Or it could mean that you have thought about the things involved in the current critical incident before and the emotional shock is thereby much less for you. You, too, are normal. Don't worry that you may be missing something. As those who have gone the other route could tell you, you have not missed anything you would want to make up!

SOME PREVENTATIVE MEASURES

You do not have to wait until a critical incident occurs to start working on controlling your stress level and reducing your emotional risks. Your employer can do a lot to help you and your peers in your efforts, too. Your department can, for example, lead the way by encouraging its command staff members to present a consistently supportive attitude toward police personnel recovering from a stressful experience. The department also can help by providing immediate, professional counseling for officers who have been involved in critical incidents such as the use of deadly force.

Ongoing psychological services should be extended as needed at no cost to police employees and, if need be, their families. In addition, training or orientation programs can be provided to police spouses to familiarize them with what to expect from an officer who has been involved in a high-stress situation. All of these services should, of course, be voluntary on the part of officers and their loved ones.

Police agencies also can provide their people with stress reduction training in which personnel are shown practical techniques for defusing job stress. Such training sessions should provide an opportunity for officers to discuss freely without fear of official retaliation the internal and organizational as well as external pressures brought on by their sometimes emotionally difficult jobs.

Finally, the agency can mitigate some of the stresses on its people by providing them with a fair and just internal investigations system for resolving complaints against police personnel. This process can be backed by adequate liability insurance on police employees paid for by the agency to remove from individual officers the worry of having to defend at personal expense a frivolous or vindictive lawsuit.

Still, in the end, it gets down to what you do for yourself to reduce the emotional risks of your job that will count the most in lowering your job's stress level. Fortunately, there are a number of practical steps you can take to help yourself on a continuing basis *before* trouble occurs.

Relax. Set aside a time and place for relaxing during your otherwise busy, off-duty day. Close your eyes. Put your feet up. Meditate. Nap. Or whatever else works for you. But do something to take the pressure off, even if it's for no more than 10 minutes at a time.

Watch Your Diet. Eat three balanced meals a day. Don't skip meals, even though you may be working a difficult shift. Watch *what* you eat, too. Take it easy on the salt and animal fats.

Watch What You Drink. Nobody said you couldn't have a beer. Or two. But put realistic limits on your alcohol consumption. Being under the influence does more than aggravate your emotional situation if you are having problems. It also keeps you from responding capably if you are suddenly confronted with a crisis demanding action of some kind. Remember, too, that alcohol dependence can sneak up on you before you know what has taken place. In summary: if you drink, be sure you drink in moderation.

Too much caffeine can hurt you, too. You might try alternating the high-test stuff with decaffeinated brew.

Again, Exercise. Stay with a regular aerobic exercise program of some kind, whether walking, jogging, swimming, or something else is your style. You'll do more than improve your endurance and strength while you control your body weight. By exercising regularly, you'll also stir up production of some bodily chemicals that make you feel better mentally.

Sleep. Get enough of it. Different people need different amounts to feel good and stay alert. Most adults need at least eight hours a night (or day). Experiment a little to see what's right for you and stick with it. For many people, taking a nap right before they go to work is not all that helpful, but see what works best for you.

Don't Smoke. Not anything. If you already smoke, stop. If you have never started, don't. You do not need the added damage to your body that smoking can cause. In spite of rumors to the contrary, smoking won't do anything to benefit your state of mind, either.

Talk. It's been mentioned before, but it's important. Share your feelings by talking with your loved ones and coworkers. Let them in on whatever it is that is troubling you. They may be able to help. Don't bottle up inside you something you really know needs aired. Talking could make you feel better. Give it a try.

Alone Is O.K., Too. You need to spend time with the people who are important to you. You need to socialize. You also need time reserved for you and you alone. Leave yourself some space. Enjoy your own company from time to time. You don't want to be a hermit, but most everyone needs the opportunity to enjoy some solitude on occasion. It's just plain healthy for you.

Passive Is Not a Dirty Word. You're a cop, right? You *have* to be in charge. You have to take the lead. But not really. Recognize that sometimes you have to accept what you cannot reasonably expect to change. Pull in your horns over the nonvital issues. You really don't have to win every argument. Let somebody else do the worrying for a change. Try a little bit of passivity. Give in occasionally. You might even find it results in a noticeable drop in your blood pressure.

Slow Down. You really don't have to be the world's fastest driver, talker, or doer of anything. Ease off a little. Try—really try—to do your job and live your life just a little more slowly when you can. Handle one crisis at a time and don't expend mental energy by worrying about one that hasn't developed yet. Stop long enough to stand back and look at yourself every once in a while. You may even see some little things you want to change. Slow down and live longer and better.

Get Help. If you feel stress building toward a point where you can no longer handle it or its consequences, admit to yourself that you need some skilled assistance and go for it. You would not try to treat an infection by yourself if it was clearly getting out of hand. Don't try to cure yourself when it is equally clear that your emotional processes are getting seriously out of hand. Avail yourself of the professional counseling help offered within or outside of your agency. Never hesitate to seek the assistance you need. Later you will thank yourself for your decision in favor of self-preservation. Getting professional aid when you need it is *that* important.

It has been said that how you handle stress determines to a great extent how long you are going to live. Handling the emotional risks of your job successfully calls for you to recognize that just about *however* you respond following a critical incident is *normal* for you. Recognizing that you are, in fact, *normal* is a big part of maintaining your sanity when the rest of the world appears to be in danger of losing touch with reality.

Your mental and emotional efforts at self-help are well worth it. There are a great number of personal benefits for you in living an emotionally healthy, stress-controlled life. You will have more self-confidence. You will maintain a more positive outlook on life. You will be generally happier both on and off the job. You almost certainly will enjoy a better sex life. You will be less likely to experience major, chronic back or stomach discomforts. You will have a better appetite. You probably will just plain *feel* better all around. You will be more likely to survive a serious illness or injury. You will be likely to live longer as well as better.

All in all, there are more than a couple of good reasons to work at reducing your emotional risks. What more could a survival-smart, law enforcement professional ask?

A RISK REDUCTION CHECKLIST FOR
REDUCING YOUR EMOTIONAL RISKS

1. Following a critical incident, you may experience absolutely normal, although very disturbing, physical, behavioral, and mental reactions to a very abnormal situation.
2. Remember that you are also quite normal if you experience little or no physical or mental reaction to a critical incident. Don't worry about that, either.

3. Practice a number of self-administered, emotional first aid techniques to minimize the traumatic effects of a critical incident or cumulative stress.
4. Follow a stress-reduction regimen that includes adequate sleep, relaxation, a healthy balanced diet, exercise and recreation, talking it out, and, where indicated, a call for professional counseling assistance.

Two officers were killed answering a domestic violence call at about 3 p.m. A 911 caller reported that a woman had been abducted from a business and assaulted. The abductor placed the victim in a vehicle, which police traced to a mobile home. As the two officers approached the home, an adult male exited the structure with a 12-gauge shotgun and fired several rounds of buckshot at the officers, both of whom were wearing body armor. The officers returned fire at the subject, but both were hit fatally, including wounds to the head. The killer fled the scene in a vehicle that crashed. He was justifiably killed by other officers.

* * * * *

A 14-year veteran officer was killed at about 5:30 a.m. while he and other officers were attempting to serve a search warrant at a residence. When the officer approached a male subject, the man fired four rounds from a .38-caliber revolver. The officer received multiple wounds, including a fatal one in the head.

* * * * *

A 29-year-old officer was slain at 1:40 a.m. at the scene of a domestic violence call. The officer and three of his peers took cover outside a house and called the occupants out. A woman and her two sons exited onto the front porch. The victim officer went to cover the rear of the residence. Unknown to the officers, an intoxicated male adult had left the residence and was hiding in an unattached garage. He later stated that he saw the officer's flashlight beam and heard his portable radio. He fired one round from a 12-gauge shotgun, which hit the officer in the head. The killer subsequently surrendered.

Appendix

OFFICERS KILLED; LESSONS LEARNED

As many law enforcement officers will attest, the lessons they remember the most were often the most painful. Inasmuch as few experiences in a peace officer's life will prove as painful as the loss of a comrade, there are lessons to be learned from these tragedies. And as most law enforcement officers will agree, many times the tragedies occur because of a mistake or momentary lapse by an otherwise excellent peace officer.

For many years, one of the best sources available for accounts of tragic mistakes made by law enforcement officers has been the annual *Law Enforcement Officers Killed and Assaulted* reports compiled and published by the Federal Bureau of Investigation. These reports contain summaries of the known circumstances surrounding each officer death resulting from felonious causes occurring that year. Many contain hints as to why the officer became the victim of a cold-blooded killer. For that reason, these real-life anecdotes are invaluable to the student of officer safety. For that same reason, a selection of those reports is included here. Each condensed report is accompanied by suggestions of what may have gone wrong or lessons that might be learned from that fatal encounter.

In examining the following examples of personal tragedies, it is important to remember that these officers did not choose to die, nor did they kill themselves. In each case, their death was brought about by the actions of a heartless, violent criminal. With that kept in mind, an examination of violent deaths and the survival lessons that may be learned from them can take place.

Case #1: A metropolitan area police patrolman was dispatched to a call where a neighbor's dog was reportedly chasing children. After speaking with the complainant, the officer went to the home of the dog's owner and attempted to contact him in the front yard. The man ran into the house and refused to come out. The officer summoned assistance, and, when help arrived, the officers made entry. The man fled into another room, reappeared with a 12-gauge shotgun, and shot the originally dispatched officer fatally in the back as he attempted to seek cover. The suspect was wounded and captured by the other officers.

Fatal Flaws

False assumptions concerning the relative danger of a "minor" call?
Poor tactics—forced entry over a vicious dog call?
Body armor?

Case #2: The body of a 41-year-old highway patrol trooper was found in his patrol car, which was partially submerged in a lake in a rural area. The trooper had been beaten about the head and face, apparently with a flashlight, and had then been shot twice in the back of the head with his own sidearm. Investigation revealed that after stopping a suspected drunk driver the night before, the officer was attacked by the motorist he had arrested but not handcuffed. The officer had started for the county jail when he was attacked.

Fatal Flaws

Failure to maintain radio contact?
Failure to use a backup for an arrest?
No handcuffing?
Weapon retention practices?

Case #3: At approximately 2 a.m., two officers responded to a trailer park where a man was reported yelling for help. The officers encountered a subject whom they recognized from an "assist the fire department" call about an hour earlier. A struggle immediately ensued, and each officer was in turn disarmed and shot fatally in the head with his own handgun.

Fatal Flaws

Proper use of backup (coordination)?
Weapon retention?
Additional assistance required but not called?

Case #4: The chief deputy of a rural sheriff's office responded at about 2 a.m. to a report that an intoxicated man was threatening his ex-wife. The deputy arrived alone and was approaching the door of a mobile home when he was struck fatally in the chest by a single round from a .22-caliber rifle. Other officers responding to a second call found the adult male killer dead inside the home from a self-inflicted wound.

Fatal Flaws

No backup officer?
Poor approach and positioning?
Complacency?

Case #5: At about 3 a.m., a police lieutenant radioed that he was stopping a vehicle believed to have fled from a just-occurred robbery of a convenience store. He requested backup. Before assistance arrived, the lieutenant approached the suspect vehicle and had the male exit the car. While he was attempting to handcuff the male, a female suspect got out of the vehicle and shot the officer once in the chest with a handgun. The lieutenant died of the wound.

Fatal Flaws

Failing to wait for backup?
Use of cover?
Lack of body armor?

Case #6: Shortly after midnight, an off-duty officer in a large American city left his residence to investigate a noise disturbance in a nearby park. He encountered several young men and identified himself as a police officer. He was then beaten to death with fists, baseball bats, a tire iron, and a cement block. Five suspects, ages 19 through 23, were later charged with murder.

Fatal Flaws

Poor decision making?
No backup?
No weapon?

Case #7: A foot pursuit resulted in a 24-year-old patrol officer losing his life just after midnight. The officer and his car partner came upon five males standing by a vehicle in an area known for drug dealing. The five fled on foot, and the two officers chased the closest subject. One officer then went back to the patrol car in an attempt to head off the fleeing subject. He heard a single gunshot and eventually found his partner fatally injured after being shot in the head with a .22-caliber handgun at close range. The officer had caught up with the offender and was struggling with him when he was shot.

Fatal Flaws

Poor tactics—splitting from one's partner on a foot chase?
Arrest-control tactics?
Failing to watch their hands?

   Case #8: Shortly after 9 a.m., a 24-year law enforcement veteran was slain by an auto thief. The officer had stopped a suspicious vehicle and summoned a second officer to the scene after obtaining the suspect's driver's license and then determining the vehicle to be stolen. The primary officer then returned to the vehicle and engaged in conversation with the suspect while the second officer took a position at the rear of the suspected stolen car. The suspect emerged with a handgun and grabbed the first officer, using him as a shield from the second. When the first officer attempted to escape, he was shot fatally. The mortally wounded officer returned fire, killing his assailant.

Fatal Flaws

Poor use of a cover officer?
Poor approach and positioning?

   Case #9: At about midnight, a veteran highway patrolman stopped a vehicle for suspected drunk driving. The officer found a man and woman in the car and placed the woman driver in his own car to issue a summons. She got out of his car, possibly with the assistance of her male companion. The officer confronted the pair and was then shot fatally in the chest and throat by the male subject. It was later learned that earlier that date the man had murdered two other people.

Fatal Flaws

Not waiting for a backup officer?
Lack of information?
Losing control of the scene and situation?

   Case #10: At 5:45 p.m., a city police detective was killed while transporting a parole violator to the police station. The detective had arrested the man on a warrant and was transporting him unhandcuffed. Upon arriving at the station, the man bolted from the car and eventually took, then released, a pedestrian as a hostage. The officer caught and struggled with the subject. During the fight, the detective's drawn handgun discharged, wounding the subject. The man took the weapon away from the officer and shot him three times. Both men died of their wounds.

Fatal Flaws

Failure to handcuff?
Poor arrest-control tactics?
Weapon retention?

Case #11: A 58-year-old patrolman responded to a single-car accident, learned the involved vehicle was stolen and abandoned, and then located and picked up a man walking nearby. The subject, seated in the back seat of the patrol car, shot the officer fatally in the back of the head with a handgun while being driven back to the accident scene. Three other officers were subsequently wounded by the fleeing killer before he was captured.

Fatal Flaws

Complacency?
Ignoring danger signs?
Poor or no search?
No handcuffing?

Case #12: A police sergeant was looking for suspects from a just-occurred robbery when he boarded a bus where one of the three parties was believed to have fled. The sergeant located a subject matching a robber's description, searched him, and was escorting him off the bus when the man produced a handgun and shot the officer fatally.

Fatal Flaws

Poor search?
No handcuffing?
Failing to wait for backup?

Case #13: At about 1 a.m., a state trooper was killed during a high-speed vehicle chase. While assisting other officers in pursuing a fleeing van, the trooper attempted to position his moving vehicle in front of the van in an attempt to stop it. The van's driver deliberately struck the left rear quarter panel of the patrol car, causing it to spin out of control and crash. The 13-

year officer was killed instantly.

Fatal Flaws

Poor positioning?
Poor decision making?

Case #14: A veteran highway patrolman stopped a male traffic violator who had three children in his car. The violator had been placed, unsecured, in the right front seat of the patrol car when the radio dispatcher announced that the car was reported stolen. The officer exited his car, walked around to the right side, and was struggling with the subject in an attempt to handcuff him when he lost control of his handgun and was killed with it.

Fatal Flaws

Complacency?
Poor positioning of unsecured violator?
Poor weapon retention practices?
Poor radio discipline?

Case #15: A 46-year-old police sergeant was murdered by a robbery suspect at about 10:20 a.m. After being flagged down by a robbery victim, the sergeant began pursuing a car containing multiple suspects. He was shot to death when he pulled his unmarked patrol car alongside the fleeing vehicle.

Fatal Flaws

Failing to obtain backup?
Poor vehicle positioning?

Case #16: A 56-year-old sheriff's deputy was killed at approximately 10:00 a.m. while transporting three inmates back to prison from a court appearance. The inmates apparently cut through their restraining belts, overpowered the deputy in the vehicle, and then shot him fatally with his own sidearm.

Fatal Flaws

Poor or no search?
Lack of alertness?
No backup (too many prisoners for one officer)?

Weapon retention?

Case #17: Shortly after 4 a.m., a young patrol officer observed a vehicle speeding from a just-occurred stickup and began to pursue it. Shortly thereafter, the suspects' vehicle crashed and the officer radioed that he was getting out to investigate the now-stationary vehicle. An arriving backup found the officer lying dead between his car and the wrecked vehicle. He had been shot twice in the forehead at close range with a .22-caliber weapon.

Fatal Flaws

Rushing when the situation does not require speed?
Fail to wait for backup?
Fail to use cover?

Case #18: At about 11:30 p.m., a patrol officer stopped to check an occupied vehicle parked on an isolated roadway. A female jumped from the car screaming for help and a male occupant fled into a wooded area. Pursuing the man on foot, the officer shortly thereafter radioed that the subject was in custody. Seconds later, gunfire was heard, and the officer was found mortally wounded in the head with his own handgun, which was now missing. It was subsequently learned that the female was a gas station attendant who had just been held up and was forced to drive her own car to the spot where the officer encountered her and the suspect.

Fatal Flaws

Failure to wait for backup?
Poor weapon retention?
Lack of information?

Case #19: At about midnight, a patrolman responded with a backup to a report of two suspicious pedestrians, one reportedly carrying a bag of burglary tools. While the 16-year veteran questioned the pair, he held his flashlight in one hand and his portable radio in the other. One subject dropped his bag to the ground, reached inside, and fired a 12-gauge shotgun through the bag. The officer was killed.

Fatal Flaws

Keep watching their hands?
Use of cover?

Proper use of a backup (contact and cover)?

Case #20: A sheriff's deputy was with two other officers in an alley attempting to talk an armed, known-suicidal man into custody. It was approximately 10:20 p.m. The officer, holding a flashlight, stepped into the open from a place of cover in order to talk with the subject. The man killed the deputy with a blast from a 12-gauge shotgun.

Fatal Flaws

Cowboy tactics?
Poor use of cover?

INDEX

243

wounded, 186
wounds, 183
wraparound, 103

Z

ZOG, 213